Spanish Ultimate
Year 2

D1649220

Presented By

Alpha Omega Publications ®

Spanish Ultimate Year 2
2004 Edition

Project Coordinator: James Blair

Development Manager: Dave Higginbotham

Editors: Heather Monson, C. Ray Graham, Richard Tice, Leticia Cabrera, Gustavo Cabrera, Debbie Haws

Editorial Assistants: Jocelyn Spencer Rhynard, Erik D. Holley, Julia Blair, Dell Blair, James Blair, Margaret Young, Ingrid Kellmer, Andy Bay, Ben Blair, Jennifer Rey, Raquel Lodeiro, Shauna Palmer, Gretchen Hilton, Emily Spackman

Translators: Robert Blair, Dell Blair, Raquel Decker

Voice Talent: Dell Blair, James Blair, Julia Blair, Robert Blair, Raquel Decker, Carlos Ramirez, Julio Salazar, Margaret Young

Layout & Design: Erik D. Holley

Illustrators: Heather Monson, Apryl Robertson

Story Writer: Heather Monson

Musicians: Paul Anderson, Marty Hughes, Scott Mills

Recording Engineers: Wade Chamberlain, Bruce Kirby, John Brady

Power-Glide Language Courses, Inc.
1682 W 820 N, Provo, UT 84601

www.power-glide.com

Contents

NOTE

To track your progress through the course, place a ✔ in the ○ after you complete a semester, module, section, or activity. As a general guide, semesters take approximately 3 1/2 months to complete, modules take approximately 1 month, and sections take approximately 1 week. These times are just estimates—you're welcome to learn at your own pace!

Introduction

Using This Course

Welcome to Power-Glide Foreign Language Courses! You hold in your hands a very powerful and effective language learning tool. Power-Glide courses are designed so that individual students working alone can use them just as well as students in classrooms. However, before starting, we'd like to offer a few tips and explanations to help you get the most from your learning experience.

The course is divided into semesters, modules, sections, and activities. Each page has a tab denoting how it fits into the course structure, and students can use these tabs to navigate their way through the course.

Each semester has three modules. Each module has two or three sections, and each section begins with a page or two of adventure story, ends with a section quiz, and has several language activities in between.

Sections are followed by quizzes, and modules are followed by tests which we encourage students to use to solidify their mastery of the materials presented in the modules and sections. These quizzes and tests are very helpful for students seeking credit for their course work.

In this course, students will find a variety of different activities. These activities include Diglot Weave™ stories, counting and number activities, storytelling activities, activities designed to build conversational ability, audio-off activities for building reading comprehension, Spanish-only activities for building listening comprehension, and much more. Word puzzles found at the beginning of some sections help the student to think and problem-solve Spanish.

These different activity types accommodate different types of learning, and all are learner-tested and effective. Students will no doubt notice that each activity begins with a new picture. These pictures are drawn from Spanish cultures and countries and are included for students' interest.

How to Use the Appendices

- Appendix A contains student answers for self quizzes, exercises, and section puzzles. Students using this appendix will receive immediate feedback on their work.

- Appendix B contains the Scope and Sequence for this course. This appendix outlines the specific language learning objectives for each section and is useful for students seeking credit or teachers looking to schedule curriculum.

- Appendix C is an index of marginalia, or information found in the margins throughout the course. In an effort to squeeze even more fun, useful information into this course, we have included cultural information on different Spanish-speaking countries.

- Appendix D is a removable sheet designed for use by teachers or parents for grading purposes. Answers to module tests and section quizzes may be used by teachers to grade and track a student's progress through the course.

Students are encouraged to familiarize themselves with these appendices, as they can be valuable resources for finding information quickly.

Getting the Most Out of This Course

- Recognize the audio on and audio off symbols.
- Understand the text.
- Speak and write.

Audio Symbols

The audio-on and audio-off symbols, as mentioned previously, are highlighted bars like those below. Watch for them to know when to use your audio CDs.

When you see this bar, press play on your CD.

When you see this bar, press pause on your CD. Do not push stop. Pausing will allow you to continue the track where you left off, rather than at the beginning of the disc.

Understanding the Text

1. Look over the material and compare the Spanish to the English.

2. Listen to the audio tracks while following the written text.

3. Listen to the audio tracks a couple of times without looking at the written text.

4. Use the pause button to stop the audio for a moment if you want more time to practice.

Speaking

1. Read the story or material out loud in chorus with the audio, and keep the meaning in mind.

2. Turn the audio off, read each sentence out loud in Spanish, and then look away and repeat the same sentence without looking. Think of the meaning.

3. Now cover up the Spanish, look at the first English sentence, and try to say it in Spanish. Check to see if you did it right. Repeat this process for all the sentences in the activity.

4. Play the recording of the text, but pause the audio after each English sentence and say the Spanish yourself.

5. Using notes of key words only, try to say the Spanish sentences without using your activity book. It's okay to put the sentences into your own words, just keep them in Spanish as much as possible.

Writing

To write, just follow the same directions for speaking, but write your sentences instead of speaking them.

Course Conventions

Objectives

Each activity has a shaded box letting learners know what they will learn during the activity.

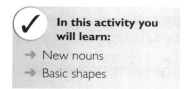

Sections also have objectives boxes. These section objectives are drawn from the activity objectives within the section. Appendix B contains a list of all the activity objectives for your convenience when reviewing for quizzes or tests.

Performance Challenges

While optional, students are encouraged to try performance challenges to fill out each activity and reinforce its content. Performance challenge boxes are located at the end of activities and look like this:

Not all activities have performance challenges and some have multiple challenges. Each performance challenge is labeled for use by an individual student or study group. If an activity has multiple performance challenges, the student may choose one or more to work on.

Audio Indicators

Some portions of this course have corresponding audio. The shaded audio boxes at the beginning of sections and selected activities indicate which audio disc and track to use. The sample audio box below indicates that disc 1, track 12 contains the audio for the given activity.

Recall the audio symbols described earlier.

You will use these bars together with the shaded audio box as you move through the course.

Here is a sample scenario for how to use the audio indicators:

- If an activity has audio, you will see the shaded audio box indicating which disc and track to use. In this example, we'll suppose that the audio box indicates disc 1, track 1.

- At the first audio-on bar you reach in the activity, insert audio disc 1 into your CD player and play track 1.

- When you reach the audio-off bar, press *pause.*

- The activity may or may not have more audio. If it does, you will see another audio-on bar. When you reach it, press *play.*

- When you reach another audio-off bar, press *pause* again.

- When you have finished your study session, press *stop* on your CD player.

Tracking Progress

The Table of Contents lists each semester, module, section, and activity in the course with a preceding checkmark circle. To track your progress through the course, place a ✓ in the ○ after you complete a semester, module, section, activity, semester test, module test, or section quiz. As a general guide, semesters take approximately 3 1/2 months to complete, modules take approximately 1 month, and sections take approximately 1 week. These times are just estimates—you're welcome to learn at your own pace!

The Power-Glide Difference

A Few of the Unique Features of Power-Glide

(And What They Mean To The Learner)

1. **Language specific.** Unlike most language training programs, Power-Glide courses are designed for speakers of specific languages, rather than the "one size fits all" approach. This takes advantage of what each language community knows and doesn't know, avoids wasted effort, and also allows special techniques to address language-specific problems.

2. **Based on up-to-date information/research on linguistics and learning methodology.** While the Power-Glide method is revolutionary, it is based on solid research and the most up-to-date information on the relevant disciplines.

3. **Involves learners in immediate use of the language in real situations.** Power-Glide courses avoid the drudgery of rote memorization of words and rules by immediately involving the learners in practical use of the language in real situations. This keeps interest, confidence, and motivation high.

4. **Uses adventure stories and activities.** From the beginning, the students are involved in an adventure story and activities that keep them engaged.

5. **Uses multiple methods of learning: music, stories, activities, and more.** People have different learning styles. By using various methods, music, stories, etc., everyone's style is addressed and learning is accelerated.

6. **Uses the Diglot Weave™ method.** Students start with familiar stories in their own language and gradually transition word by word, into the new language. The context provides the meaning and thus makes the learning an almost effortless, natural process.

7. **Takes learners from the known to the unknown along the easiest path.** While learning a foreign language can be challenging, it does not need to be brutal. The Power-Glide method guides the learners through the most productive and gentle paths.

8. **Uses memory devices and phonemic approximations.** Learning the right pronunciation and

remembering the words and phrases of another language are greatly facilitated by using memory devices and similar sounding words from the student's own language. This also reduces the "fear" of speaking the new language that many people experience.

9. **Doesn't require teachers.** One of the greatest advantages of Power-Glide courses is the fact that the teacher, parent, or facilitator doesn't need to know the language in order to assist the learner in the process. The one assisting also learns as an unexpected by-product of their teaching others.

10. **Many other linguistic strategies.** The variety of methods used increase motivation, retention, joy of learning, and desire to use the target language.

What People Are Saying About Power-Glide

Stephanie Heese, reviewer, *The Review Corner*:

"Speaking and thinking spontaneously in a foreign language is challenging, but is an important goal that is hard to achieve with traditional programs. In Power-Glide courses, emphasis is not on mechanics and rote learning. This course aims to teach children in a manner that simulates natural language acquisition."

Herbert Horne, linguist, former teacher for Wycliffe Bible Translators, and current homeschool co-op administrator:

"Thirty years ago, in Guatemala, I used Dr. Blair's materials and they were the best I had ever seen. Now that I could 'test' the materials with more than 40 students in various classes, I am even more convinced that they are the best language teaching materials in existence today."

Susan Moore, reviewer, *Editor's Choice*:

"Most curriculum developers seem to have forgotten what it was like to sit endlessly in a classroom listening and pretending to be interested in boring subject material, but not Dr. Blair."

Linda Rittner, Director, Pleasant Hill Academy:

"As one who designs educational programs for individual students in our school, I must tell you how impressed I have been with the Power-Glide material. I was able to examine the second year course material for our community college. Your course is more comprehensive!"

Anne Brodbeck, reviewer for Mary Pride's, *Practical Homeschooling*:

"Unlike other higher-priced courses, the approach does not contain repetitive drills, is not strictly hearsay, and does not promise subliminal learning. It is fast-paced and takes full concentration. The use of the full-sized textbook included with the [audio] makes it a more comprehensive course than others with twice the number of [audio CDs]."

Nancy Lande, author, *Homeschooling: A Patchwork of Days*:

"I really love the way that a concept is presented, used in various examples and then left for the student to take the next leap and apply key information in different ways. You can actually watch the light bulb flash brightly above your child's head! She gets it!"

Cafi Cohen, author, *And What about College? How Homeschooling Leads to Admissions to the Best Colleges and Universities*:

"I've been chipping away at Spanish for 20+ years and have purchased umpteen zillion programs. I was immediately impressed by how much conversational fluency I felt I gained in the two short hours of my flight home."

Semester I

(COLOMBIA)

ISLAS
DEL MAIZ

CA

é

Puerto
Limón

Bocas
del Toro

Colón

Panama

olfito

David

Balboa

PANAMA

Santiago

La Palma

Module 1.1

Throughout this module we'll be learning about the culture of Panamá.

Keep these tips in mind as you progress through this module:

1. Read instructions carefully.
2. Repeat aloud all the Spanish words you hear on the audio CDs.
3. Learn at your own pace.
4. Have fun with the activities and practice your new language skills with others.
5. Record yourself speaking Spanish on tape so you can evaluate your own speaking progress.

La Casa
del Señor
Espinoza

Isla
Verde

Day One, 00:30 Hours

Una llamada por socorro

Just a few *horas* ago, you successfully completed an adventure on *Isla de Providencia*. With only moments to spare, you met the small boat which carried you across choppy waters to your rendezvous with the submarine. Now safely aboard the submarine while a storm rages on the surface, you have the recipe that turned out to be the object of your quest neatly folded in your pocket. In your bag, you also carry two bottles of the magnificent salsa—a parting gift from Violeta. In the hallway just below the main hatch, you and your fellow agent wait for the submarine captain to debrief you.

Finally, you are summoned to the bridge, where the captain greets you, then leads you to a small ready room just off the bridge. "Well, your boss, *su jefe*, finally let me know what you've been doing," he tells you with a gruff *sonrisa*. "Let me tell you, she was *muy feliz* to hear you finished before we picked you up. Good work. Now, for the paperwork, we need as complete and accurate account as you can provide of your mission, so—"

"Excuse me, sir," one of the crew pokes his head into the ready room.

"Yes, what is it?" asks the captain.

"Message coming through, sir—some sort of shortwave radio. It's all *en español*, sir."

The captain gives you and your fellow agent a significant look. "We'll see what we can do," you state, then follow the captain back to the bridge. Another crew member hands you a headphone set, and you hear the following:

¡Socorro! ¡Ayúdeme por favor! Mi nombre es Raul Alvarez. Trabajo para Don Julio Roberto Espinoza. ¡El ha sido secuestrado! No podría parar los secuestradores. Si puede oírme, por favor, ¡ayúdeme!

You listen to the message again, then summarize what it's saying.

"So, a Mr. Julio Roberto Espinoza has been kidnapped?" the captain asks, thoughtfully stroking his mustache. "Who is he?"

✓ **In this section you will:**

→ Comprehend the meaning of a story.
→ Understand a telephone conversation.
→ Understand and use small talk.
→ Understand new vocabulary in a conversation.
→ Master object pronouns with finite and infinite verbs.
→ Build fluency through repetition.
→ Follow instructions in Spanish.
→ Identify objects from a description.

⊙ Disc 1   Track 1

SECTION 1.1.1

"I've heard of him before," the crewman volunteers. "He's a famous author and journalist. His work has been translated into *docenas de idiomas*, and he's won literary prizes all over *el mundo*."

"Yeah, I remember reading about him!" your fellow agent volunteers. "He's from *Panamá* originally—there was an article on him a couple of weeks ago. Doesn't he have a home on one of the little islands around here?"

Another crew member checks a series of computerized maps. "Here," she replies, pointing to a dot on one of the maps. "Just off the coast of Venezuela, on *Isla Verde*." She checks distance. "We could reach it by morning. We'd still be in the storm, but we'd be south of the worst of it."

"Do they have a port big enough for us to surface?" the captain asks.

The crew member zooms in on the island's shores. "Yes. It'll be a tight squeeze, but we should fit, sir."

The captain shakes his head. "A tight squeeze in stormy waters…it's asking for trouble. Are any other ships nearby?"

"Negative, sir," the crew member replies.

"We'll go, then," the captain decides, "*pero* we can't surface for more than a few *minutos*. We'll need to drop someone off and get back below the surface." He turns to look at you and your fellow agent. "I can't spare any of my own crew," he tells you. "Are you two up for another assignment?"

You nod.

"As long as we can get some sleep before starting," your fellow agent adds.

The captain nods. "*Muy bien*, I'll contact your boss and get approval."

"While you're in contact with her, sir," you request, "could you request some additional Spanish materials? It sounds like we're going to need them."

The captain grins. *"Sí, por supuesto."*

You pass the night in the sub's only empty bunks and wake ready for your new adventure. After a light breakfast, you do a bit of research about *Panamá*, the missing author's homeland.

Day One, 06:30 Hours

The surfaced sub tosses and rolls with the waves, despite the crew's best attempts to hold it steady. The captain sees you to the main hatch. "We can't accompany you, but we'll provide whatever support we can," he tells you. "Call us if you need help."

You thank the captain. He nods. "Now, for this assignment, your boss suggested you have more local-sounding code names, so you," he says, pointing to you, "will be Agent *Mosca*, and you," he adds, pointing to your fellow agent, "will be Agent *Araña*."

"Spider and fly, huh?" you say with a grin.

"Glad I'm the spider," says your fellow agent, grinning back.

It's time. You open the main hatch. Outside, it's windy, and a heavy rain is falling. The submarine is slippery and wet as waves splash over its top. Very carefully, you and *Araña* move to the edge of the sub and scramble up a ladder onto the dock. You look back from the dock—the sub is already closed up and starting to submerse again.

"Come on, *vámonos*," suggests *Araña*, looking longingly at a sheltered cabin on the beach nearby.

You hesitate—you hate to waste time that could be spent finding the house of the missing Mr. Espinoza. However, the rain is coming down so heavily that you can't see more than thirty feet away. Finding an unfamiliar house on an unfamiliar island in weather like this is beyond even your skills. Reluctantly, you follow *Araña* to the cabin.

It's unlocked and appears to be there for no other purpose than sheltering passersby from the weather. You and *Araña* dry off as best you can, then settle down to study the new Spanish materials your boss sent you until the storm eases.

ACTIVITY

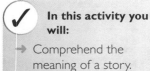

✓ **In this activity you will:**
→ Comprehend the meaning of a story.

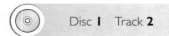

Disc **I**   Track **2**

In the Aquarium

Panama Culture Overview

Panama's national motto is "For the benefit of the world," which reflects Panama's strategic position and the services that it provides for other nations through the Panama Canal. This small Central American country isn't all about its famous canal, though. Visitors to Panama can find some of the best fishing, snorkeling, and wildlife watching in the Americas. Adventures abound in this proud nation, which respects its seven indigenous peoples and celebrates its colonial heritage with colorful local festivals.

INSTRUCTIONS   Listen to and read the following story.

◀))

English	Spanish
Look at that big fish.	*Mira ese pez tan grande.*
It's a shark.	*Es un tiburón.*
Sharks live in the ocean.	*Los tiburones viven en el océano.*
They have very large mouths.	*Tienen bocas muy grandes.*
And they have a lot of sharp teeth.	*Y tienen muchos dientes agudos.*
Sharks are dangerous, they say.	*Los tiburones son peligrosos, dicen.*
Some sharks attack people.	*Algunos tiburones atacan a la gente.*
A big shark can take off your leg in one bite.	*Un tiburón grande puede quitarte la pierna de una mordida.*
Are you afraid of sharks?	*¿Tienes miedo de los tiburones?*
Are all sharks big?	*¿Son grandes todos los tiburones?*

English (cont.)	Spanish
No, some are small, like those fish there, but others are as big as a bus.	No, algunos son pequeños, como los peces esos, pero otros son grandes como un autobús.
Would you like to play with a shark?	¿Te gustaría jugar con un tiburón?
It's dangerous to play with a shark.	Jugar con un tiburón es peligroso.

This activity is packed with different sentence structures, from simple imperatives ("Look at that big fish") to more complicated infinitive phrases ("It's dangerous to play with a shark").

Performance Challenge

Individual   Using two sentences in the activity as models, write ten sentences of your own using simple imperatives and infinitive phrases.

1. ....

2. ....

3. ....

4. ....

5. ....

6. ....

7. ....

8. ....

9. ....

10. ....

Performance Challenge

Group   Plan a field trip to a local aquarium or fish hatchery. Write a list of the names of animals or items that can be found at that location in Spanish. Split the students into teams and give them each a list. Have them go on a scavenger hunt, working as teams to find each item.

A Small Child Answers the Phone

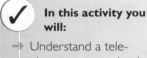

In this activity you will:

→ Understand a telephone conversation in Spanish.

Disc **I** Track **3**

INSTRUCTIONS Listen to this conversation. Try to learn its vocabulary and sentence patterns. A small child's voice answers the telephone in a muffled whisper, as if in a closet.

	English	Spanish
Whisper:	Hellooo.	*Alooo.*
Caller:	Hello. Is your mother there?	*Alo. ¿Está tu mamá?*
Whisper:	Yeees.	*Síí.*
Caller:	May I talk with her?	*¿Puedo hablar con ella?*
Whisper:	Nooo.	*Nooo.*
Caller:	Why not?	*¿Por qué no?*
Whisper:	She's busssyy.	*Está ocupadaaa.*
Caller:	Is your father there?	*¿Está tu papá?*
Whisper:	Yeees.	*Síí.*
Caller:	May I talk with him?	*¿Puedo hablar con él?*
Whisper:	Nooo.	*Nooo.*
Caller:	Why not?	*¿Por qué no?*
Whisper:	He's busssyy.	*Está ocupadooo.*
Caller:	Well, is anyone else there?	*Bueno, ¿está alguien más?*
Whisper:	Yeees.	*Síí.*
Caller:	Who?	*¿Quién?*

	English (cont.)	Spanish
Whisper:	Mmm.	*Mmm.*
Caller:	Who? Tell me.	*¿Quién? Dígame.*
Whisper:	Some neighbors and some police.	*Algunos vecinos y la policía.*
Caller:	Oh, is there something wrong?	*Oh, ¿hay algo malo allí?*
Whisper:	Nooo.	*Nooo.*
Caller:	Well could I talk with one of them?	*Bueno, ¿puedo hablar con uno de ellos?*
Whisper:	Nooo.	*Nooo.*
Caller:	Why not?	*¿Por qué no?*
Whisper:	They're all busssyy.	*Todos están ocupadoos.*
Caller:	Well what are they doing?	*Bueno, ¿Qué están haciendo?*
Whisper:	They're looking for me.	*Me están buscando.*

Performance Challenge

Individual   In this activity, there are many examples of how to ask permission in Spanish. Following the example set in these sentences, write five sentences of your own, asking for permission to do something. Then ask at least one of those questions to a parent, teacher, or friend.

Performance Challenge

Group   Divide the group into two teams, have each team sit in a semicircle. Play the game "*Teléfono*" using phrases from the conversations in this activity. The group whose phrase is the most correct at the end of the chain, wins.

Encounter at the University

✔ **In this activity you will:**

→ Understand and use small talk.

→ Understand new vocabulary in a conversation.

Disc **I**   Track **4**

INSTRUCTIONS   Listen to this simple, meaningful conversation. By working through the activity, you will build your confidence and fluency.

	English	Spanish
•:	Hi!	*¡Hola!*
••:	Sir?	*¿Señor?*
•:	Hey, I have a question.	*Oye, tengo una pregunta.*
••:	Yes.	*¡Sí!*
•:	Where are you going?	*¿Adónde vas?*
••:	Over there.	*Allá.*
•:	Oh, me too.	*Oh, yo también.*
••:	What a coincidence!	*¡Qué coincidencia!*
•:	Listen, I have an idea.	*Oye, tengo una idea.*
••:	Tell me.	*Dígame.*
•:	Let's go together, okay?	*Vamos juntos, ¿está bien?*
••:	Okay. Why not? With pleasure.	*Está bien. ¿Por qué no? Con mucho gusto.*
•:	I'm Vincent. You're Rosa, right?	*Me llamo Vicente. Tú te llamas Rosa, ¿verdad?*
••:	No. I'm [called] Nancy.	*No, me llamo Nancy.*
•:	Nancy, delighted to make your acquaintance.	*Nancy, encantado de conocerte.*
••:	It's a pleasure for me.	*Es un placer para mí.*
•:	What are you studying here?	*¿Qué estudias?*
••:	Music. I'm a pianist.	*Música. Soy pianista.*

	English (cont.)	Spanish
•:	Very interesting. I am too.	*Muy interesante. Yo también.*
••:	My husband is also a pianist, you know?	*Mi esposo también es pianista ¿sabes?*
•:	Truly?!	*¿De veras?*
••:	Yes, it's true.	*Sí, es cierto.*
•:	What is his name?	*¿Cómo se llama él?*
••:	Don Quixote. Do you know him?	*Don Quixote. ¿Lo conoces?*
•:	You're making a joke!	*¡Estás bromeando!*
••:	No. It's the truth.	*No. Es verdad.*
•:	Oh, I forgot!	*¡Oh, se me olvidó.*
••:	What did you forget?	*¿Qué?*
•:	Excuse me. I have to go home.	*Perdóneme. Tengo que ir a casa.*
••:	So soon?	*¿Tan pronto?*
•:	Yes. Excuse me.	*Sí. Disculpe.*
••:	But of course.	*¿Cómo no?*
•:	Good-bye. Until later! My compliments to your husband.	*Adiós. ¡Hasta la próxima! Mis felicitaciones a su esposo.*
••:	Thanks. Thanks much. Good-bye.	*Gracias. Muchas gracias. Adiós.*
•:	Good luck!	*¡Buena suerte!*

Performance Challenge

Individual   This activity presented you with a conversation between two people. Using the vocabulary and grammar you've learned up to now, write a conversation of your own. It should be at least four lines long. Once you have written it, perform it with a friend, sibling, or classmate.

Performance Challenge

Group   Split your group up into team. Give them a list of words that can be found at a university. Go on a scavenger hunt. The first team to find all of the words on their list, wins.

ACTIVITY 4

Chatter at a Royal Ball

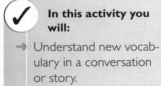

In this activity you will:

→ Understand new vocabulary in a conversation or story.

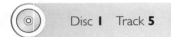

Disc **1**   Track **5**

Getting Ready for *Conversación*

INSTRUCTIONS   Learn this new vocabulary to use in conversation.

English	Spanish
to understand	*entender*
to attend	*asistir* (not "assist"!)
including the queen	*incluso la reina*
almost	*casi*
They do speak it.	*Sí lo hablan.*
(He) only speaks it there.	*Lo habla solamente allá.*
in fact	*de hecho*
church	*iglesia*
there	*allá*
not everyone	*no todos*
Almost without an accent.	*Casi sin acento.*
How is [it] that…?	*¿Cómo es que…?*

Conversación 11

	English	Spanish
•:	The prince speaks Chinese, right?	*Sólo el príncipe habla chino, ¿verdad?*
••:	No. He doesn't speak it. He understands it a bit, but he doesn't speak it.	*No, él no lo habla. Lo entiende un poco, pero no lo habla.*
•:	Then it's the princess that speaks it.	*Entonces es la princesa que lo habla.*

English (cont.)	Spanish
●●: Only her. She doesn't speak it much. In fact, she only speaks it at church. But she speaks it almost without an accent.	Sólo ella. No lo habla mucho. De hecho, lo habla solamente en la iglesia. Pero lo habla casi sin acento.
●: How is it that she speaks it at church?	¿Cómo es que lo habla en la iglesia?
●●: Apparently she likes to speak it there. She doesn't like to speak it in the palace, it seems.	Aparentemente le gusta hablarlo allá. No le gusta hablarlo en el palacio, parece.
●: And who does she talk Chinese with at church?	¿Y con quién habla chino en la iglesia?
●●: Well, she knows many Chinese who attend church, including the queen of Canton.	Pues ella conoce a muchos chinos que asisten a la iglesia, incluso la reina de Cantón.
●: Oh, did the princess know the queen of Canton?	¿Conoce la princesa a la reina de Cantón?
●●: Yes, she knows her well.	Sí, la conoce bien.
●: And she knows the king of Canton too and all the royal family.	Y conoce al rey de Cantón también y a toda la familia real.
●●: How interesting!	¡Qué interesante!
●: Really.	De veras.

These chatter activities may seem a bit nonsensical, but if you pay attention, you'll see they're presenting a lot of useful words and phrases in context, where they're easy to understand and remember.

Performance Challenge

Individual   This activity presented you with several useful new verbs and phrases. Choose at least five of these new verbs and phrases, study how they are used in the conversation, then use them in sentences of your own.

Performance Challenge

Group   Give each group a familiar story that contains royalty (i.e. The Princess and the Pea, Rapunzel, The Lion King), ask them to tell, or dramatize the story using as many Spanish words as possible.

Focus on the Language 15-16

INSTRUCTIONS Use these exercises to master more Spanish grammar patterns.

In this activity you will:

→ Master object pronouns with finite and infinite verbs.

Focus 15

Object pronouns with finite verbs. Note how the object pronoun comes before the finite verb.

English	Spanish
He sees the duchess.	*Él ve a la duquesa.*
Yes, he sees her.	*Sí, él la ve.* (NOT *El ve la.*)
He sees the duke.	*Él ve al duque.*
Yes, he sees him.	*Sí, él lo ve.* (NOT *El ve lo.*)

Observe Closely

English	Spanish
Does Juan know the duchess?	*¿Juan conoce a la duquesa?*
Yes, he knows her.	*Sí, la conoce.*
And does he know the duke too?	*¿Y conoce al duque también?*
Yes, he knows him.	*Sí lo conoce.*
He knows the plan, doesn't he?	*El sabe el plan, ¿no?*
Yes, he knows it well.	*Sí, lo sabe bien.*

Translate Orally Into Spanish

1. Roberta knows Roberto.
2. Roberto knows Ana.
3. He knows the princess.
4. Roberto knows her.
5. Alberta knows him.

Facts and Figures on Panama

- The country's full name is the Republic of Panama.
- Panama's official language is Spanish, but about 14% of the population speaks English natively. Many more speak English as a second language, and indigenous languages are also spoken.
- Panama's population hovers around 2.8 million and is growing by 1.3% annually.
- Panama City is Panama's capital.
- Omelets and tortillas are popular national foods in Panama.
- Baseball is Panama's most popular sport. Other favorites include boxing, baseball, and soccer.
- The Panama Canal runs through *Lago Gatún*.
- Panama's government is a constitutional republic.
- Panama's federal government consists of a president, two vice presidents, and a unicameral legislature.

6. She knows the prince.

7. Who knows María?

8. Who does María know?

9. Who knows whom?

10. Who knows him?

11. He doesn't know her.

12. Do they know Roberto and Alberto?

13. Yes, (they) know them.

Focus 16

Object pronouns with infinitive verbs. Note how the object pronoun comes after the infinitive verb.

English	Spanish
He hopes to see the duchess.	Él espera ver a la duquesa.
Yes, he hopes to see her.	Sí, él espera verla. (NOT *El espera la ver.)
He desires to see the duke.	Él desea ver al duque.
Yes, he desires to see him.	Sí, él desea verlo. (NOT *El desea lo ver.)

Observe Closely

INSTRUCTIONS   Examine these sentence structures closely.

English	Spanish
Does Juan expect to know the plan?	¿Juan espera saber el plan?
Yes, he expects to know it.	Sí, él espera saberlo.
Does he want to sing the song?	¿Él quiere cantar la canción?
Yes, he wants to sing it.	Sí, él quiere cantarla.

Further Observation

INSTRUCTIONS   Examine these sentence structures closely

English	Spanish
She speaks Chinese.	Ella habla chino.
She speaks it.	Ella lo habla.
She wants to speak it.	Ella quiere hablarlo.

English (cont.)	Spanish
She speaks Chinese and Spanish.	*Ella habla chino y español.*
She speaks them.	*Ella los habla.*
She wants to speak them.	*Ella quiere hablarlos.*
He doesn't speak Chinese.	*Él no habla chino.*
He doesn't speak it.	*Él no lo habla.*

Translate Orally From Spanish

1. *¿Qué es lo que él toma?*
2. *Él toma jugo.*
3. *Lo toma mucho.*
4. *Le gusta tomarlo.*
5. *Ellos cantan un canto fúnebre.*
6. *Lo cantan más o menos bien.*
7. *¿Qué es lo que él toma?*

Performance Test

INSTRUCTIONS Translate orally into Spanish. Don't be overly concerned with your pronunciation. Mark anything that you want to come back later to review.

1. Which one (of them) speaks Chinese?
2. Only the princess speaks it.
3. Speaks it in the church.
4. She knows many Chinese.
5. Knows them well.
6. Talks with them there.
7. Who knows?
8. Who knows it?
9. Who knows the duke?
10. Who knows the king?
11. Who knows them? (Ana and María)
12. Who knows them? (Juan and José)
13. Who knew many things?
14. Who used to speak with her?
15. The princess used to cry a lot.
16. Did the prince used to cry with her?
17. (They) used to sing and cry.
18. (They) didn't used to attend church.

19. (They) didn't know the prince.
20. Nor (did they know) the king.
21. Robert likes the princess.
22. And she doesn't like him.

Performance Challenge

Individual   After carefully studying each grammar focus, use the grammar principles you learned in making sentences of your own. Write at least three sentences for each focus.

Performance Challenge

Group   Have the students find the lyrics to their favorite song. Then have them translate as many of the lyrics into Spanish as possible. Ask for volunteers to perform their songs for the class.

The Farmer and the Turnip

INSTRUCTIONS Listen to and read this story. Use it to increase vocabulary and comprehension. By studying this story, you will build fluency with using the past tense and you will learn the names for different animals.

A Folktale From Russia

✔ **In this activity you will:**
→ Build fluency through repetition.

◎ Disc **1**   Track **6**

English	Spanish
Once upon a time there was a farmer,	*Había una vez un campesino,*
and the farmer planted some seeds,	*y el campesino plantó unas semillas,*
and he watered them,	*y les echó agua,*
and the sun shone.	*y brilló el sol.*
And after a time, a tiny plant grew out.	*Y después de un tiempo, creció una plantita.*
And he watered it,	*Y le echó agua,*
and the sun shone,	*y brilló el sol,*
and the little plant grew.	*y la plantita creció.*
And he watered it,	*Y le echó agua,*
and the sun shone,	*y brilló el sol,*
and the little plant grew even more.	*y la plantita creció aún más.*
And he watered it,	*Y le echó agua,*
and the sun shone,	*y brilló el sol,*
and the little plant grew and grew.	*y la plantita creció y creció.*
And finally, one day the farmer said:	*Y por fin, un día el campesino dijo:*
The plant is ripe.	*La planta está madura.*

Geography of Panama

Panama occupies the isthmus that links Central America to South America. Panama borders the Caribbean Sea to the north, Colombia to the west, the Pacific Ocean to the south, and Costa Rica to the east. Much of the country is covered in rainforests, and two mountain ranges run down its length. Some of these peaks are volcanic, with *Volcán Barú* being the highest at 11,400 feet. Panama has an amazing variety of flora and fauna, as well as large tracts of land set aside for their preservation. Panama has two seasons, a dry season which lasts from January to mid-April and a rainy season that stretches from mid-April to December. Rainfall is heavier on the Caribbean side, but most people live on the Pacific side of the country. Temperatures are generally hot in the coastal lowlands (between 70°F and 90°F) and cooler in the highlands (between 50°F and 64°F).

English *(cont.)*	Spanish
So the farmer took hold of the plant,	*Entonces el campesino tomó la planta,*
and tugged and tugged and tugged,	*y estiró y estiró y estiró,*
but the plant didn't come out.	*pero la planta no salió.*
So the farmer called his wife:	*Entonces el campesino llamó a su esposa:*
"Wife, come here, wife."	*"Esposa, ven aquí, esposa."*
And so the wife came and took hold of the farmer,	*Y entonces la esposa vino y tomó al campesino,*
and the farmer grabbed the plant,	*y el campesino agarró la planta,*
and they tugged, and they tugged, and they tugged,	*y estiraron, y estiraron, y estiraron,*
but the plant didn't come out.	*pero la planta no salió.*
So the farmer called his daughter:	*Entonces el campesino llamó a su hija:*
"Daughter, come here, daughter."	*"Hija, ven aquí, hija."*
And so the daughter came and took hold of the wife.	*Y entonces vino la hija y tomó a la esposa.*
And the wife grabbed on to the farmer,	*Y la esposa agarró al campesino,*
and the farmer grabbed the plant,	*y el campesino agarró la planta,*
and they tugged and tugged and tugged,	*y estiraron, y estiraron, y estiraron,*
but the plant didn't come out.	*pero la planta no salió.*
So they called the dog: "Dog, come here, dog."	*Entonces llamaron al perro: "Perro, ven aquí, perro."*
So the dog came,	*Entonces vino el perro,*
and the dog grabbed on to the daughter,	*y el perro agarró a la hija,*
and the daughter grabbed on to the wife,	*y la hija agarró a la esposa,*
and the wife grabbed on to the farmer,	*y la esposa agarró al campesino,*
and the farmer grabbed the plant,	*y el campesino agarró la planta,*
and they tugged, and they tugged, and they tugged,	*y estiraron, y estiraron, y estiraron,*
but the plant didn't come out.	*pero la planta no salió.*

English (cont.)	Spanish
So the farmer called the cat: "Cat, kitty-kitty, come here, cat."	Entonces el campesino llamó al gato: "Gato, miau-miau-miau, ven aquí, gato."
So the cat came, and the cat grabbed on to the dog,	Entonces vino el gato, y el gato agarró al perro,
and the dog grabbed on to the daughter,	y el perro agarró a la hija,
and the daughter grabbed on to the wife,	y la hija agarró a la esposa,
and the wife grabbed on to the farmer,	y la esposa agarró al campesino,
and the farmer grabbed the plant,	y el campesino agarró la planta,
and they tugged, and they tugged, and they tugged,	y estiraron, y estiraron, y estiraron,
but the plant didn't come out.	pero la planta no salió.
Then, at that moment, a little mouse came by.	Entonces, en ese momento, pasó un ratoncito.
And the mouse said: "What goes on here?"	Y el ratoncito dijo: ¿Qué pasa aquí?
And the farmer explained that they	Y el campesino explicó que
were not able to get the plant out.	no podían sacar la planta.
Then the mouse said: "I can help."	Entonces el ratoncito dijo: "Yo puedo ayudar."
And they all laughed at him: "Ha-ha-ha-ha.	Y todos se rieron de él: "Ja-ja-ja-ja.
You, so small, how are you going to help?"	Tú, tan pequeño, ¿cómo vas a ayudar?"
But the mouse convinced them.	Pero el ratoncito les convenció.
And so the mouse grabbed on to the cat,	Y entonces el ratoncito agarró al gato,
and the cat grabbed on to the dog,	y el gato agarró al perro,
and the dog grabbed on to the daughter,	y el perro agarró a la hija,
and the daughter grabbed on to the wife,	y la hija agarró a la esposa,

English (cont.)	Spanish
and the wife grabbed on to the farmer,	*y la esposa agarró al campesino,*
and the farmer grabbed the plant,	*y el campesino agarró la planta,*
and they tugged and tugged and tugged,	*y estiraron, y estiraron, y estiraron,*
and the plant came out.	*y la planta salió.*

This activity taught several family- and animal-related vocabulary words. It also showed you some great examples of how to use simple imperative and past tense verbs.

Performance Challenge

Individual   Read through the story again and write down all the characters that appear in the story. Use at least four of them to write a short story of your own. Ask a parent, teacher, or classmate if you have difficulty coming up with an idea for your story. Rough out some ideas below.

....

....

....

....

....

....

....

....

....

....

....

....

Performance Challenge

Group   Have the students choose three of their favorite plants (vegetables, flowers, trees) and create seed packets for each. Include a drawing of the plant, how to care for it, and what the typical growing behavior of the plant is, in Spanish.

ACTIVITY 7 • A SPANISH LESSON

A Spanish Lesson

7

INSTRUCTIONS   Listen to and learn these sentences. In this lesson, you will work with the past and present tenses. You will also work with instructions: insert, extract, pick up, and lay down.

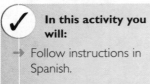

In this activity you will:

→ Follow instructions in Spanish.

Disc **I**   Track **7**

English	Spanish
How do you say "bag" in Spanish?	*¿Cómo se dice "bag" en español?*
Is it "*caja*" or "*bolsa*"?	*¿Es "caja" o "bolsa"?*
It's "*bolsa.*"	*Es "bolsa."*
How do you say "*caja*" in English?	*¿Cómo se dice "caja" en inglés?*
In English it's "box."	*En inglés se dice "box."*
How do you say "pencil" in Spanish?	*¿Cómo se dice "pencil" en español?*
Is it "*lapicero*" or "*lápiz*"?	*¿Es "lapicero" o "lápiz"?*
"*Lápiz.*"	*"Lápiz."*
What does "*lapicero*" mean?	*¿Qué quiere decir "lapicero"?*
"*Lapicero*" means "pen" (ballpoint pen).	*"Lapicero" quiere decir "pen."*
A block of wood. Another block.	*Un trozo de madera. Otro trozo.*
On the table there are various blocks of wood.	*En la mesa hay varios trozos de madera.*
Here, for example, is one block.	*Aquí, por ejemplo, hay un trozo.*
It is standing on the table.	*Está parado sobre la mesa.*
Here is another block of wood.	*Aquí hay otro trozo de madera.*
Now, please pay attention.	*Ahora, ponga atención, por favor.*
Watch. Observe what I do.	*Mire. Observe lo que hago.*
I take this block and lay it down.	*Tomo este trozo y lo acuesto.*
I lay it on the table.	*Lo acuesto sobre la mesa.*
What did I do?	*¿Qué hice?*

English (cont.)	Spanish
I took the block and laid it down.	Tomé el trozo y lo acosté.
I laid it on the table.	Lo acosté sobre la mesa.
Here it is, laid out on the table.	Aquí está, acostado sobre la mesa.
The two blocks are on the table.	Los dos trozos están en la mesa.
The one is standing and the other is lying.	El uno está parado y el otro está acostado.
Put down. Insert (place inside).	Poner. Meter.
Pick up. Extract (remove from inside).	Tomar. Sacar.
Here we have a book, a bag, and a box.	Aquí tenemos un libro, una bolsa, y una caja.
Again, please pay attention.	Otra vez, ponga atención, por favor.
Observe what I do.	Observe lo que hago.
I take one piece of wood, a red one,	Tomo un trozo de madera, un rojo,
and I place it on the book.	y lo pongo sobre el libro.
I again take another piece of wood, a black piece.	Otra vez tomo un trozo de madera, un trozo negro.
I put it in this box.	Lo pongo en esta caja.
Better said, I stand it in the box.	Mejor dicho, lo paro en la caja.
Lastly, I take a white piece and put it inside this bag.	Al fin, tomo un trozo blanco y lo meto en la bolsa, en esta bolsa.
You should remember the position of each of the pieces.	Se debe recordar la posición de cada uno de los trozos.
Remember, the red one is lying on the book,	Recuerda, el rojo está acostado sobre el libro,
the black one is standing in the box,	el negro está parado en la caja,
and the white one is in the bag.	y el blanco está en la bolsa.
Do you have a book?	¿Tiene Ud. un libro?
Show me. Fine.	Enséñeme. Bien.
Now take the book and stand it up.	Ahora, tome el libro y párelo.
Stand it up on the table.	Párelo sobre la mesa.
Yes, stand it there.	Sí, párelo allí.
Right.	Correcto.

The Panama Canal

Panama's most famous landmark is 80 kilometers (about 50 miles) long and effectively chops the small nation into eastern and western parts. The idea of building a canal was first proposed during the Spanish colonialism of the 16th century, but the first to attempt it were the French in 1880. This failed attempt resulted in bankruptcy for all its financiers and in the death of some 22,000 workers from yellow fever and malaria. The United States bought the rights to build the canal from a Frenchman, despite vigorous objections from the Colombian government (Panama at that time was part of Colombia). On November 3, 1903, Panama declared its independence, with overt support from the USA. In 1904, the United States began construction on the canal. It was an effort unprecedented in American history to that point. Approximately $352,000,000 went into the construction of this engineering marvel between its beginning in 1904 and its completion in 1914. Between this effort and the earlier French effort, more than 80,000 people took part in building the canal. The canal continues to be a major thoroughfare for seagoing vessels, accommodating over 12,000 vessels each year.

English (cont.)	Spanish
What did you do?	¿Qué hizo?
You took your book and stood it on the table.	Usted tomó su libro y lo paró en la mesa.
Now take your book again	Ahora tome el libro otra vez
and lay it on the chair.	y acuéstelo sobre la silla.
Right, take it and lay it there.	Correcto, tómelo y acuéstelo allí.
Exactly. Very good.	Exactamente. Muy bien.
What did you do?	¿Qué hizo?
You first took the book and stood it on the table.	Primero usted tomó el libro y lo paró en la mesa.
Then you laid it on the chair.	Después lo acostó sobre la silla.

Performance Challenge

Individual   This activity presented some classroom vocabulary as well as simple descriptions of actions. Using this activity as a model, describe the things that are on your desk and different ways you can move and arrange them.

Performance Challenge

Group   Set up a pen pal program for your students. Try to find students the same age as yours. Ask each student to include a description about a typical day at school in the first letter, and to ask at least five questions about the recipient's school and what a typical day there might be like.

Focus on a Scene

ACTIVITY 8

✓ **In this activity you will:**

→ Identify objects from a description.

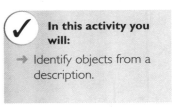

Disc **1**   Track **8**

INSTRUCTIONS   Try to understand the following descriptions. Match the words with items in the picture. Translate the description into English. Check your answers in Appendix A, on page 331.

◀))

Description

En este diseño hay varias cosas. En el centro del diseño hay una maleta. Y a un lado de la maleta vemos a dos adultos, un hombre, y una mujer. Al otro lado hay dos infantes. A la izquierda, en uno de los extremos del diseño, hay dos casas. A la derecha en el otro extremo, hay cuatro edificios grandes. Tal vez es un centro de una ciudad. Arriba hay un reloj. El reloj indica 9:05. Abajo hay una calle, y encima de la calle hay un carro y un chofer. Delante del carro hay un semáforo.

◀▶

Your Translation

....

ACTIVITY 8

....
....
....
....
....
....
....
....
....
....
....
....
....
....
....
....
....
....

Performance Challenge

Individual   This activity described a picture. Look around your house or classroom for a picture you can describe. Then describe it, using as much Spanish and as many details as you can.

Performance Challenge

Group   Split the group into pairs. Put each player back-to-back. Give one player paper and pens and give the other a picture. The one with the picture must describe what they see in Spanish so the other can draw it. Give a time limit. Have the group vote on the closest match.

You have completed all the activities for

**Section 1.1.1
Day One, 00:30 Hours**

and are now ready to take the section quiz. Before continuing, be sure you have learned the objectives for each activity in this section.

Section Quiz

INSTRUCTIONS   Select the most correct answer for the following questions. Check your answers in Appendix D, on page 346.

1. **¿Dónde viven los tiburones?**

   A. *En el océano.*

   B. *En una casa.*

   C. *En la calle.*

   D. *En el cielo.*

2. **¿Cuántos dientes tienen un tiburón?**

   A. *Uno.*

   B. *Ninguno.*

   C. *Un tiburón tiene muchos dientes.*

   D. *Más de un millón.*

3. **¿A quién busca la gente?**

   A. *Busca una torta.*

   B. *Busca al niño del cuento.*

   C. *Busca al jefe.*

   D. *Busca el caballo.*

4. **¿Qué estudia Vicente?**

   A. *La música.*

   B. *La geología.*

   C. *El atletismo.*

   D. *La biología.*

5. **¿Está casada o soltera la muchacha?**

   A. Está soltera.

   B. Está casada.

6. **¿Quién habla chino?**

   A. El niño.

   B. El sirviente.

   C. El rey.

   D. Sólo la princesa.

7. **¿Dónde habla chino?**

   A. En el castillo.

   B. En la iglesia.

   C. En la casa.

   D. En el dormitorio.

8. **¿Conoce la princesa a la reina de Canton?**

   A. No, no la conoce.

   B. Sí y a toda la familia real.

9. **¿Quién le ayuda al campesino primero?**

   A. El vecino.

   B. El padre.

   C. La esposa.

   D. La hija.

10. **¿Cuántas persona hay en el cuento?**

    A. Hay cinco personas.

    B. Hay dos personas y tres animales.

    C. Hay cuatro personas.

    D. Hay tres personas y tres animales.

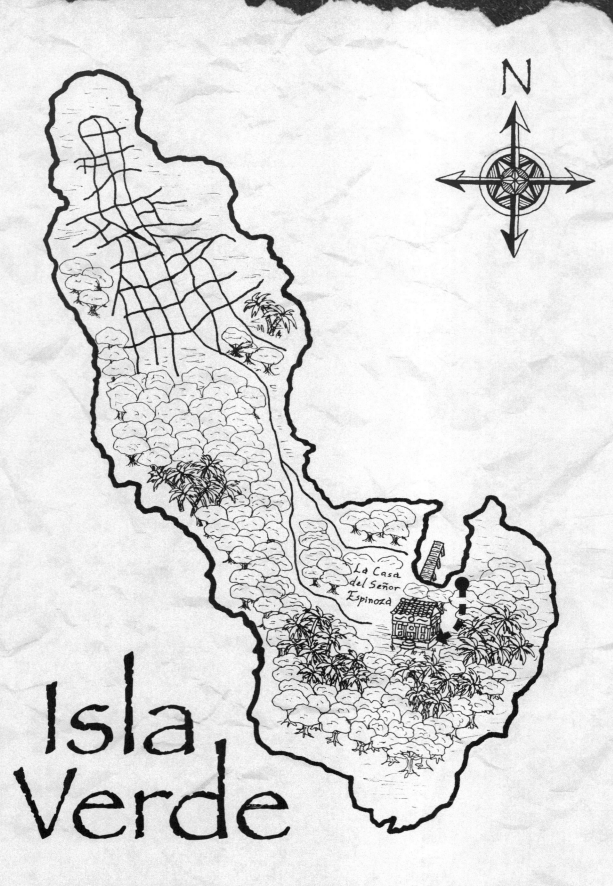

Day One, 12:30 Hours

La primera pista

Time in the tiny seaside cabin passes quickly, with rain lashing at the roof and winds shaking the thin walls. Eventually, though, the storm passes, and the rain stops. You put away your Spanish activities, get to your feet, and peer out the cabin's only glass window. It looks inward, on the island. Now that the rain has stopped, you can see a large, whitewashed *casa* through the thick trees. "We can probably get directions there," you say, pointing it out to Agent *Araña*.

"*¡Qué buena idea!*" he replies, gathering his things and opening the door.

You don't see any roads leading from the beach to the whitewashed house, but you do find a recently trampled path through the thick undergrowth. Following this path, you come to the low wall surrounding *la casa blanca*. You push through the thick vegetation to reach the front gate and ring the old-fashioned bell.

A slender, distraught-looking older man opens the front door of the house and cautiously peers outside. "Hello!" you call to him. "*¿Es usted Raúl Álvarez?*" He nods and cautiously ventures out of the doorway. "We got your message," you continue. "We've come to help."

Hearing these words, Raul hurries down the path to meet you. "*¡Bienvenidos!*" he exclaims. "*¡Muchas gracias por haber venido!*"

Raul leads you into the house. It's in disarray. Shelves are emptied, pictures torn from walls, tables and chairs overturned. Every drawer in sight has been opened, and its contents scattered. The back door has been smashed in, and the door to the kitchen's walk-in pantry is also torn off its hinges.

Whoever took *el famoso* Julio Roberto Espinoza was obviously looking for something—and didn't find it. Quietly, Raul explains what happened. Last night, he was cleaning up after dinner when, without warning, a group of people with their faces hidden broke in through the back door, forced him into the pantry, and locked him there. He heard crashes and sounds of a fight. One of the kidnappers kept asking "*¿Dónde está el diario?*" and *Señor* Espinoza kept answering, "*¡Nunca te diré!*"

In this section you will:

→ Understand the story of "The Three Bears" in Spanish.
→ Describe objects of different sizes and shapes.
→ Expand grammar skills.
→ Understand new vocabulary in a conversation or story.
→ Understand enough vocabulary to comprehend a lesson about geography and geometry.
→ Understand pronoun and verb use.
→ Identify and describe objects.
→ Recognize how much Spanish you can comprehend, say, read, and write.
→ Learn Spanish action verbs.
→ Use small talk phrases.

 Disc 1   Track 9

After a time, the noises faded, and Raul redoubled his efforts to escape. Eventually, he broke the door off its hinges (thankfully, neither door nor hinges were very sturdy) and escaped to find his master gone and the house in ruin.

You ask him if he found anything unusual in the house—anything the kidnappers or *Señor* Espinoza might have left behind. Raul hesitates, thinking, then nods. He leads the way up a broad flight of stairs to a small room that looks like a study. On a large desk facing the window, *la ventana*, is a computer and a pile of notebooks. Scribbled on the cover of one notebook are the words *preguntas de un niño*—questions of a child. Raul explains that he isn't sure what this is referring to. The notebook contains research notes for *Señor* Espinoza's latest short story collection—it has no questions from any child.

The Spanish words ring a bell, though—you remember seeing them in the Spanish activities your boss sent you. You check the table of contents. Sure enough, it's one of the activities you haven't done yet. Coincidence? You think not. Hoping that the activity will provide some hints for the author's mysterious clue, you catch Agent *Araña*'s attention and nod significantly at Raul. *Araña* catches the hint.

He thanks Raul for his help and asks him to go try again to contact any local authorities who might visit this small island. Then you and *Araña* pull out your study materials and get to work.

Story Time: The Story of the Three Bears

INSTRUCTIONS Listen to and learn this familiar story in Spanish. In this story you will learn how to use words to describe different sizes of objects and things.

In this activity you will:
→ Understand the story of "The Three Bears" in Spanish.
→ Describe objects of different sizes and shapes.

 Disc **1** Track **10**

English	Spanish
A family of bears.	*Una familia de osos.*
A big bear. The daddy.	*Un oso grande. El papá.*
A middle-sized bear. The mama.	*Un oso mediano. La mamá.*
A tiny bear. The little son.	*Un oso chiquito. El hijito.*
The morning.	*La mañana.*
The mama prepares breakfast.	*La mamá prepara el desayuno.*
Puts it on the table.	*Lo pone en la mesa.*
Calls: Daddy Bear, Little Bear.	*Llama: Papá Oso, Osito.*
Come and eat.	*Vengan a comer.*
The food is very hot.	*La comida está muy caliente.*
Too hot.	*Demasiado caliente.*
The Bear family goes out.	*La familia de osos sale de la casa.*
They walk in the woods.	*Caminan en el bosque.*
A little girl walks through the woods.	*Una niñita anda por el bosque.*
She sees a house.	*Ve una casita.*
It's the house of the bears.	*Es la casa de los osos.*
She knocks at the door.	*Golpea la puerta.*

English *(cont.)*	Spanish
There is no one home.	*No hay nadie en la casa.*
So she enters.	*Entonces entra.*
She sees three plates of food.	*Ve tres platos de comida.*
She is hungry.	*Tiene hambre.*
She tries papa bear's plate.	*Prueba el plato del papá oso.*
It's a big plate, right?	*Es un plato grande, ¿verdad?*
Ahh! The food is too hot.	*¡Ay! La comida está demasiado caliente.*
She tries mama bear's plate.	*Prueba el plato de la mamá osa.*
It's a middle-sized plate, right?	*Es un plato mediano, ¿verdad?*
Ahh! It's too cold.	*¡Ay! Está demasiado fría.*
She tries baby bear's plate.	*Prueba el plato del osito chiquito.*
It's a little plate, right?	*Es un plato chiquito, ¿verdad?*
Hmm. Perfect.	*Mmm. Perfecto.*
She eats all the food.	*Se come toda la comida.*
She sees three chairs.	*Ve tres sillas.*
She sits in papa's chair.	*Se sienta en la silla del papá.*
It's big, right?	*Es grande, ¿verdad?*
Ahh! It's too hard.	*¡Ay! Es demasiado dura.*
She sits in mama's chair.	*Se sienta en la silla de la mamá.*
It's too soft.	*Es demasiado suave.*
She sits in baby's chair.	*Se sienta en la silla del osito chiquito.*
It's a tiny chair, right?	*Es una silla chiquita, ¿verdad?*
Hmm. Perfect.	*Mmm. Perfecto.*
But the chair breaks.	*Pero la silla se rompe.*
She goes to the bedroom.	*Ella va al dormitorio.*
She sees three beds.	*Ve tres camas.*
She lies down on papa's bed.	*Se acuesta en la cama del papá.*
It's too hard.	*Es demasiado dura.*
She lies down on mama's bed.	*Se acuesta en la cama de la mamá.*
Too soft.	*Demasiado suave.*

English (cont.)	Spanish
She lies on baby's bed.	Se acuesta en la cama del nene.
Hmm. Perfect.	Mmm. Perfecto.
And she falls asleep.	Y se duerme.
Now the bears return home.	Los osos ya vuelven a su casa.
The daddy looks at his plate.	El papá mira su plato.
He says: Someone has tasted my food.	Dice: Alguien ha probado mi comida.
The mama looks at her plate and says:	La mamá mira el plato suyo y dice:
Someone has tasted my food, too.	Alguien ha probado mi comida también.
The baby looks at his plate:	El osito mira el plato suyo:
Someone has tasted my food, too.	Alguien ha probado mi comida también.
And ate it all.	Y se la comió toda.
The little bear cries.	El osito llora.
The bears see the chairs.	Los osos ven las sillas.
Papa looks at his chair and says:	El papá mira su silla y dice:
Someone has sat in my chair.	Alguien se ha sentado en mi silla.
Mama looks at her chair and says:	La mamá mira la silla suya y dice:
Someone has sat in my chair, too.	Alguien se ha sentado en mi silla también.
The baby looks at his chair and says:	El osito mira la silla suya y dice:
And someone has sat in my chair, too,	Y alguien se ha sentado en mi silla también,
and has broken it.	y la ha roto.
The little bear cries.	El osito llora.
The bears go to the bedroom.	Los osos van al dormitorio.
The daddy looks at his bed and says:	El papá mira su cama y dice:
Someone has lain on my bed.	Alguien se ha acostado en mi cama.
The mama looks at her bed and says:	La mamá mira su cama y dice:
Someone has lain on my bed too.	Alguien se ha acostado en mi cama también.
The baby looks at his bed and says:	El osito mira su cama y dice:
And someone lay on my bed too.	Y alguien se ha acostado en mi cama también.

English *(cont.)*	Spanish
And is still there.	*Y todavía está allí.*
The little girl wakes up.	*La niñita se despierta.*
She sees the bears.	*Ve a los osos.*
She is extremely frightened, and she screams.	*Está sumamente asustada y grita.*
She jumps from the bed and runs out.	*Brinca de la cama y sale corriendo.*
And she never returns to the woods.	*Y nunca vuelve al bosque.*

Performance Challenge

Individual   This activity presented a familiar story in simple Spanish. Choose your own favorite story and try to tell it, using as much Spanish vocabulary as you can.

Performance Challenge

Group   Have students write a two act play where the first act is the story of the three bears and the second act is a new, additional story using the same characters. Have them perform it in Spanish for each other, other students, or family and friends.

Chatter at a Royal Ball

INSTRUCTIONS Use this conversation to learn more vocabulary and review sentence patterns.

Resumen

✓ **In this activity you will:**
→ Expand grammar skills.

 Disc 1 Track 11

English	Spanish
In the royal family not everyone speaks Chinese.	*En la familia real no todos hablan chino.*
In fact, only the princess speaks it.	*De hecho, sólo la princesa lo habla.*
And she speaks it only at church.	*Y ella lo habla solamente en la iglesia.*
(The prince doesn't speak it, but he understands it a bit.)	*(El príncipe no lo habla, pero lo entiende un poco.)*
Of course the Chinese speak Chinese, including those that attend church, but they're not of the royal family.	*Claro que los Chinos hablan chino, incluso los que asisten a la iglesia, pero ellos no son de la familia real.*
In reality, not all Chinese speak Chinese.	*En realidad, no todos los Chinos hablan chino.*
Those that attend church with the princess do speak it, but they speak it with a Castilian accent.	*Los que asisten a la iglesia con la princesa sí lo hablan, pero lo hablan con el acento castellano.*
In the castle where they live, they always speak in Spanish.	*En el castillo donde viven, siempre hablan en español.*
They don't like to speak Chinese there.	*No les gusta hablar en chino allá.*
It's that the king doesn't like Chinese.	*Es que al rey no le gusta el chino.*
Nor does the queen.	*A la reina tampoco.*

Panama City

Panama's capital city is a thriving, modern metropolis of 700,000 people which stretches along the Pacific coast from the ruins of *Panamá Viejo* to the Panama Canal. Any visit to the city should include an excursion to *San Felipe*, the old district whose colonial architecture remains a grand sight to see. Other excellent spots to visit include the presidential palace, the *Plaza de Bolívar*, the 17th century Metropolitan Church, and the History Museum of Panama. The ruins of *Panamá Viejo* make a fine day trip for those interested in history, and those with an interest in nature can investigate the Summit Botanical Gardens and Zoo, the rainforests in *Parque Nacional Sobrerania*, and the sizable *Parque Nacional Metropolitana*.

English (cont.)	Spanish
He doesn't understand it.	*Él no lo entiende.*
Nor does the queen.	*La reina tampoco.*

Performance Challenge

Individual Go back to the previous chatter activity (Activity 4) and write a summary of it, using as much Spanish as you can.

....

....

....

....

....

....

....

....

....

....

....

....

....

Performance Challenge

Group Assign a student to be the "Guesser." Assign another student to be the King/Queen. Have the Guesser deduct who the King/Queen is by asking questions in Spanish. Take turns until each student has had a chance to be either the Guesser or the King/Queen.

Chatter at a Royal Ball

Getting Ready for *Conversación*

INSTRUCTIONS Use this conversation to learn more vocabulary and review sentence patterns.

English	Spanish
to eat	*comer*
to drink	*beber*
to cover	*cubrir*
fat / stout	*gordo/a*
to get fat	*engordar*
unfortunately	*desgraciadamente*
principally	*principalmente*
How disgusting!	*¡Que disgusto!*
butter covered with chocolate	*mantequilla cubierta de chocolate*
If I'm not mistaken.	*Si no me equivoco.*
of course	*desde luego*
to be mistaken	*equivocarse*
butter	*mantequilla*
everyone	*todo el mundo*
each day	*cada día*
at least	*por lo menos*
very often	*muy a menudo*

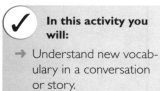

In this activity you will:
→ Understand new vocabulary in a conversation or story.

Disc **I**   Track **12**

Conversación 12

	English	Spanish
•:	Who's that fat little lady there talking with?	¿Con quién está hablando la gordita esa?
••:	With her cats…and with her son, the fat duke.	Con sus gatos…y con su hijo, el duque gordo.
•:	What are they drinking?	¿Qué están bebiendo?
••:	What they're drinking is cream, if I'm not mistaken.	Lo que están bebiendo es crema, si no me equivoco.
•:	Cream? Cream from milk? Well then, of course they're fat.	¿Crema? ¿Crema de leche? Pues desde luego que son gordos.
••:	What is the duke eating?	¿Qué es lo que está comiendo el duque?
•:	Butter…covered with chocolate.	Mantequilla…cubierta de chocolate.
••:	How disgusting!	¡Qué disgusto!
•:	He eats at least a kilogram of butter and chocolate every day.	Come por lo menos un kilo de mantequilla y chocolate cada día.
••:	Really?	¿Sí?
•:	Unfortunately, it's the truth. Everybody knows it.	Desgraciadamente, es la verdad. Todo el mundo lo sabe.
••:	My goodness!	¡Ay caray!

Review: A Servant Answers Her Small Child's Questions

INSTRUCTIONS   Orally translate these sentences.

1. Mama, why is the duke so fat?
2. It's because he eats and drinks so much.
3. What is it he eats?
4. Butter and chocolate, principally.
5. And what is it he drinks?
6. Cream. Nothing but cream.
7. Do you eat butter, Mama?
8. Not much. I eat very little butter. Almost never.
9. Do you drink cream?

10. No, I don't drink cream. Never.

★ **Performance Challenge**

Individual   This activity presented you with several useful new verbs and phrases. Choose at least five of these new verbs and phrases, study how they are used in the conversation, then use them in sentences of your own.

....

....

....

....

....

....

....

....

....

....

....

....

....

....

★ **Performance Challenge**

Group   Bring Mexican chocolate to class. Make hot chocolate and share the treat with the students. Teach them about Mexican chocolate, how it differs from the chocolate found in the United States, and how it is used in cooking.

A Geography Lesson

In this activity you will:

→ Understand enough vocabulary to comprehend a lesson about geography.

  Disc **1**   Track **13**

INSTRUCTIONS   Listen to and read the following lesson. You will learn African and South American geography.

English	Spanish
This continent here is Africa.	*Este continente de aquí es África.*
Africa is very large, but it doesn't measure even half as large as Eurasia.	*África es muy grande, pero no mide ni la mitad de Eurasia.*
In the northern part of Africa is Egypt.	*En la parte norte de Africa se encuentra Egipto.*
Through Egypt flows a great river called the Nile.	*Por Egipto pasa un gran río llamado el Nilo.*
The great Egyptian civilization developed here over 6,000 years ago.	*La gran civilización egipcia se desarrolló aquí hace más de 6,000 años.*
Here you see another great continent.	*Aquí puede verse otro continente.*
This is South America.	*Ésta es Sudamérica.*
Here is found another great river.	*Aquí se encuentra otro gran río.*
It is the largest river in the world.	*Es el río más grande del mundo.*
It is called the Amazon River.	*Se llama el Río Amazonas.*
It flows east through Brazil.	*Corre hacia el este a través de Brasil.*
Brazil is a very large country.	*Brasil es un país muy grande.*
It's the largest nation in South America.	*Es el país más grande de Sudamérica.*
It is as large as the continental U.S.	*Es tan grande como Los Estados Unidos.*
It is almost as large as China.	*Es casi tan grande como China.*
But its population is relatively small.	*Pero su población es relativamente pequeña.*

English (cont.)	Spanish
Most of Brazil is covered with forest, and in the forest live a great variety of animals.	*La mayor parte de Brasil está cubierta por selva, y en la selva vive una gran variedad de animales.*
There are many snakes and reptiles.	*Hay muchas culebras y reptiles.*
Not many people live in the forest.	*No mucha gente vive en la selva.*
The large cities of Brazil are on the coast.	*Las ciudades más grandes de Brasil están en la costa.*
This is São Paulo, Brazil's largest city and one of the largest cities in the world.	*Éste es San Pablo, la ciudad más grande del Brasil y una de las más grandes del mundo.*
And here is Rio de Janeiro, one of the most beautiful cities in the world.	*Y aquí está Río de Janeiro, una de las ciudades más bellas del mundo.*
In the western part of South America is found a great mountain chain.	*En la parte oeste de Sudamérica encontramos una gran cadena de montañas.*
There are many peaks above 5,000 meters.	*Tienen muchos picos sobre los 5.000 metros.*
In ancient times a civilization developed in this area: the Inca Civilization.	*En la antigüedad se desarrolló una civilización en esta área: la civilización incaica.*

Performance Challenge

Individual   This lesson presented you with a variety of useful geography-related words. Using as many of these words as you can, describe your state or province, or choose another location to describe. Share your description with a parent, teacher, or friend.

Performance Challenge

Group 1   Lay butcher paper out on the floor. Have students draw and label a large map with as many features as they can in Spanish. Hang the map on the wall and have each student talk about all the places in the world they have visited, in Spanish. Mark the places with a stickers.

Performance Challenge

Group 2   Play geography bingo in Spanish. For each space on a card, have students answer questions, completely in Spanish, about geography of the world.

A Geometry Lesson

INSTRUCTIONS   Listen to this lesson and learn its vocabulary.

English	Spanish
Answer this question.	*Contesta esta pregunta.*
How many corners does a square have?	*¿Cuántas esquinas tiene un cuadrado?*
Four. A square has four corners.	*Cuatro. Un cuadrado tiene cuatro esquinas.*
It has four sides and four corners.	*Tiene cuatro lados y cuatro esquinas.*
Look! Four sides and four corners or angles.	*Mira, cuatro lados y cuatro esquinas o ángulos.*
Answer these questions.	*Contesta estas preguntas.*
Does a circle have corners?	*¿Tiene esquinas un círculo?*
No, a circle doesn't have corners.	*No, un círculo no tiene esquinas.*
Does a circle have straight lines?	*¿Tiene líneas rectas un círculo?*
No. It doesn't have straight lines.	*No, no tiene líneas rectas.*
Crooked lines?	*¿Líneas chuecas?*
No, it doesn't have crooked lines either.	*No, tampoco tiene líneas chuecas.*
It has only one curved line.	*Tiene solo una línea curva.*
Does a square have any curved lines?	*¿Tiene líneas curvas un cuadrado?*
No it doesn't.	*No, no tiene líneas curvas.*
It has only straight lines, perpendicular lines.	*Sólo tiene líneas rectas, líneas perpendiculares.*
It has four straight lines and four right angles.	*Tiene cuatro líneas rectas y cuatro ángulos rectos.*

✓ **In this activity you will:**

→ Understand enough vocabulary to comprehend a lesson about geometry.

 Disc **1**   Track **14**

English (cont.)	Spanish
In which box are there two squares?	¿En qué caja hay dos cuadrados?
In the first or in the second?	¿En la primera o la segunda?
Does the first box contain circles or squares?	¿La primera caja contiene círculos o cuadrados?
It contains two squares.	Contiene dos cuadrados.
The second contains two circles.	La segunda contiene dos círculos.
Touch the box that contains a triangle in which there is a star.	Toca la caja que contiene un triángulo en el que hay una estrella.
Point to the box that contains a star.	Apunta a la caja que contiene una estrella.
Point to the box that contains nothing.	Apunta a la caja que no contiene nada.
There is nothing in it. It is empty.	No hay nada en ella. Está vacía.

Performance Challenge

Individual   In this lesson, different shapes were described. Choose a shape that wasn't included in this lesson and try to describe it, using as much Spanish as you can.

Performance Challenge

Group   Create cards with geometric shapes on them. Lay the shapes on the floor in a specific order. Give the students a time limit to memorize where the shapes are, then cover the cards. Have teams try to recreate the pattern of shapes. The team that gets the most correct, wins.

Questions From a Child

INSTRUCTIONS   Listen to this conversation, and learn its pronouns and verb forms.

English	Spanish
Mama, why is it that birds eat insects?	Mamá, ¿por qué es que los pájaros comen insectos?
Because they like to eat them.	Porque a ellos les gusta comerlos.
Do I eat insects?	¿Como yo insectos?
No, you don't eat insects.	No, tú no comes insectos.
You and Daddy, do you eat insects?	¿Tú y papá, comen ustedes insectos?
No, we don't eat insects.	No, nosotros no comemos insectos.
Why?	¿Por qué?
Because we are not birds.	Porque no somos pájaros.

Conjugation of the verb *comer,* "to eat"

Comer			
yo	como	nosotros	comemos
tú	comes	ustedes	comen
el / ella / Ud	come	ellos / ellas	comen

In this activity you will:

→ Understand pronoun and verb use.

Disc 1   Track 15

Sights to See in Panama

Naturally, no trip to Panama would be complete without a visit to its famous canal, but there's much more to see and do in this small nation than that. The capital city has a number of interesting sites and attractions (see separate entry).

Isla Taboga, just twelve miles south of Panama City, is home to a lovely beach, verdant protected rain forest, and one of the largest brown pelican colonies in Latin America. Settled even before the capital city, *Isla Taboga* has a small church that is said to be the second-oldest in the Western Hemisphere. Also, the famous conquistador Francisco Pizarro set sail from *Isla Taboga,* bound for Peru, in 1524.

Those wanting an alpine retreat instead would do well to investigate Boquete, a small town located in a craggy mountain valley not far from *Volcán Barú.* Known for its refreshing climate and pristine environment, Boquete is the place to go for outdoor activities such as walking, horseback riding, and birdwatching.

Performance Challenge

Individual   This brief conversation presents a series of simple yes / no questions. Using this conversation as a model, write at least five yes / no questions of your own in Spanish.

1. ....
....

2. ....
....

3. ....
....

4. ....
....

5. ....
....

Performance Challenge

Group   Choose a variety of Power-Glide Flash Cards and place them in a hat. Create teams and have them play twenty questions using the Spanish words from the hat.

Focus on a Scene

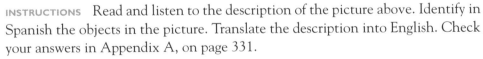

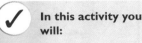

✓ In this activity you will:

→ Identify and describe objects.

 Disc **1** Track **16**

INSTRUCTIONS Read and listen to the description of the picture above. Identify in Spanish the objects in the picture. Translate the description into English. Check your answers in Appendix A, on page 331.

Description

En este diseño hay varios objetos. Encima del diseño hay un tren que va de la izquierda hacia la derecha. Debajo del tren y al centro del dibujo hay tres instrumentos para comunicación a larga distancia. El instrumento de la izquierda de los tres es una carta. El instrumento a la derecha es un televisor. Y el instrumento de en medio es un teléfono. Debajo de la línea horizontal, vemos dos modos de transporte. Uno es más rápido que el otro. Estos son un avión y un camión. El avión está a la izquierda del camión y se dirige hacia la izquierda. El camión se dirige hacia la derecha. En la base a la izquierda vemos dos géneros de armas: una pistola y un cuchillo. La pistola está a la izquierda del cuchillo. Al lado opuesto de las armas vemos dos géneros de animales: una tortuga y un dinosaurio. El último está a la derecha.

Your Translation

....

....

....

....

....

....

....

....

....

....

....

....

....

....

Performance Challenge

Individual   Look around your house or classroom for a picture you can describe. Then describe it, using as much Spanish and as many details as you can.

Performance Challenge

Group   Have your students write a play for small children about a turtle, a dinosaur, a train, and an airplane. Perform the play for the younger children once in English and then a second time in Spanish (or use a Spanish translator while performing the English).

Review

INSTRUCTIONS This review will show you how much Spanish you've already learned. Before you begin, go back and review anything that you marked in the previous lessons. Make sure you understand it. Then, when you're ready, look at the following sentences.

- 1st time through: Compare the Spanish forms and their meaning with the English. (Read the Spanish out loud, then look away and say the phrase while thinking about its meaning and form.)
- 2nd time through: Cover the English and see if you can translate the Spanish into English.
- 3rd time through: Cover the Spanish and see if you can translate the English into Spanish.

 In this activity you will:

➔ Recognize how much Spanish you can comprehend, say, read, and write.

Group A

- ○ 1st time through
- ○ 2nd time through
- ○ 3rd time through

English	Spanish
Anna doesn't know the queen.	*Anna no conoce a la reina.*
I know it. I know that she doesn't know her.	*Lo sé. Sé que ella no la conoce.*
She doesn't know the king either.	*No conoce al rey tampoco.*
I know it. I know she doesn't know him.	*Lo sé. Sé que ella no lo conoce.*
I know she doesn't know them.	*Sé que no los conoce.*

Group B

- ○ 1st time through
- ○ 2nd time through

Pie de Limón: A Recipe of Panama

Crust

- 2 cups crushed vanilla wafers or graham crackers
- 1 stick butter, melted
- dash cinnamon

Mix the crushed wafers with the melted butter and cinnamon and press into bottom and sides of a 9-inch pie pan. Bake at 350 degrees for 10 minutes. Let cool.

Filling

- 1 1/2 cups sweetened condensed milk
- 2/3 cup lemon juice
- 4 large egg yolks

Beat milk and egg yolks together, gradually adding the lemon juice. The mix will curdle slightly. Pour mix into baked crust and bake at 350 degrees for another 10 minutes. The center of the pie should be firm to the touch. Cool completely, then chill. Serve cold with whipped cream.

○ 3rd time through

English	Spanish
The princess is not eating.	*La princesa no está comiendo.*
She is not drinking cream, either.	*No está tomando crema, tampoco.*
The prince drinks cream all the time.	*El príncipe toma crema todo el tiempo.*
The princess never drinks cream.	*La princesa nunca toma crema.*
The duke does nothing but eat.	*El duque no hace nada mas que comer.*
They do nothing but eat.	*Ellos no hacen nada mas que comer.*

Group C

○ 1st time through
○ 2nd time through
○ 3rd time through

English	Spanish
Does the prince speak Chinese?	*¿El príncipe habla chino?*
No, only the princess speaks it.	*No, solamente lo habla la princesa.*
She doesn't speak it often.	*No lo habla a menudo.*
She speaks it only in church.	*Lo habla solamente en la iglesia.*
She knows the Chinese people.	*Conoce a la gente china.*
She knows some Chinese people.	*Conoce a algunos chinos.*
She knows the truth.	*Ella sabe la verdad.*
She knows a lot of things.	*Sabe muchas cosas.*

Group D

○ 1st time through
○ 2nd time through
○ 3rd time through

English	Spanish
The Chinese attend church.	*Los chinos asisten a la iglesia.*
Some Chinese attend church.	*Algunos chinos asisten a la iglesia.*
The Chinese used to live in China.	*Los chinos vivían en China.*

English (cont.)	Spanish
Now some Chinese live in the castle.	*Ahora, algunos chinos viven en el castillo.*
Some princes lived here.	*Algunos príncipes vivían aquí.*
Where do the princes of Cali live?	*¿Dónde viven los príncipes de Cali?*
One of them lives here.	*Uno de ellos vive aquí.*

Group E

○ 1st time through
○ 2nd time through
○ 3rd time through

English	Spanish
What is it she likes?	*¿Qué es lo que a ella le gusta?*
She likes butter and cream.	*A ella le gusta mantequilla y crema.*
No, what is it she likes to do?	*¿No, qué es lo que le gusta hacer?*
Oh, she likes to sing.	*Oh, a ella le gusta cantar.*
What is it she prefers to do, eat butter or drink cream?	*¿Qué es lo que prefiere hacer, comer mantequilla o tomar crema?*
She prefers to eat.	*Prefiere comer.*
What is it she doesn't like?	*¿Qué es lo que no le gusta?*
She doesn't like water.	*No le gusta el agua.*
What is it she doesn't like to do?	*¿Qué es lo que no le gusta hacer?*
She doesn't like to sleep.	*No le gusta dormir.*

Group F

○ 1st time through
○ 2nd time through
○ 3rd time through

English	Spanish
The cat drinks juice when the dog sings.	*El gato toma jugo cuando el perro canta.*
The dog drinks juice when the cat sings.	*El perro toma jugo cuando el gato canta.*

English *(cont.)*	Spanish
The cat drinks only when the dog sings.	*El gato toma solamente cuando el perro canta.*
The dog drinks only when the cat sings.	*El perro toma solamente cuando el gato canta*
That's shocking!	*¡Qué impresionante!*
In reality, it's no big thing.	*En realidad, no es gran cosa.*
I agree.	*Estoy de acuerdo.*

Performance Challenge

Individual   This activity reviewed some of the vocabulary words and verb conjugations that you've learned so far. Choose three of the sentences in this activity to use as models. Then, write three sentences of your own.

1. ....

   ....

2. ....

   ....

3. ....

   ....

Performance Challenge

Group   Have a "Pronunciation Competition" where students volunteer to read the phrases out loud one at a time. Have the teacher or facilitator be the judge and assign points for accent and fluency. The student with the most points at the end of the story, wins.

Focus on Action

Scatter Chart

INSTRUCTIONS   Familiarize yourself with these 13 new action pictographs:

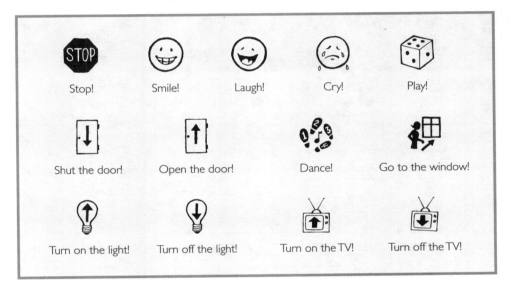

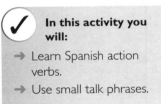

In this activity you will:

→ Learn Spanish action verbs.
→ Use small talk phrases.

Self Quiz

INSTRUCTIONS   Without looking at the scatter chart above, do you remember what the new action pictographs represent? Say what each pictograph represents out loud.

INSTRUCTIONS Review the pictographs. See the word equivalents below.

INSTRUCTIONS Learn the Spanish vocabulary for the new action pictographs.

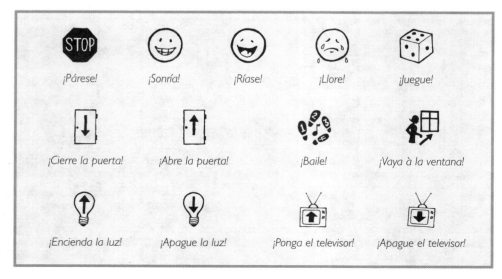

INSTRUCTIONS   Read and act out the following Spanish phrases, using your new vocabulary.

1. *¡Póngase de pie!*
2. *¡Cante y baile!*
3. *¡Cierre la puerta!*
4. *¡Lea y cuente!*
5. *¡Ríase y llore!*
6. *¡Párese y salte!*
7. *¡Coma y beba!*
8. *¡Ríase y llore!*
9. *¡Lea y escriba!*
10. *¡Juegue y trabaje!*
11. *¡Siéntese y sonría!*
12. *¡Lea, cuente y escriba!*
13. *¡Ande y abra la puerta!*
14. *¡Cierre los ojos y hable!*
15. *¡Encienda la luz y cante!*
16. *¡Vaya a la ventana y párese!*
17. *¡Póngase de pie y ande!*
18. *¡Siéntese, pinte y escriba!*
19. *¡Acuéstese y cierre los ojos!*
20. *¡Apague el televisor y siéntese!*
21. *¡Abra los ojos, levántese y corra!*
22. *¡Despiértese, levántese y trabaje!*
23. *¡Vaya a la puerta, párese y sonría!*
24. *¡Acuéstese, cierre los ojos y duerma!*
25. *¡Apague la luz y ponga la televisión!*
26. *¡Cierre la puerta y abra la puerta!*
27. *¡Encienda la luz, ponga el televisor y baile!*
28. *¡Apague la luz, acuéstese y duerma!*

ACTIVITY 17

INSTRUCTIONS   Look at the pictographs below. How many of these commands can you say in Spanish?

★
Performance Challenge

Individual   Study this activity's pictographs to review the vocabulary until you can associate the picture directly with the Spanish word, without thinking of the English equivalent first.

★
Performance Challenge

Group   Choose a caller to play Simon Says in Spanish. Use as many of the actions described in the lesson. Keep going until only one player is left standing.

You have completed all the activities for

Section 1.1.2
Day One, 12:30 Hours

and are now ready to take the section quiz. Before continuing, be sure you have learned the objectives for each activity in this section.

Section Quiz

INSTRUCTIONS   Select the most correct answer for the following questions. Check your answers in Appendix D, on page 346.

1. *¿Qué pasa cuando la niña se despierta?*
   A. *Come el desayuno.*
   B. *Se asusta, brinca, grita, y va corriendo.*
   C. *Se asusta, grita, y vuelve a dormir.*
   D. *No hace nada.*

2. *¿Cuándo vuelve al bosque?*
   A. *Nunca vuelve al bosque.*
   B. *Al día siguiente.*
   C. *La próxima semana.*
   D. *Vuelve cuando puede.*

3. *¿Qué hablan en el castillo?*
   A. *A veces hablan chino.*
   B. *Siempre hablan del reino.*
   C. *Siempre hablan español.*
   D. *A veces hablan español.*

4. *¿Qué come el duque?*
   A. *Manzanas cubiertas de chocolate.*
   B. *Carne con cebollas.*
   C. *Mantequilla cubierta de chocolate.*
   D. *Papas fritas.*

5. **¿Cuál es el río más grande del mundo?**

   A. El Río Mississippi.

   B. El Río Amazonas.

   C. El Nilo.

   D. El Congo.

6. **¿Dónde está el Nilo?**

   A. Está en Africa.

   B. Está en Asia.

   C. Está en Norteamérica.

   D. Está en Australia.

7. **¿Cuántas esquinas tiene un cuadrado?**

   A. Un cuadrado no tiene esquinas.

   B. Un cuadrado tiene seis esquinas.

   C. Un cuadrado tiene cuatro esquinas.

   D. Un cuadrado tiene dos esquinas.

8. **¿Por qué es que los pájaros comen insectos?**

   A. Porque a ellos no les gusta comerlos.

   B. Porque tortugas son demasiado grandes.

   C. Porque tienen sabor feo.

   D. Porque a ellos les gusta comerlos.

9. **¿Qué hace el gato cuando el perro canta?**

   A. El gato nada.

   B. El gato come naranjas.

   C. El gato toma jugo.

   D. El gato tira piedras.

10. **¿Qué hace el duque gordo?**

    A. No hace nada mas que comer.

    B. Corre en las calles.

    C. Canta desde su balcón.

    D. Siempre va a nadar.

You have completed all the sections for

Module 1.1

and are now ready to take the module test. Before continuing, be sure you have learned the objectives for each activity in this module.

Module Test

INSTRUCTIONS   True or False: The following phrases or sentences are translated correctly. Check your answers in Appendix D, on page 345.

1. *Mira ese pez grande.* = Look at that big fish.

   A. True

   B. False

2. *Es un tiburón.* = It's a snake.

   A. True

   B. False

3. *¿Son grandes todos los tiburones?* = Are all sharks big?

   A. True

   B. False

4. *Un tiburón grande puede quitarte la pierna en una bocadita.* = A large shark can take your arm off in one bite.

   A. True

   B. False

5. *Algunos tiburones atacan a la gente.* = Some sharks attack people.

   A. True

   B. False

6. hello = *allo*

   A. True

   B. False

7. **yes = *sí***

   A. True

   B. False

8. **She's busy. = *Está lista.***

   A. True

   B. False

9. **Is your father there? = *¿Está tu papá?***

   A. True

   B. False

10. **yes = *nos vemos***

    A. True

    B. False

11. **May I speak with him? = *¿Puedo hablar él?***

    A. True

    B. False

12. **no = *nos vemos***

    A. True

    B. False

13. **well = *bueno***

    A. True

    B. False

14. **Is anyone else there? = *¿Hay alguien más allí?***

    A. True

    B. False

15. **tell me = *dígame***

    A. True

    B. False

....

INSTRUCTIONS　For the following questions, choose the correct Spanish translation of the English word or phrase.

16. **to eat**

　　A. *beber*

　　B. *cubrir*

　　C. *comer*

　　D. *desgraciadamente*

17. **to drink**

　　A. *cada día*

　　B. *cubrir*

　　C. *mantequilla*

　　D. *beber*

18. **to cover**

　　A. *equivocarse*

　　B. *por lo menos*

　　C. *desgraciadamente*

　　D. *cubrir*

19. **unfortunately**

　　A. *por lo menos*

　　B. *equivocarse*

　　C. *desgraciadamente*

　　D. *todo el mundo*

20. **of course**

　　A. *cada día*

　　B. *desde luego / por supuesto*

　　C. *por lo menos*

　　D. *equivocarse*

21. **to be mistaken**

　　A. *mantequilla*

　　B. *todo el mundo*

　　C. *equivocarse*

　　D. *desgraciadamente*

22. **butter**

    A. *por lo menos*

    B. *cada día*

    C. *cubrir*

    D. *mantequilla*

23. **everyone**

    A. *todo el mundo*

    B. *por lo menos*

    C. *desde luego / por supuesto*

    D. *comer*

24. **each day**

    A. *equivocarse*

    B. *por lo menos*

    C. *cada día*

    D. *mantequilla*

25. **at least**

    A. *todo el mundo*

    B. *por lo menos*

    C. *cubrir*

    D. *desde luego / por supuesto*

Module 1.2

Throughout this module we'll be learning about the culture of Uruguay.

Keep these tips in mind as you progress through this module:

1. Read instructions carefully.
2. Repeat aloud all the Spanish words you hear on the audio CDs.
3. Learn at your own pace.
4. Have fun with the activities and practice your new language skills with others.
5. Record yourself speaking Spanish on tape so you can evaluate your own speaking progress.

N

La Casa
del Señor
Espinoza

Isla Verde

Day One, 16:00 Hours

Hacia la tierra firme

🔊

You finish a set of activities and look again at the hastily scribbled clue from *Señor* Espinoza—*preguntas de un niño*. The activity with that title talked about birds and insects. You stand up and walk around the messy study. Atop a low table, one of very few things in the room not overturned, is a thriving ant farm. Insects… You look more closely.

What looks like the corner of a sheet of paper is poking out of the soil in the ant farm. Pulling some tweezers from your pocket, you tug the paper free, careful to avoid disturbing the ants. It looks like half of a map of South America, with locations marked and numbered in red. You show it to Agent *Araña*.

He groans. "If they're sending us after another recipe…"

"I doubt it," you reply with a wry grin. "The kidnappers were demanding some sort of journal or diary, remember?"

"Maybe it's a whole cookbook this time," *Araña* says, grinning.

You shake your head. "The question is, why would anyone kidnap a harmless author?"

"Wrong on two counts, *Mosca*," says *Araña*. "The pen is mightier than the sword. Espinoza has penned some pretty scathing articles over the years—I'm sure he's made some enemies. And the real question is, how are we going to get to the first location? Mainland Venezuela is a bit far to swim."

You nod. "Well, your question, unlike mine, is answered easily enough. Let's ask Raul where we can rent a motorboat."

You find Raul downstairs, having failed again to contact the local authorities. Everything but the shortwave radio he used to contact you seems to be cut off. When you ask Raul about a boat, he informs you he can do better than that and leads you to a large side yard, where a small helicopter is parked. Raul explains that *Señor* Espinoza used this to get from the island to the mainland for book signings. Raul served as pilot, and his piloting license is still current.

✓ **In this section you will:**

→ Build fluency for negative voice.

→ Use small talk phrases.

→ Expand your comprehension toward complete understanding.

→ Use objects with command voice.

→ Understand new vocabulary in a conversation.

→ Use the grammar "*le*" and "*se*."

 Disc **2**   Track **1**

Minutes later, the helicopter lifts off, and you, *Araña*, and Raul rush toward the first location marked on the map. Having seen aerial views of the ocean many times before, you and *Araña* decide your time would be better spent learning more Spanish. When it grows too dark for you to see clearly, Raul entertains you with stories of his own homeland, Uruguay.

Openers and Rejoinders

INSTRUCTIONS Learn these short sentences.

English	Spanish
I'm out of here.	*Ya me voy.*
Good-bye.	*¡Qué te vaya bien!*
Tomorrow I take my exams.	*Mañana tomo mis exámenes.*
Good luck!	*¡Buena suerte!*
Thanks a lot.	*Muchas gracias.*
No problem.	*No hay por qué.*
Congratulations!	*¡Felicitaciones!*
For what? I haven't done anything.	*¿Por qué? No he hecho nada.*
We're there!	*¡Ya llegamos!*
Finally!	*¡Por fin!*
It's going to rain.	*Va a llover.*
So it seems. / It seems so.	*Así parece. / Parece que sí.*
I have a question.	*Tengo una pregunta.*
What is it?	*¿Cuál es?*
I'm going to the fair.	*Yo voy a la feria.*
Me too.	*Yo también.*
Good luck.	*¡Qué te vaya bien!*
Thanks. Same.	*Gracias. Igualmente.*
Excellent! Remarkable!	*¡Excelente! ¡Fantástico!*
Yes. Marvelous! Fantastic!	*Sí. ¡Maravilloso! ¡Fantástico!*

In this activity you will:
→ Use small talk phrases.

Disc **2** Track **2**

English (cont.)	Spanish
Thanks for your time.	*Gracias por su tiempo.*
Any time.	*Cualquier hora.*
See you tomorrow, then.	*Nos vemos mañana entonces.*
Until then.	*Hasta entonces.*
It's getting late.	*Ya es tarde.*
Yes. Let's go home.	*Sí. Vamos a casa.*
Bring me a drink, please.	*Tráeme un refresco, por favor.*
Right away.	*En seguida.*
Please carry my coat.	*Por favor, lleve mi saco.*
With pleasure.	*Con mucho gusto.*
I like this.	*Me gusta ésto.*
Me too.	*A mí también.*
Your suitcase is heavy. Let me help you.	*Su maleta es pesada. Permítame ayudarle.*
There's no need. It's light.	*No hay necesidad. Es ligera.*
And another thing, you owe me five dollars.	*Y otra cosa, me debes cinco dólares.*
Since when?	*¿Desde cuándo?*

Performance Challenge

Individual   This activity taught you a number of useful openers and rejoinders. Focus on three of them and look for opportunities to use those three in your regular conversations this week.

Performance Challenge

Group   Write a one act play about two people meeting for the first time in Spanish. Use as many phrases from the lesson as you can. Then act it out for the class. The team who is able to use the most material from the lesson, wins.

Story Time: Little Red Riding Hood

 In this activity you will:

→ Expand your comprehension toward complete understanding.

 Disc **2** Track **3**

INSTRUCTIONS Listen to and read this story. Work toward full comprehension.

English	Spanish
Here is a little girl.	*Aquí está una niñita.*
She is called Red Riding Hood.	*Se llama Caperucita Roja.*
Here is her mother.	*Aquí está su mamacita.*
Here is her grandma.	*Aquí está su abuelita.*
Here is her mother's house.	*Aquí está la casa de su mamacita.*
Here is her grandma's house.	*Aquí está la casa de su abuelita.*
Here is the forest.	*Aquí está el bosque.*
Here is a wolf.	*Aquí está un lobo.*
Well.	*Bueno.*
The grandma is sick.	*La abuelita está enferma.*
Mother sends Red Riding Hood with a basket of cookies.	*La mamacita manda a Caperucita Roja con una canasta de galletas.*

Uruguay Culture Overview

Covering just 72,930 square miles and having a population of under 3.5 million, Uruguay is the smallest Hispanic nation in South America. However, what it lacks in size, it makes up for in personality. Uruguay's east coast sports some of the finest beaches in South America, earning it the title of the Uruguayan Riviera. The cooler western highlands hold most of the country's agricultural industries and also a variety of colonial remnants. With its pleasant capital city and its generally laid-back populace, Uruguay is a delightful place to visit.

English	Spanish
In the woods the wolf asks her:	En el bosque, el lobo le pregunta:
"Where are you going?	"¿Adónde vas?
What is your name?"	¿Cómo te llamas?"
Red Riding Hood tells him, and he goes away.	Caperucita Roja le contesta, y él se aleja.
He runs to the grandma's house.	Él corre a la casa de la abuelita.
He knocks on the door.	Toca a la puerta.
The grandma asks:	La abuelita pregunta:
"Who is it?"	"¿Quién es?"
The wolf answers:	El lobo responde:
"Red Riding Hood."	"Caperucita Roja."
"Come in."	"Adelante."
Grandma sees the wolf and runs from the house.	La abuelita ve al lobo, y corre de la casa.
The wolf gets in bed.	El lobo se mete en la cama.
Red Riding Hood comes.	Caperucita Roja viene.
She enters and sees the wolf.	Entra y ve al lobo.
She thinks it's her grandma.	Piensa que es su abuelita.
She asks: "Why do you have such big ears?"	Pregunta: "¿Por qué tienes las orejas tan grandes?"
The wolf answers: "To hear you better."	El lobo responde: "Para oírte mejor."
"Why do you have such big teeth?"	"¿Por qué tienes los dientes tan grandes?"
"To eat you better."	"Para comerte mejor."
Red Riding Hood screams:	Caperucita roja grita:
"Oh, it's the wolf!"	"¡Ay, es el lobo!"
At that moment the grandma enters with a dog.	En ese momento entra la abuelita con un perro.
The wolf runs out and escapes.	El lobo sale corriendo y se escapa.
Then Red Riding Hood and the grandma and the dog eat the cookies.	Entonces Caperucita Roja y la abuelita y el perro se comen las galletas.

Performance Challenge

Individual   This activity presented a familiar story in Spanish. Choose a favorite story—or make up one of your own—and tell it in simple Spanish. Rough out some ideas below.

....
....
....
....
....
....
....
....
....
....
....
....
....
....
....
....

Performance Challenge

Group   Have a "cookie exchange" where each student brings their favorite cookie and the recipe for it written in Spanish. Pass around the cookies and the recipes to take home and enjoy.

A Spanish Lesson

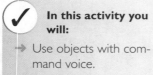

In this activity you will:

→ Use objects with command voice.

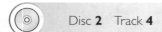

Disc **2**   Track **4**

INSTRUCTIONS   Listen to these sentences and use them to learn new vocabulary in Spanish. You will learn to work with objects and the commanding voice.

English	Spanish
Take your pencil. Take it.	*Toma tu lápiz. Tómalo.*
Put your pencil here. Put it here.	*Pon tu lápiz aquí. Ponlo aquí.*
Take your white paper. Take it.	*Toma tu papel blanco. Tómalo.*
Put your paper here. Put it here.	*Pon tu papel aquí. Ponlo aquí.*
Take my red pencil. Take it.	*Toma mi lápiz rojo. Tómalo.*
Put my pencil here. Put it here.	*Pon mi lápiz aquí. Ponlo aquí.*
Take my red paper. Take it.	*Toma mi papel rojo. Tómalo.*
Put my red paper here.	*Pon mi papel rojo aquí.*
Excellent!	*¡Excelente!*
Here there is a pencil.	*Aquí hay un lápiz.*
And here there are two pencils.	*Y aquí hay dos lápices.*
How many pencils? Two.	*¿Cuántos lápices? Dos.*
Put this one in the box.	*Pon éste en la caja.*
Put it in.	*Ponlo.*
Put these in the box too.	*Pon éstos en la caja también.*
Put them in.	*Ponlos.*
Take a paper and put it in this box.	*Toma un papel y ponlo en la caja.*
Take another paper and put it in the same box.	*Toma otro papel y ponlo en la misma caja.*
Take two pencils and put them in this sack.	*Toma dos lápices y ponlos en esta bolsa.*
Take another pencil and put it in the same sack.	*Toma otro lápiz y ponlo en la misma bolsa.*

English (cont.)	Spanish
In the sack there is a pencil.	*En la bolsa hay un lápiz.*
Take it out.	*Sácalo.*
Take one pencil from the sack and put it in the box.	*Toma un lápiz de la bolsa y ponlo en la caja.*
Take one paper from the box and put it in the sack.	*Toma un papel de la caja y ponlo en la bolsa.*
I take the red paper out and put it in the box.	*Yo saco el papel rojo y lo pongo en la caja.*
Pick up the box. Pick it up.	*Toma la caja. Tómala.*
Give it to me.	*Dámela a mí.*
Pick up the pencil. Pick it up.	*Toma el lápiz. Tómalo.*
Give it to me.	*Dámelo a mí.*
Pick up your pencils. Pick them up.	*Toma tus lápices. Tómalos.*
Give them to me.	*Dámelos a mí.*
Pick up the sack. Pick it up.	*Toma la bolsa. Tómala.*
Give it to me.	*Dámela a mí.*
Pick up the sheets. Pick them up.	*Toma las hojas. Tómalas.*
Give them to me.	*Dámelas a mí.*
Yes, give them to me, please.	*Sí, dámelas a mí, por favor.*

This activity focused on using the command voice and giving directions in Spanish.

Performance Challenge

Individual   Using this activity as a model, write five similar sentences of your own. Then, if possible, use those sentences with a classmate or friend. Can he or she understand and follow your directions? Can you understand and follow his or hers?

1. ....

....

2. ....

....

3. ....

....

4. ....

....

5. ....

....

Performance Challenge

Group   Find a Spanish newspaper and circle all the adjectives on one page. Use these words to write your own news story. Be as creative as you can!

Chatter at a Royal Ball

Getting Ready for *Conversación*

INSTRUCTIONS   Using the list of new words and sample sentences, learn the following conversation.

In this activity you will:

→ Understand new vocabulary in a conversation.

Disc **2**   Track **5**

Some Words

INSTRUCTIONS   Study these words for the following sentences.

English	Spanish
to buy	*comprar*
to sell	*vender*
to remember	*acordarse*
to call oneself / be named	*llamarse*
to write	*escribir*
to continue, keep on	*seguir*
leave / abandon / quit	*dejar*
to let / allow	*dejar*
to doubt	*dudar*
I doubt it.	*Lo dudo.*
recently	*recientemente*

Facts and Figures on Uruguay
- Uruguay's official name is la *República Oriental del Uruguay.*
- The government of Uruguay is a republic, with a president, a vice president, and a bicameral legislature.
- Uruguay was the first South American country to give women the right to vote.
- Uruguay's main industries include tourism, tires, cement, hides, beef, wool, fishing, footwear, and textiles.

Some Sentences

INSTRUCTIONS   Study these sentences in preparation for the conversation.

English	Spanish
Leave me in peace.	*Déjeme en paz.*
Let me think.	*Déjeme pensar.*
He buys a cat.	*Él compra un gato.*

English (cont.)	Spanish
He buys him / her a cat.	*Él le compra un gato.*
He buys himself a cat.	*Él se compra un gato.*
What do you call yourself / What's your name?	*¿Cómo se llama Ud.?*
I am called / My name is Carlos.	*Me llamo Carlos.*
He calls himself José.	*Él se llama José.*
What do you call yourself, sonny?	*¿Cómo te llamas, hijito?*
María, do you remember that?	*¿María, te acuerdas de eso?*
I remember that I was with you.	*Me acuerdo que yo estaba contigo.*
I don't remember when.	*No me acuerdo cuándo.*
He remembers that.	*Él se acuerda de eso.*
He lived in Madrid.	*Él vivía en Madrid.*
He lived there for two years.	*Él vivió allá por dos años.*
(He) must be crazy.	*Tiene que estar loco.*
She had to speak Spanish there.	*Ella tenía que hablar español allá.*
She had to sell the dog?	*¿Ella tuvo que vender el perro?*
Just go ahead / Go right ahead / Continue, please.	*¡Siga, no más!*
She keeps on doing that: buying and selling cats…and writing checks.	*Ella sigue haciendo eso: comprando y vendiendo gatos…y escribiendo cheques.*
Now (she) has quit doing that.	*Ya ha dejado de hacer eso.*

Conversación 13

◀))

	English	Spanish
•:	What has happened to the queen that lived in Ventura and bought and sold cats?	*¿Qué le ha pasado a la reina que vivía en Ventura y compraba y vendía gatos?*
••:	Bought and sold cats?	*¿Compraba y vendía gatos?*
•:	One time she sold her cat and bought herself an enormous dog, don't you remember?	*Una vez vendió su gato y se compró un perro enorme, ¿no te acuerdas?*

English *(cont.)*	Spanish
••: Just a moment…let me think…	*Un momento…déjame pensar…*
•: I think she was called Anita…the queen, not the dog.	*Creo que se llamaba Anita…la reina, no el perro.*
••: Anita…yes, now I remember her. She lived there ten years I think.	*Anita…sí, ahora me acuerdo de ella. Ella vivió allá diez años, creo.*
•: And now?	*¿Y ahora?*
••: She doesn't live there now. And now she doesn't sell cats anymore.	*Ya no vive allá. Y ya no vende gatos.*

Performance Challenge

Individual   This activity presented you with several useful new verbs and phrases. Choose at least five of these new verbs and phrases, study how they are used in the conversation, then use them in sentences of your own.

1. ....
....

2. ....
....

3. ....
....

4. ....
....

Performance Challenge

Group   Split students into groups. Give each group a children's book in English that has to do with either royalty, dogs/cats, or a foreign country. Have them rewrite the ending of the stories, then create a Diglot-Weave using their story.

Focus on the Language 17-18

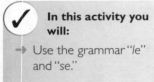

In this activity you will:

→ Use the grammar "*le*" and "*se*."

INSTRUCTIONS   Use these exercises to learn Spanish grammar patterns.

Focus 17

The use of *le*

English	Spanish
What has happened to her?	*¿Qué le ha pasado?*
What has happened to her?	*¿Qué le ha pasado a ella?*
What has happened to him?	*¿Qué le ha pasado?*
What has happened to him?	*¿Qué le ha pasado a él?*
What (to him / to her) has happened?	*¿Qué le ha pasado?*

> **NOTE**
>
> It is usual to include the word *le* before the verb as well as the *a* + pronoun after the verb. If context is clear and no particular emphasis is intended, the *a* + pronoun is left off the end.

Observation and Practice

INSTRUCTIONS   Read these sentences then cover the Spanish and orally translate from the English.

English	Spanish
What (to her) has happened to the queen?	*¿Qué le ha pasado a la reina?*
And the prince, what (to him) has happened to him?	*Y al príncipe, ¿qué le ha pasado a él?*
What (to him) has happened to the king?	*¿Qué le ha pasado al rey?*

English *(cont.)*	Spanish
And the princess, what (to her) has happened to her?	*Y a la princesa, ¿qué le ha pasado a ella?*
And what has happened to the cat?	*¿Y qué le ha pasado al gato?*

INSTRUCTIONS   Translate the following sentences into Spanish.

1. What has happened to the queen?

   ....

2. What has happened to the princess?

   ....

3. What has happened to her?

   ....

4. What has happened to him?

   ....

5. What has happened to the king?

   ....

6. What has happened to the prince?

   ....

7. The princess has suffered a lot.

   ....

8. Now she's eaten the chocolates.

   ....

9. She's already eaten the chocolates.

   ....

10. But she has cried a lot.

    ....

11. And the queen has cried with her.

    ....

Performance Self Quiz

INSTRUCTIONS   Translate the following conversation into English.

1. •: *¿Qué le ha pasado a la reina?*

   ....

2. ● ●: *La reina que vivía en Ojai y vendía gatos…*

....

3. ●: *Ella está escribiendo cheques falsos.*

....

4. ● ●: *Y al rey, ¿qué le ha pasado a él?*

....

5. ●: *¿A aquel que tenía una pistola?*

....

6. ● ●: *Está viviendo una vida santa.*

....

7. ●: *También está dirigiendo el coro de las madres.*

....

8. ● ●: *¿Qué le ha pasado al príncipe?*

....

9. ●: *El príncipe tuvo un ataque.*

....

10. ● ●: *El comió demasiado chocolate.*

....

11. ●: *Ahora él lo come con los angelitos.*

....

12. ● ●: *¿Y a la princesa? ¿Qué le ha pasado a ella?*

....

13. ●: *¿A cuál princesa?*

....

14. ● ●: *A aquélla que sabía hablar ruso.*

....

15. ●: *Ella también escribía tonterías.*

....

16. ● ●: *Ella está viviendo en Siberia.*

....

Focus 18

The use of *se* meaning "for himself (herself, themselves)"

English	Spanish
She bought me a cat.	*Ella me compró un gato.*
She bought herself a cat.	*Ella se compró un gato.*
He bought himself a cat.	*Él se compró un gato.*
They have bought themselves a cat.	*Ellos se han comprado un gato.*
He wants to buy himself a cat.	*Él quiere comprarse un gato.*

Observation and Practice

INSTRUCTIONS   Read these sentences then cover the Spanish and orally translate from the English.

English	Spanish
He bought himself a dog.	*Él se compró un perro.*
He ate all of it himself.	*Él se comió todo.*
They have eaten all of it themselves.	*Ellos se han comido todo.*
He takes a swallow.	*Él se toma un trago.*

Performance Challenge

Individual   After carefully studying each grammar focus, use the grammar principles you learned in sentences of your own. Write at least three sentences for each focus.

Focus 17

1. ....

   ....

2. ....

   ....

3. ....

   ....

Focus 18

1. ....

....

2. ....

....

3. ....

....

Performance Challenge

Group   Organize a singing contest where each learner must choose a song that contains at least three questions. Have them each translate as much of the song into Spanish as they can. Next, have each student (or student group) perform their songs.

You have completed all the activities for

**Section 1.2.1
Day One, 16:00 Hours**

and are now ready to take the section quiz. Before continuing, be sure you have learned the objectives for each activity in this section.

Section Quiz

INSTRUCTIONS   Select the most correct answer for the following questions. Check your answers in Appendix D, on page 346.

1. *Qué le vaya bien.*
    A. *Me gusta ésto.*
    B. *¡Por fin!*
    C. *Tráeme un refresco, por favor.*
    D. *Gracias. Igualmente.*

2. *Mañana tomo mis exámenes.*
    A. *¡Buena suerte!*
    B. *Por favor, lleve mi saco.*
    C. *Esta maleta está pesada.*
    D. *Ya me voy.*

3. *¿A dónde va la Caperucita Roja?*
    A. *A la casa del lobo.*
    B. *A visitar a su abuela.*
    C. *A la escuela.*
    D. *A andar en bicicleta.*

4. *¿Con qué entra la abuelita?*
    A. *Con un cuchillo.*
    B. *Con un perro grande.*
    C. *Con el gato.*
    D. *Con fresas frescas.*

5. **¿Cuántos lápices hay?**

   A. *Hay dos lápices.*

   B. *Hay tres lápices.*

   C. *Hay un lápiz.*

   D. *Hay cinco lápices.*

6. **¿Cómo se llamaba la reina?**

   A. *Se llamaba Veronica.*

   B. *Se llamaba Carola.*

   C. *Se llamaba Miriam.*

   D. *Se llamaba Anita.*

7. **¿Qué hacía con los cheques?**

   A. *Llenaba los cheques.*

   B. *Falsificaba los cheques.*

   C. *Rompía los cheques.*

   D. *Tiraba los cheques.*

8. **¿Qué le ha pasado al rey con la pistola?**

   A. *Se fue a cazar.*

   B. *Corre por el bosque.*

   C. *Está viviendo una vida santa.*

   D. *Se convirtió en león.*

9. **¿Qué le pasó a la princesa que hablaba chino?**

   A. *Está viviendo en Siberia.*

   B. *Se casó.*

   C. *Vive en el castillo.*

   D. *Se fue a la China.*

10. **¿Dónde vivía la reina?**

    A. *Vivía al lado del lago.*

    B. *Vivía en Ojai.*

    C. *Vivía cerca de las montañas.*

    D. *Vivía en España.*

N

Coro

O Maracaibo

Barquisimeto

Valencia

★ Caracas

O Carúpano

O Cumaná

Barcelona

Lago
Maracaibo

Mérida

Pico Bolívar

Los
Llanos

Río Orinoco

O Tucupita

O Ciudad Guyana

Ciudad Bolívar

San
Cristóbal

Los Andes

San Fernando
de Apure

Embalse
de Guri

Guyana

Salto Aponguao

Salto Angel

Puerto
Ayacucho

Venezuela

O Santa Elena
de Ualrén

Colombia

Parque Nacional
Parima-Tapirapecó

Brazil

Parque Nacional
Serranía la Neblina

Venezuela

Day One, 22:00 Hours

Un día en Coro

Well past dark, Raul lands the helicopter in an open field just outside a town near Venezuela's Caribbean coast. *"El pueblo se llama Coro,"* Raul informs you. You check the half-map against your current location. The first spot on the map appears to be somewhere in this town.

"Muchísimas gracias, Raúl," you say, as you and *Araña* climb out of the helicopter. *"No se preocupe—encontraremos a su amo."*

With a smile and a wave, Raul takes off. You and *Araña* walk into town and find lodgings at the first inn you find.

The next morning, you examine the map more closely, looking for some sort of hint. You hold it up to the bright morning sunlight and notice something you hadn't seen before. There's some very fine print running around the edges of the map. You'd mistaken them earlier for decorative lines. By the bright morning light, you can read the tiny text. It's numbered just like the locations on the map, with numbers and wording going beyond what's written on this half of the map. Next to the number one, you read, *"¿Qué se comió el cerdo?"*

"What's that supposed to mean?" *Araña* asks.

"No sé," you reply, *"pero* I'll bet we can find out if we study a little more."

Araña nods. "Okay. We'd better hurry. Those kidnappers have a full day's head start on us already, and with no idea of what they're after, we need to close that gap, or the trail will go cold."

You agree. Then, seated on a little balcony overlooking *Coro*'s superb colonial architecture, you and *Araña* get to work.

✓ **In this section you will:**

→ Understand past perfect tense.

→ Use more small talk on a formal level.

→ Make distinctions among verbs and use them correctly.

→ Use numbers and math terms in a math setting.

→ Ask and answer questions in imperfect tense.

→ Master grammar patterns.

→ Create a mini-story using both written and oral skills.

 Disc **2** Track **6**

SECTION **1.2.2**

A Hungry Giant

ACTIVITY 23

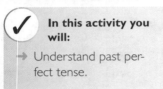

In this activity you will:

→ Understand past perfect tense.

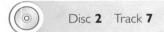

Disc **2** Track **7**

INSTRUCTIONS Listen to and read the following story. Use it to increase vocabulary and comprehension skills.

Geography of Uruguay

Uruguay borders Argentina to the west, Brazil to the north, the Atlantic ocean to the east, and the broad estuary of the *Río de la Plata* to the south. Two low mountain ranges—the *Cuchilla de Haedo* and the *Cuchilla Grande*—run north to south across the country, though coastal areas are flatter. Five rivers drain into the *Río Uruguay*, which forms the country's western border with Argentina and drains into the *Río de la Plata*. When left to itself, most of the country is covered in grasslands, with forest along its rivers and streams. Wild life is scarce, although birdwatchers can occasionally catch a glimpse of a rhea (an ostrich-like bird). Uruguay's climate is temperate, even in winter. Frost is rare, and snow in the lowlands is almost unheard of. Rainfall is evenly distributed over both the calendar year and the country.

English	Spanish
Have you ever seen a giant?	*¿Has visto alguna vez a un gigante?*
Do you know how big a giant is?	*¿Sabes lo grande que es un gigante?*
Do you know how much a hungry giant can eat?	*¿Sabes lo mucho que puede comer un gigante hambriento?*
Well I haven't ever seen a giant, but one time my father saw one.	*Bueno, yo nunca he visto a un gigante, pero una vez mi padre vio a uno.*
Anyway, he told me he saw one.	*Como quiera, me dijo que vio a uno.*
This happened when he was a boy just my age.	*Esto pasó cuando él era un niño justo mi de edad.*
One morning before breakfast, he took a walk and saw a fly caught in a spider's web.	*Una mañana antes del desayuno, daba un paseo y vio una mosca que estaba atrapada en una telaraña.*
He watched as the spider came and ate the fly.	*Observó como la araña vino y se comió la mosca.*

English *(cont.)*	Spanish
Good, thought my father. The spider ate the fly. I don't like flies.	*Qué bueno, pensó mi papá. La araña se comió la a mosca. No me gustan las moscas.*
A moment later there came a bird and ate the spider.	*Un momento después vino un pájaro y se comió a la araña.*
Good, thought my father. The bird ate the spider. I don't like spiders.	*¡Qué bueno!, pensó mi papá. El pájaro se comió a la araña. No me gustan las arañas.*
But the next moment a cat came along and ate the bird.	*Pero poco después vino un gato y se comió al pájaro.*
And my father thought: Too bad, the cat ate the bird. I like birds.	*Y mi papá pensó: ¡Qué lástima [que] el gato se comió al pájaro! Me gustan los pájaros.*
But the next moment a snake came along and ate the cat.	*Pero poco después vino una serpiente y se comió al gato.*
And my father thought: Too bad. I like cats.	*Y mi papá pensó: ¡Qué lástima! Me gustan los gatos.*
But the next moment a pig came along and ate the snake.	*Pero poco después vino un chancho y se comió a la serpiente.*
And my father thought: Good, the pig ate the snake. I don't like snakes.	*Y mi papá pensó: ¡Qué bueno que el chancho se comió a la serpiente! No me gustan las serpientes.*
Before long a leopard came along and ate the pig.	*Poco después vino un leopardo y se comió al chancho.*
And my father thought: Wow! A leopard ate the pig. This is exciting!	*Y mi papá pensó: ¡Caramba! Un leopardo se comió al chancho. ¡Qué emocionante!*
A while later a crocodile came along and ate the leopard.	*Más tarde vino un cocodrilo y se comió al leopardo.*
And my father thought: Wow! A crocodile ate the leopard. This is really exciting!	*Y mi papá pensó: ¡Caramba! Un cocodrilo se comió al leopardo. Esto sí que es emocionante.*
What will happen next?	*¿Qué más pasará?*
Before long a hippopotamus came along and ate the crocodile.	*Poco después vino un hipopótamo y se comió al cocodrilo.*

English (cont.)	Spanish
And my father thought: Wow! A hippopotamus ate the crocodile. What will happen next?	Y mi papá pensó: ¡Caramba! Un hipopótamo se comió al cocodrilo. ¿Qué más pasará?
A moment later a whale came along and ate the hippopotamus.	Después de un momento vino una ballena y se comió al hipopótamo.
And my father thought: Wow! This is too much. Just imagine:	Y mi papá pensó: ¡Caramba! Esto ya es demasiado. ¡Imagínate!:
A whale has eaten a hippopotamus,	Una ballena se ha comido a un hipopótamo,
the hippopotamus had eaten a crocodile,	el hipopótamo se había comido a un cocodrilo,
the crocodile had eaten a leopard,	el cocodrilo se había comido a un leopardo,
the leopard had eaten a pig,	el leopardo se había comido a un chancho,
the pig had eaten a snake,	el chancho se había comido a una serpiente,
the snake had eaten a cat,	la serpiente se había comido a un gato,
the cat had eaten a bird,	el gato se había comido a un pájaro,
the bird had eaten a spider,	el pájaro se había comido a una araña,
and the spider had eaten a fly.	y la araña se había comido a una mosca.
That's amazing. I've never seen such a thing.	¡Es increíble! Jamás había visto tal cosa.
Just then a hand reached down from the sky and picked up the whale.	En ese preciso momento una mano bajó del cielo y levantó a la ballena.
My father looked up just as the giant swallowed it whole.	Mi papá miró hacia arriba en el momento justo en que el gigante se la tragaba entera.
And he thought: Wow! This is the first time I've seen a giant.	Y él pensó: ¡Caramba! Es la primera vez que veo a un gigante.
Maybe he's still hungry. I'd better get out of here.	Tal vez todavía tenga hambre. ¡Mejor me voy!
And he ran home as fast as he could.	Y corrió a su casa tan rápido como pudo.
And there, as he ate a big bowl of oatmeal,	Y allí, mientras comía un tazón de avena,
he thought of the fly	pensaba en la mosca

English (cont.)	Spanish
and the spider	y *la araña*
and the bird	y *el pájaro*
and the cat	y *el gato*
and the snake	y *la serpiente*
and the pig	y *el chancho*
and the leopard	y *el leopardo*
and the crocodile	y *el cocodrilo*
and the hippopotamus	y *el hipopótamo*
and the whale.	y *la ballena.*
But most of all he thought of the giant and how hungry he must have been.	*Pero más que nada pensaba en el gigante y en lo hambriento que debía haber estado.*

Performance Challenge

Individual   The repetitive nature of this story makes it easy to remember the new vocabulary. Without looking at the story, write down (in Spanish!) as many of the animals that appeared in the story as you can remember.

....

....

....

....

....

....

....

....

....

....

....

....

....

....

....

....

....

....

....

....

Performance Challenge

Group   Play "Mother May I" in Spanish, using as many words as you can from the story. Have the students take "giant" steps, or advance like the animals in the story might.

Second Meeting at the University

INSTRUCTIONS   Listen to and read this conversation. Use the English in the left column to help you understand the Spanish in the right column.

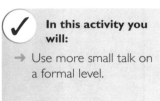

In this activity you will:
→ Use more small talk on a formal level.

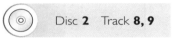

Disc **2**   Track **8, 9**

	English	Spanish
	It is spring. April.	*Es la primavera. Abril.*
N:	Vincent?	*¿Vicente?*
V:	Rose, hello.	*Rosa, hola.*
N:	Hi, Vincent. You forgot my name. It's Nancy.	*Hola, Vicente. Olvidaste mi nombre, me llamo Nancy.*
V:	Nancy, forgive me. I suppose I have Rose in my head.	*Nancy, perdóneme. Supongo que tenía Rosa en mi mente.*
N:	Who is this Rose?	*¿Quién es esta Rosa?*
V:	She's just a friend…many years ago. So be it. How are things?	*Ella es una amiga no más…hace muchos años. Bueno pues, ¿cómo van las cosas?*
N:	Quite well, thanks.	*Bastante bien, gracias.*
V:	And how is your husband?	*¿Y cómo está su esposo?*
N:	Fine. Everything's fine with us. How are you doing? Everything okay? I haven't seen you for a long time.	*Bien, Todo está bien con nosotros. Ud. ¿Cómo le va? ¿Está todo bien? No le he visto por mucho tiempo.*
V:	I haven't seen you since fall. By the way, happy new year!	*No le he visto desde el otoño. Desde luego [or A propósito], ¡Feliz año nuevo!*
N:	Same to you. Are you coming from work?	*Igualmente. ¿Vienes del trabajo?*

ACTIVITY 24

English (cont.)	Spanish
V: No, from a singing lesson. I'm going to the library.	*No, de una lección de cantar. Voy a la biblioteca.*
N: Still working at the post office?	*¿Todavía está trabajando en el correo?*
V: No. I quit in February. To tell the truth, they fired me.	*No, renuncié de allí en Febrero. Para decir la verdad, me echaron.*
N: That's too bad! What happened? Why did they fire you?	*¡Qué lástima! ¿Que pasó? ¿Por qué le echaron?*
V: Because I couldn't come on time.	*Porque no podía llegar a tiempo.*
N: How could you not have arrived on time?	*¿Como que no podía llegar a tiempo?*
V: I always study until midnight in the library. I can't get up at five in the morning.	*Siempre estudio hasta la media noche en la biblioteca. No puedo levantarme a las cinco de la mañana.*
N: I understand that.	*Entiendo eso.*
V: But now my father is angry with me.	*Pero ahora mi padre esta enojado conmigo.*
N: Why is that?	*¿Por qué?*
V: He says I'm a fool. I should've bought an alarm clock.	*Dice que soy tonto. Debía de haber comprado un despertador.*
N: In my opinion, it would have been better to go to bed earlier.	*En mi opinión, hubiera sido mejor acostarse más temprano.*
V: And get poor grades in my courses?	*¿Y sacar malas calificaciones en mis cursos [clases]?*
N: Such is life! Are you looking for a job?	*¡Así es la vida! ¿Estás buscando un trabajo?*
V: Of course. Otherwise I'd have no money.	*Por supuesto, de otro modo no tendría dinero.*
N: Where do you work now?	*¿Dónde trabajas ahora?*
V: At the bookstore.	*En la librería.*
N: That's where my sister works.	*Allí trabaja mi hermana.*
V: Really. I didn't know. What's her name?	*De veras, no lo sabía. ¿Cómo se llama?*
N: Rose. Her name is Rose, believe it or not!	*Rosa, su nombre es Rosa, ¡créalo o no!*

English *(cont.)*	Spanish
V: You're kidding!	*¡Está bromeando!*
N: No, I'm not kidding. I'm telling the truth. She works in the computer section.	*No, no estoy bromeando. Digo la verdad. Ella trabaja en la sección de computadoras.*
V: Introduce me to her, will you?	*¿Preséntemela por favor?*
N: I will do that some day.	*Lo haré algún día.*
V: Got to go now. I'm going to a piano lesson. Nice to see you again.	*Tengo que irme ahora. Voy a una lección de piano. Tanto gusto verle de nuevo.*
N: So long.	*Hasta luego.*

INSTRUCTIONS   Listen to the same conversation again, this time in Spanish only.

Performance Challenge

Individual   Using the vocabulary and grammar you've learned up to now, write a conversation of your own. It should be at least four lines long. Once you have written it, perform it with a friend, sibling, or classmate.

....

....

....

....

....

....

....

Performance Challenge

Group   Have each student research and write about Spanish New year or *El Año Nuevo*. Then have them describe their own family's traditions for the holiday, and their goals for the current year.

Observing Closely How Spanish Works

In this activity you will:

- Make distinctions among verbs and use them correctly.

INSTRUCTIONS Spend some time observing closely how Spanish works in the following. The first time through go from Spanish to English; then from English to Spanish. Use these exercises to learn new grammar principles.

English	Spanish
The queen knows how to sell cats.	*La reina sabe vender gatos.*
She sold me a cat.	*Me vendió un gato.*
She used to sell cats in Ojai.	*Vendía gatos en Ojai.*
She quit selling cats.	*Dejó de vender gatos.*
Now she has to sell chocolates?	*¿Ahora tiene que vender chocolates?*
The king knows how to direct hymns.	*El rey sabe dirigir himnos.*
He directed the national anthem.	*Dirigió el himno nacional.*
He quit directing the men's choir.	*Dejó de dirigir el coro de hombres.*
He began to direct the mothers' choir.	*Comenzó a dirigir el coro de las madres.*
He's going to direct a funeral song.	*Va a dirigir un canto fúnebre.*
He did it. He already did it.	*Lo hizo. Ya lo hizo.*
He didn't want to do it.	*No quiso hacerlo.*
He had to do it.	*Tuvo que hacerlo.*
That princess speaks Russian.	*Aquella princesa habla ruso.*
She learned it in Siberia.	*Lo aprendió en Siberia.*
She learned Arabic there also.	*Aprendió el árabe allá también.*
She knew the Arabs.	*Conocía a los árabes.*

English *(cont.)*	Spanish
She met King Hussein.	*Conoció al rey Hussein.*
She used to write nonsense to him.	*Le escribía tonterías.*
She has to do it. She's crazy.	*Tiene que hacerlo. Está loca.*
She's going to live in Siberia.	*Va a vivir en Siberia.*
She prefers to live there, I think.	*Prefiere vivir allá, creo.*
That prince eats too much.	*Aquel príncipe come demasiado.*
He likes to eat.	*Le gusta comer.*
He has to quit eating too much.	*Tiene que dejar de comer tanto.*
He has to begin eating only a little.	*Tiene que comenzar a comer sólo un poco.*
He didn't want to eat it, but he ate it.	*No quiso comerlo, pero lo comió.*
He had to eat the chocolates.	*Tuvo que comer los chocolates.*
Poor thing. What a pity! Really!	*¡Pobrecito! ¡Qué lástima! ¡De veras!*

Making Distinctions

INSTRUCTIONS   Study the different verb forms below. Learning them will give you the foundation that you need to move forward. Practice saying them out loud.

English	Spanish
buys it	*lo compra*
(he) used to buy it	*lo compraba*
(he) bought it	*lo compró*
wants to buy it	*quiere comprarlo*
has bought it	*lo ha comprado*
sells them	*los vende*
(he) used to sell them	*los vendía*
(he) sold them	*los vendió*
wants to sell them	*quiere venderlos*
has sold them	*los ha vendido*
sings hymns	*canta himnos*
(he) used to sing hymns	*cantaba himnos*

Montevideo

With a population of 1.4 million, Montevideo is Uruguay's only large city. Many members of the upper crust in Argentina and Brazil come to Montevideo for their summer holidays, to enjoy the nearby white sand beaches and the city's own unique style. Popular destinations within the city itself include the *Mercado del Puerto*, the *Museo Histórico Nacional*, the *Palacio Legislativo*, and the *Teatro Solís*. The *Mercado del Puerto* was the finest in Latin America when it first opened for business in 1868. While it can no longer make that claim, it remains an impressive wrought-iron structure in which one can find a variety of excellent seafood restaurants and traditional grills. Housed in the *Ciudad Vieja*, the *Museo Histórico Nacional* is actually spread over four traditional houses. Appropriately, most of these houses once belonged to national heroes. The *Palacio Legislativo* features a neoclassical architecture designed by Victor Meano. This *Palacio* makes a grand sight at night when it's brightly lit. Guided tours are also available in both English and Spanish. The *Teatro Solís*, with its superb acoustics, varied performers, and 19th century architecture, was named for the first Spaniard to enter what is now Uruguay.

English (cont.)	Spanish
(he) sang a hymn yesterday	*cantó un himno ayer*
knows how to sing hymns	*sabe cantar himnos*
has to sing hymns	*tiene que cantar himnos*
has sung hymns	*ha cantado himnos*
(he) lives in Ojai	*vive en Ojai*
used to live in Ojai	*vivía en Ojai*
lived in Ojai two years	*vivió en Ojai dos años*
wants to live in Ojai	*quiere vivir en Ojai*
has to live in Ojai	*tiene que vivir en Ojai*
has lived in Ojai	*ha vivido en Ojai*
is living in Ojai	*está viviendo en Ojai*
used to attend church	*asistía a la iglesia*
attended church (one occasion)	*asistió a la iglesia*
has attended church	*ha asistido a la iglesia*
has to attend church	*tiene que asistir a la iglesia*
is attending church	*está asistiendo a la iglesia*
used to direct the hymns	*dirigía los himnos*
directed the hymns	*dirigió los himnos*
has directed the hymns	*ha dirigido los himnos*
knows how to direct the hymns	*sabe dirigir los himnos*
is directing the hymns	*está dirigiendo los himnos*
eats too much	*come demasiado*
used to eat too much	*comía demasiado*
ate too much	*comió demasiado*
has eaten too much	*ha comido demasiado*
is going to eat too much	*va a comer demasiado*
writes to him	*le escribe*
used to write to him	*le escribía*
wrote to him	*le escribió*
has to write to him	*tiene que escribirle*

English (cont.)	Spanish
is writing to him	le está escribiendo
quit writing to him	dejó de escribirle
likes to write to him	le gusta escribirle
happens to him	le pasa
used to happen to him	le pasaba
happened to him	le pasó
has happened to him	le ha pasado
is going to happen to him	le va a pasar
is happening to him	le está pasando
talks with her	habla con ella
used to talk with her	hablaba con ella
had a talk with her	habló con ella
has talked with her	ha hablado con ella
didn't want to talk with her	no quiso hablar con ella
had to talk with her	tuvo que hablar con ella
was having to talk with her	tenía que hablar con ella
is going to do it	va a hacerlo
is doing it	lo está haciendo
did it	lo hizo
does it	lo hace
used to do it	lo hacía
had to do it	tuvo que hacerlo
has to do it	tiene que hacerlo
wants to do it	quiere hacerlo
enjoys buying a cat	le gusta comprar un gato
used to enjoy buying one	le gustaba comprar uno
enjoyed (once) buying one	le gustó comprar uno
will enjoy buying one	le va a gustar comprar uno
has enjoyed buying one	le ha gustado comprar uno

Note the similarities in the use of the infinitive in Spanish and English.

English	Spanish
To eat is to live.	*Comer es vivir.*
To eat it is to live.	*Comerlo es vivir.*
He likes to eat and drink.	*Le gusta comer y tomar.*
wants to eat	*quiere comer*
is going to eat	*va a comer*
has to eat	*tiene que comer*
had to eat	*tuvo que comer*
knows how to eat	*sabe comer*
started to eat	*comenzó a comer*
prefers to eat	*prefiere comer*

Sometimes the Spanish infinitive is not represented by an English infinitive:

English	Spanish
He quit eating.	*Dejó de comer.*

Practice

INSTRUCTIONS   Translate into Spanish.

1. She doesn't speak Spanish.

   ....

2. She doesn't know how to speak.

   ....

3. He prefers to speak Spanish.

   ....

4. She prefers not to speak.

   ....

5. He started talking.

   ....

6. He quit talking.

   ....

7. She is now going to talk Spanish.

....

8. Going to start talking Spanish.

....

9. She has to speak Spanish.

....

10. She had to speak Spanish.

....

11. She has to know how to speak.

....

12. She has to start talking.

....

13. She had to start talking.

....

14. She has to quit talking.

....

15. She had to quit talking.

....

16. He had to quit talking.

....

17. He used to have to talk Spanish.

....

18. She didn't used to have to talk.

....

19. She didn't know how.

....

20. She was beginning to talk Spanish.

....

Performance Challenge

Individual   This activity showed you how to use a variety of verb conjugations in context. Choose one of the verbs used in this activity and look at the different ways it is used and conjugated within the activity. Then write your own sentences, using the different forms of the verb you chose.

1. ....
....

2. ....
....

3. ....
....

4. ....
....

5. ....
....

Performance Challenge

Group   Break students into groups. Have them write a one act puppet show using as many of the words in these conversations as possible. Have them create their own puppets and perform their scenes for each other and perhaps a group of children.

The Skillful Calculator

INSTRUCTIONS Listen to and read this story. Learn its vocabulary and sentence structures.

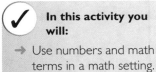

In this activity you will:
→ Use numbers and math terms in a math setting.

Disc **2**   Track **10**

English	Spanish
A poor man passes by a bakery.	*Un pobre pasa por una panadería.*
He sees and smells the bread rolls.	*El ve y huele los panecillos.*
He is hungry, but he has no money.	*Tiene hambre, pero no tiene dinero.*
He enters the bakery and asks a new employee:	*Entra en la panadería y le pregunta a una empleada nueva:*
Say…how much are the rolls?	*Este…¿A cómo son los panecillos?*
A dozen for eleven pesos.	*A una docena por once pesos.*
Mmm, a dozen for eleven pesos.	*Mmm, una docena por once pesos.*
Could you give me eleven for ten pesos?	*¿Me puede dar once por diez?*
Mmm, surely.	*Mmm, claro.*
Then ten for nine?	*Entonces, ¿diez por nueve?*
Well…uh…yes, it's possible.	*Pues…este…sí, se puede.*
Then nine for eight?	*¿Entonces, nueve por ocho?*
All right.	*Está bien.*
Then eight for seven?	*¿Entonces, ocho por siete?*
But of course.	*Claro pues.*
Then seven for six?	*¿Entonces siete por seis?*
Yes.	*Sí.*
How about six for five?	*¿Qué tal seis por cinco?*

English (cont.)	Spanish
Why not?	¿Por qué no?
And five for four?	¿Y cinco por cuatro?
I think so.	Pienso que sí.
Perhaps four for three?	¿Tal vez cuatro por tres?
Fine.	Está bien.
How about three for two?	¿Qué tal tres por dos?
Why yes.	Sí pues.
Then two for one peso?	¿Entonces dos por un peso?
Yes.	Sí.
Then just give me one.	Entonces, déme sólo uno.

Performance Challenge

Individual   This activity presented several different ways of agreeing to something. Go through the activity again and make a written list of all the ways you can find.

....

....

....

....

....

....

Performance Challenge

Group   Organize a restaurant. Divide students into two groups. Have one group act as waiters and waitresses and the other group act as restaurant patrons. Have them order, eat, and pay for their food all in Spanish. Once complete, have the groups trade roles.

Questions and Answers

INSTRUCTIONS Listen to and read these useful questions and answers.

English	Spanish
May I?	¿Puedo?
Yes, you may.	Sí, puede.
May I come in?	¿Puedo entrar?
Come in, please.	Adelante, por favor.
Understood?	¿Entendido?
Yes, understood.	Entendido.
What happened?	¿Qué pasó?
Nothing of importance.	Nada de importancia.
What's happening here?	¿Qué pasa aquí?
Nothing is happening.	No pasa nada.
What's new?	¿Qué [hay] de nuevo?
Nothing much.	No mucho.
What's new?	¿Qué hay de nuevo?
Nothing.	Nada especial.
Don't you believe it?	¿No lo crees?
No, I can't believe it.	No, no puedo creerlo.
May I come in?	¿Puedo entrar?
Surely. Please come in.	Sí, claro. Pase adelante.
Shall we go on?	¿Seguimos?
Of course. Go right ahead.	¿Cómo no? Siga, no más.

In this activity you will:

→ Ask and answer questions in imperfect tense.

  Disc **2**   Track **11**

119

ACTIVITY 27

English *(cont.)*	Spanish
Can it be done?	*¿Se puede?*
It certainly can. Of course.	*Sí se puede. Claro que sí.*

Performance Challenge

Individual   This activity presented several useful questions and answers. Focus on three of them and look for opportunities to use those three in your regular conversations this week.

Performance Challenge

Group   Have your students write riddles in both Spanish and English. Create a riddle book to be shared with friends, family, and other students.

Focus on the Language

INSTRUCTIONS   Use these exercises to master new grammar patterns. Look at the following verbs in the imperfect. Note the parallel between the endings *-aba* and *-ía* (shortened from *-iba*)

Infinitive	Imperfect	English
hablar	*hablaba*	used to speak
tomar	*tomaba*	used to drink
amar	*amaba*	used to love
asistir	*asistía*	used to attend
saber	*sabía*	used to know
conocer	*conocía*	used to know

Have you noticed any patterns? What type of verbs take *-aba* as the ending? What type of verbs take *-ía* as the ending?

Infinitives ending in *-ar*, take *-aba* to indicate the imperfect, whereas infinitives ending in *-er* or *-ir* take *-ía* to indicate the imperfect.

Study Task

INSTRUCTIONS   Take a few minutes now to review the key vocabulary presented in the sentences below. Make three passes through each of these sentences.

1st time through: Compare the Spanish forms and their meaning with the English. (Suggestion: read the Spanish out loud, then look away and say it, thinking of its meaning and form.)

2nd time through: Cover the English and see if you can translate the Spanish into English.

3rd time through: Cover the Spanish and see if you can translate the English into Spanish.

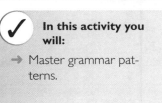

In this activity you will:

→ Master grammar patterns.

Garampiñada: A Recipe of Uruguay

☕ Equal parts of peanuts, sugar, and water (may substitute brown sugar or add a bit of cinnamon if desired)

Directions

Combine all ingredients and cook at a low boil, stirring occasionally, until water is evaporated. Eat warm or cold. This snack is often sold by street vendors, who make it fresh while you wait.

Group A

○ 1st time through
○ 2nd time through
○ 3rd time through

	English	Spanish
1.	(He) knows things and knows José.	*Sabe cosas y conoce a José.*
2.	(They) know things and (they) know José.	*Saben cosas y conocen a José.*
3.	(He) used to know things and (he) used to know José.	*Sabía cosas y conocía a José.*
4.	(They) used to know things and (they) used to know José.	*Sabían cosas y conocían a José.*
5.	(He) knows it; (he) knows her.	*Lo sabe; la conoce.*
6.	(He) doesn't know much yet. Only a little.	*Él todavía no sabe mucho. Sólo un poco.*

Group B

○ 1st time through
○ 2nd time through
○ 3rd time through

	English	Spanish
1.	Used to attend, but no longer attends.	*Asistía, pero ya no asiste.*
2.	She used to attend and used to speak Chinese a little.	*Ella asistía y hablaba un poco de Chino.*
3.	Still attends and still knows José.	*Todavía asiste y todavía conoce a José.*
4.	Ana doesn't know the queen yet.	*Ana todavía no conoce a la reina.*
5.	Doesn't know the king either.	*Tampoco conoce al rey.*
6.	I believe (she) doesn't know them.	*Creo, que no los conoce.*
7.	But they know her.	*Pero ellos la conocen a ella.*

Group C

○ 1st time through
○ 2nd time through

○ 3rd time through

English	Spanish
1. He is talking with her.	*Él está hablando con ella.*
2. The princess is not drinking juice.	*La princesa no está tomando jugo.*
3. She doesn't drink it yet.	*Ella todavía no lo toma.*
4. She is only drinking water.	*Ella está tomando agua no más.*
5. He alone is drinking it.	*Sólo él lo está tomando.*
6. He alone drinks them.	*Sólo él los toma.*
7. They drink it.	*Ellos lo toman.*

Group D

○ 1st time through
○ 2nd time through
○ 3rd time through

English	Spanish
1. Does the prince speak Chinese?	*¿Él príncipe habla chino?*
2. No, only the princess speaks it.	*No, sólo la princesa lo habla.*
3. Doesn't speak it much.	*No lo habla mucho.*
4. Speaks it only in church.	*Lo habla sólo en la iglesia.*
5. She knows many (people).	*Ella conoce a muchos.*
6. Knows the Chinese (people).	*Conoce a los chinos.*
7. Knows a lot (of things).	*Sabe mucho.*
8. The Chinese (people) attend church.	*Los chinos asisten a la iglesia.*

Group E

○ 1st time through
○ 2nd time through
○ 3rd time through

English	Spanish
1. (They) live there in the castle.	*Viven allá en el castillo.*
2. The Chinese used to live in China.	*Los chinos vivían en China.*
3. Where do the king and queen live?	*¿Dónde viven el rey y la reina?*

English *(cont.)*	Spanish
4. It pleases me to sing.	*Me gusta cantar.*
5. It pleases him to play the drum.	*Le gusta tocar el tambor.*
6. What is it pleases her?	*¿Qué es lo que le gusta a ella?*
7. It used to please her to sing with the dog.	*Le gustaba cantar con el perro.*

Have you cemented your knowledge of the new vocabulary?

Performance Self Quiz

INSTRUCTIONS   Match the lettered Spanish phrases with the numbered English phrases, placing the letter in the blank before the corresponding number. Check your answers in Appendix A, on page 331.

	English		Spanish
___ 1.	They used to drink water.	A.	*Ellos están tomando agua.*
___ 2.	They drink water.	B.	*Ellos tomaban agua.*
___ 3.	They are drinking water.	C.	*Ellos toman agua.*
___ 4.	Are speaking Chinese well.	A.	*Ellos hablaban chino bien.*
___ 5.	They speak Chinese well.	B.	*Ellos hablan chino bien.*
___ 6.	They used to speak Chinese well.	C.	*Ellos están hablando chino bien.*
___ 7.	Attends church there.	A.	*Él asistía allá a la iglesia.*
___ 8.	He used to attend church there.	B.	*Asiste allá a la iglesia.*
___ 9.	They used to attend church a lot.	C.	*Ellos asistían mucho a la iglesia.*
___ 10.	They attend church little.	D.	*Ellos asisten un poco a la iglesia.*
___ 11.	Knows many things.	A.	*Él sabía muchas cosas.*
___ 12.	He used to know many things.	B.	*Sabe muchas cosas.*
___ 13.	They know many things.	C.	*Ellos saben muchas cosas.*
___ 14.	They used to know many things.	D.	*Ellos sabían muchas cosas.*
___ 15.	Knows many Chinese there.	A.	*Ellos conocen a muchos chinos allá.*

		English *(cont.)*		Spanish
___	16.	They know many Chinese there.	B.	*Ellos conocían a los chinos.*
___	17.	He used to know the Chinese.	C.	*Conoce a muchos chinos allá.*
___	18.	They used to know the Chinese.	D.	*Él conocía a los chinos.*
___	19.	It didn't please me to sing.	A.	*Me gusta cantar.*
___	20.	It pleases me to sing.	B.	*No me gustaba cantar.*
___	21.	It doesn't please her to eat it.	C.	*A ella no le gustar comerlo.*
___	22.	It didn't please him to eat it.	D.	*A él no le gustaba comerlo.*
___	23.	She didn't used to speak it.	A.	*Ella no lo hablaba.*
___	24.	Didn't used to understand it.	B.	*No lo entendía.*
___	25.	Now (she) understands it.	C.	*Ahora ella lo entiende.*

Performance Challenge

Individual After carefully studying each grammar focus, use the grammar principles you learned in sentences of your own. Write at least three sentences for each focus.

1. ....

....

2. ....

....

3. ....

....

Performance Challenge

Group Have each student write ten "Why" questions in Spanish. Assign each student a partner to interview using the questions they wrote. When they are done, have them introduce their partner to the class in Spanish, using the information they gathered in their interview.

ACTIVITY

29

Wrap-Up Activities

 In this activity you will:

→ Create a mini-story using both written and oral skills.

INSTRUCTIONS Create more of your own mini-story plots. You can write them out or just plan them so you can give them orally.

New Vocabulary

Persons and Samples of Associated Verbs

INSTRUCTIONS Practice translating to and from Spanish.

English	Spanish
The chief	El jefe
is the one who commands.	es el que manda.
The assistant	El ayudante
needs help.	necesita ayuda.
The old nurse	La enfermera vieja
helps the assistant.	ayuda al ayudante.
The young lawyer (advocate)	El abogado joven
falls in love with her.	se enamora de ella.
The surgeon	El cirujano
condemns the general.	condena al general.
The commander	El comandante
wins the battle,	gana la batalla,
rescues the nurse,	rescata a la enfermera,
saves the young lawyer.	salva al abogado joven.

Places and Associated Verbs

INSTRUCTIONS   Practice translating to and from Spanish.

English	Spanish
the circus	el circo
diverts himself in the circus	se divierte en el circo
the battle field	el campo de batalla
leaves the battle field	sale del campo de batalla

Concrete Objects and Associated Verbs

INSTRUCTIONS   Practice translating to and from Spanish.

English	Spanish
suitcase	maleta
carries a suitcase	lleva una maleta
coat	saco
wears a white coat	lleva un saco blanco
weapons	armas
carries weapons	llevan armas
tools / instruments	instrumentos
contains tools	contiene instrumentos
battle	batalla
wins (gains) the battle	gana la batalla

Adverbs and Adjectives

INSTRUCTIONS   Practice translating to and from Spanish.

English	Spanish
suddenly	de repente
suddenly gets up	de repente se levanta
at times	a veces
At times he speaks Japanese.	A veces él habla japonés.
many times / often	muchas veces
Often he comes alone.	Muchas veces él viene solo.
day and night	día y noche

English *(cont.)*	Spanish
sings day and night	*canta día y noche*
especially	*especialmente*
I especially like to sing.	*Especialmente me gusta cantar.*
famous	*famosa*
a very famous surgeon	*un cirujano muy famoso*
therefore (literally "for this")	*por eso*
Therefore he works alone.	*Por eso él trabaja solo.*

Verbs and Associated Nouns

INSTRUCTIONS Practice translating to and from Spanish.

English	Spanish
carries / carried	*lleva, llevaba / llevó*
He carries a suitcase.	*Él lleva una maleta.*
contains / contained	*contiene / contenía*
He is hidden in the kitchen.	*Él está escondido en la cocina.*
shouts / shouted	*grita / gritaba / gritó*
The queen shouts: HELP!	*La reina grita: ¡SOCORRO!*
finds / found / encountered	*encuentra / encontraba / encontró*
finds the queen in the park	*encuentra a la reina en el parque*
saves / saved / salvation	*salva / salvaba / salvó*
The surgeon saves the princess.	*El cirujano salva a la princesa.*
falls in love / fell in love	*se enamora / enamoraba / enamoró*
The soldier falls in love with her.	*El soldado se enamora de ella.*
marries / married	*se casa / casaba / casó*
He marries (with) her.	*Se casa con ella.*
is / was known	*se sabe / sabía*
It's not known that he's a general.	*No se sabe que él es un general.*
stops / stopped / ceased from	*cesa de / cesaba de / cesó de*
stops (from) singing	*cesa de cantar*
wins / won / gain	*gana / ganaba / ganó*
wins the hand of the young lady	*gana la mano de la jovencita*

English *(cont.)*	Spanish
returns / returned / regress	*regresa / regresaba / regresó*
leaves and doesn't return	*sale y no regresa*

Sample Mini-Story Plot

Present Tense

Hay un soldado que viene del campo de batalla. Es un soldado viejo…de hecho, un general—pero no se sabe que él es un general. Y hay una reina, una reina vieja, que vive en el castillo con el rey. El soldado viejo se enamora de la reina vieja, pero no habla nada de su amor. Él sabe que el rey es cruel y que el rey detesta a la reina. El rey detesta a la reina por que ella siempre está cantando. Ella canta día y noche. Al comandante le gusta cuando la reina canta. Le gusta escucharla cantando. De hecho, a él le gusta cantar. Muchas veces él canta en el campo de batalla. A veces él canta con los soldados. Ahora él quiere cantar con la reina. Él quiere cantar con la reina en el castillo. Pero el soldado viejo es un hombre muy bueno. La reina no conoce al soldado viejo, y él no habla nada con la reina.

Un día el rey muere. Ahora la reina está sola en el mundo. ¿Cesa la reina de cantar? No, no cesa de cantar. Un día el soldado viejo encuentra a la reina en un parque. Es el parque de un gigante—un gigante que de hecho es un cirujano muy famoso. La reina está escondida en un árbol. ¿Qué está haciendo en el árbol? De hecho, está cantando. El soldado viejo viene a donde está y dice: «¿Por qué está Ud. escondida en este árbol?» Y ¿Por qué está cantando? Y la reina responde: «Me gusta cantar. Especialmente me gusta cantar en un árbol en el parque.» El soldado viejo dice: «Pero éste es el parque del gigante, y él es un gigante cruel, ¿no?» La reina no responde. Por eso, el soldado viejo sale y no regresa. Eso es todo.

(If you didn't like the ending, try writing a continuation of the story yourself.)

Past Tense

Había un soldado que había venido (had come) del campo de batalla. Era un soldado viejo…de hecho, un general—pero no se sabía que él era un general. Y había una reina, una reina vieja, que vivía en el castillo con el rey. El soldado viejo se enamoró de la reina vieja, pero no hablaba nada de su amor. El sabía que el rey era cruel y que el rey odiaba a la reina. El rey odiaba a la reina por que ella siempre estaba cantando. Ella cantaba día y noche. Al general le gustaba cuando la reina cantaba. Le gustaba escucharla cantar. De hecho, le gustaba cantar él mismo. Muchas veces él cantaba en el campo de batalla. A veces él cantaba con los soldados. Ahora él quería cantar con la reina. El quería cantar con la reina en el castillo. Pero el soldado viejo era un hombre muy bueno. La reina no conocía al soldado viejo, y él no hablaba con la reina.

Un día el rey murió. Entonces la reina estaba sola en el mundo. ¿Cesó la reina de cantar? No, no cesó de cantar. Un día el soldado viejo encontró a la reina en un parque. Era el parque de un gigante—un gigante que de hecho era un cirujano muy famoso. La reina estaba escondida en un árbol. ¿Qué estaba haciendo en el árbol? De hecho, estaba cantando. El soldado viejo venía a donde estaba la reina y dijo: «¿Por qué estaba escondida en este árbol y por qué estaba cantando?» Y la reina respondió: «Me gusta cantar. Especialmente me gusta cantar en un árbol en el parque.» El solda do viejo dijo: «Pero éste es el parque del gigante, y él es un gigante cruel, ¿no?» La reina no respondió. Por eso, el soldado viejo salió y no regresó. Eso es todo.

Performance Challenge

Individual   This activity showed you how to write a mini-story. Working from the words and examples in the activity, write a mini-story of your own. Rough out some ideas below.

....

....

....

....

....

....

....

....

....

....

....

....

Performance Challenge

Group   Have your students write "Help Wanted" ads in Spanish for their dream occupation. Make sure that they use at least 50 words in each ad.

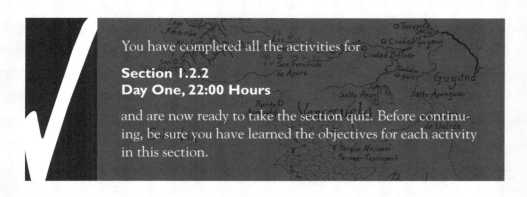

You have completed all the activities for

**Section 1.2.2
Day One, 22:00 Hours**

and are now ready to take the section quiz. Before continuing, be sure you have learned the objectives for each activity in this section.

Section Quiz

INSTRUCTIONS   Select the most correct answer for the following questions. Check your answers in Appendix D, on page 346.

1. *¿Qué comió el pájaro?*

   A. *Se comió una piedra.*

   B. *Se comió al gusano.*

   C. *Se comió a la araña.*

   D. *Se comió las semillas.*

2. *¿Qué fue que le comió a la ballena?*

   A. *El tiburón.*

   B. *El gigante hambriento.*

   C. *La araña.*

   D. *El leopardo.*

3. *¿Qué año es en la universidad?*

   A. *Es 1993.*

   B. *Es 1990.*

   C. *Es 1890.*

   D. *Es 1980.*

4. *¿Por qué lo echaron del trabajo?*

   A. *Porque no hacía sus tareas.*

   B. *Porque no podía llegar a tiempo.*

   C. *Porque fumaba demasiado.*

   D. *Porque no entendía español.*

5. **¿Dónde aprendió la princesa a hablar ruso?**

   A. Lo aprendió en Moscú.

   B. Lo aprendió en las escuela.

   C. Lo aprendió en Siberia.

   D. La princesa no habla ruso.

6. **¿Qué sabe hacer el rey?**

   A. Sabe dirigir himnos.

   B. Sabe cantar la opera.

   C. Sabe cocinar.

   D. Sabe tocar la guitarra.

7. **¿Cuánto cuestan los panecillos?**

   A. Once pesos cada uno.

   B. Once pesos la docena.

   C. Doce pesos por once.

   D. Seis pesos la media docena.

....

INSTRUCTIONS For the following questions, choose the correct English translation of the Spanish sentence.

8. **Ellos asistían mucho a la iglesia.**

   A. We attend church a lot.

   B. They attended church a lot.

   C. We will attend church tomorrow.

   D. They attended church in English.

9. **A ella no le gusta comerlo.**

   A. They do not like to eat it.

   B. We did not like to eat it.

   C. She did not like to eat it.

   D. She does not like to eat it.

10. *El comandante gana la batalla, rescata la enfermera, y salva el abogado joven.*

    A. The commander won the battle, rescued the nurse and saved the young lawyer.

    B. The commander wins the battle, rescues the nurse and saves the young lawyer.

    C. The commander will win the battle, rescue the nurse and save the young lawyer.

    D. The commander wins the battle, rescued the nurse and saves the young lawyer.

You have completed all the sections for

Module 1.2

and are now ready to take the module test. Before continuing, be sure you have learned the objectives for each activity in this module.

Module Test

INSTRUCTIONS   Choose the correct Spanish translation of the English word or sentence. Check your answers in Appendix D, on page 345.

1. **I'm out of here.**
   A. *Ya llegamos.*
   B. *Ya me voy.*
   C. *Por fin.*
   D. *Que te vaya bien.*

2. **Good luck.**
   A. *Así parece.*
   B. *Felicitaciones* (or *Felicidades*).
   C. *Que te vaya bien.*
   D. *Yo voy a la feria.*

3. **Thanks a lot.**
   A. *No he hecho nada.*
   B. *Así parece.*
   C. *Felicitaciones* (or *Felicidades*).
   D. *Muchas gracias.*

4. **Congratulations.**
   A. *Maravilloso.*
   B. *Felicitaciones* (or *Felicidades*).
   C. *Que te vaya bien.*
   D. *Va a llover.*

5. **finally**
   A. *por fin*
   B. *va a llover*
   C. *no hay porqué*
   D. *tengo una pregunta*

6. **I have a question.**
   A. *¿Cuál es?*
   B. *Va a llover.*
   C. *Tengo una pregunta.*
   D. *¿Por qué?*

7. **I'm going to the fair.**
   A. *Ya me voy.*
   B. *Tengo una pregunta.*
   C. *Que te vaya bien.*
   D. *Yo voy a la feria.*

8. **fantastic**
   A. *excelente*
   B. *maravilloso*
   C. *fantástico*
   D. *felicidades*

INSTRUCTIONS True or False: The following phrases or sentences are translated correctly.

9. ***Aquí está una niñita.* = Here is a big girl.**
   A. True
   B. False

10. ***Aquí está su abuelita.* = Here is a big girl.**
    A. True
    B. False

11. ***Aquí está la casa de su abuelita.* = Here is her grandma's house.**
    A. True
    B. False

12. **Aquí está el bosque.** = Here is the jungle.

   A. True

   B. False

13. **Aquí está un lobo.** = Here is a wolf.

   A. True

   B. False

14. **bueno** = well

   A. True

   B. False

15. **La abuelita está enferma.** = The grandma is well.

   A. True

   B. False

16. The mother sends Little Red Riding Hood with a basket of cookies. = **La mama manda a Caperucita Roja con una canasta de galletas.**

   A. True

   B. False

17. He runs to the grandma's house. = **Corre a la casa de la mama.**

   A. True

   B. False

18. The wolf gets in bed. = **El lobo se mete en la cama.**

   A. True

   B. False

19. She thinks it's her grandma. = **Piensa que es su abuelita.**

   A. True

   B. False

20. At that moment the grandma enters with a dog. = **En ese momento entra la abuelita con un perro.**

   A. True

   B. False

21. **Toma tu lápiz. Tómalo.** = Take your pencil. Take it.

   A. True

   B. False

22. *Ponlo aquí.* = Put it here.

   A. True

   B. False

23. *Toma mi papel rojo.* = Give me my red paper.

   A. True

   B. False

24. *¿Cuántos lápices?* = Where are the pencils?

   A. True

   B. False

25. *Toma un papel y ponlo en la caja.* = Take a paper and put it in the box.

   A. True

   B. False

Aruba
(NETH.)

Netherlands
Antilles
(NETH.)

ST. VINCENT AND
THE GRENADINES
GRENADA

Maracaibo

Caracas

Port-

TRI
TO

Valencia

Barquisimeto

ta

E
S

San Cristóbal

Rio

Orinoco

Ciudad
Guayana

VENEZUELA

Bogotá

G U I A N A

H I G

OLOMBIA

Boa Vista

G

A M A Z O N

Rio

Negro

Amazon

M

os

Madeira

Module 1.3

Throughout this module we'll be learning about the culture of Venezuela.

Keep these tips in mind as you progress through this module:

1. Read instructions carefully.
2. Repeat aloud all the Spanish words you hear on the audio CDs.
3. Learn at your own pace.
4. Have fun with the activities and practice your new language skills with others.
5. Record yourself speaking Spanish on tape so you can evaluate your own speaking progress.

N

Coro

Maracaibo

Caracas

Carúpano

Cumaná

Barcelona

Barquisimeto

Valencia

Lago
Maracaibo

Mérida

Pico Bolívar

Tucupita

Los
Llanos

Río Orinoco

Ciudad Guyana

Ciudad Bolívar

San
Cristóbal

Los Andes

San Fernando
de Apure

Embalse
de Guri

Guyana

Salto Aponguao

Salto Angel

Puerto
Ayacucho

Venezuela

Santa Elena
de Ualrén

Colombia

Parque Nacional
Parima-Tapirapecó

Brazil

Parque Nacional
Serranía la Neblina

Venezuela

Day Two, 12:00 Hours

El leopardo azul

The bells on the town's cathedral are chiming *mediodía* when you and *Araña* look up from your studies. "Well," says *Araña*, "we know from that story that *el leopardo* ate *el cerdo*, but I'm not sure how that helps us."

"Let's have a look around town and find out," you suggest.

You and *Araña* wander around *el pueblo de Coro* looking for anything to do with *leopardos*. You pass *el museo de arte*. Its entrance is blocked off, with police officers standing nearby. You ask them what happened.

One of the officers explains that last night, someone—or, as they suspect, several someones—broke into *el museo* and stole several items. Most were the sort of thing they expect to have stolen—a valuable painting, two examples of pre-Columbian gold work—but one stolen item really puzzles them. Whoever broke in stole a small, battered travel journal kept by one Alonso Hernández, an eccentric scholar who traveled over much of South America in late 1600's. It was neither pretty nor, as far as they knew, valuable—the museum curator had just used it to fill out an exhibit. Nonetheless, it is missing.

Wondering if the museum robbery is somehow connected to your kidnapping case, you thank the officers and move on.

"Hey, *Mosca*, look!" *Araña* whispers excitedly, nodding to the building next to the museum. It's one of the older buildings you've seen in *Coro*. It looks like someone's remodeled it into a pleasant *café*. The sign hanging over it is what really catches your attention, though—the *café* is named "*El Leopardo Azul*."

You and *Araña* walk in to investigate. Occupying the center of the *café* is a stylized statue of *un leopardo*, and tucked into a crack at the statue's base is *una hoja de papel*. You retrieve it, sit down at a quiet corner table, and carefully unfold it. It's a puzzle, in what you're starting to recognize as the handwriting of *Señor* Espinoza. The format, though, is familiar.

"Well," says *Araña*, "I don't know the words to finish that yet. Let's order some *almuerzo* and study while we eat."

In this section you will:

- → Build fluency in past tense.
- → Understand new vocabulary and grammar.
- → Expand comprehension, fluency, and use of past and present tense.
- → Follow a conversation and understand its meaning.
- → Understand directions.
- → Follow a story line with full comprehension.

   Disc **3**   Track **1**

You agree, place an order for Venezuela's tasty version of black beans and rice, and get to work.

Recipe: Venezuelan Black Beans and Rice

- 1 tablespoon olive oil
- 1 medium onion, coarsely chopped
- 1 stalk celery, sliced
- 1 red bell pepper, seeded and coarsely diced
- 1 cup long-grain white rice
- 1 1/2 cups broth
- 1 teaspoon turmeric
- 1 teaspoon oregano
- 1/4 teaspoon cumin
- 1 teaspoon salt
- 1 can black beans, mostly drained (leave about 1 tablespoon liquid)
- 4 eggs
- salt and pepper to taste
- red pepper to taste
- lemon wedges (optional)

Directions   Sauté onion in olive oil for 2-3 minutes over medium heat. Stir in celery, bell pepper, and rice. Cook, stirring frequently, for another 2-3 minutes until rice turns pale. Reduce heat to low and add broth, turmeric, oregano, cumin, salt, and beans (with remaining liquid). Stir, then cover and cook 20-30 minutes, until liquid is absorbed and rice is tender. While rice is cooking, scramble eggs in a separate pan, adding salt and pepper to taste. Scoop cooked rice and beans onto a plate, top with scrambled eggs, and sprinkle with red pepper. Garnish with lemon wedges, if desired. Serve warm.

Puzzle

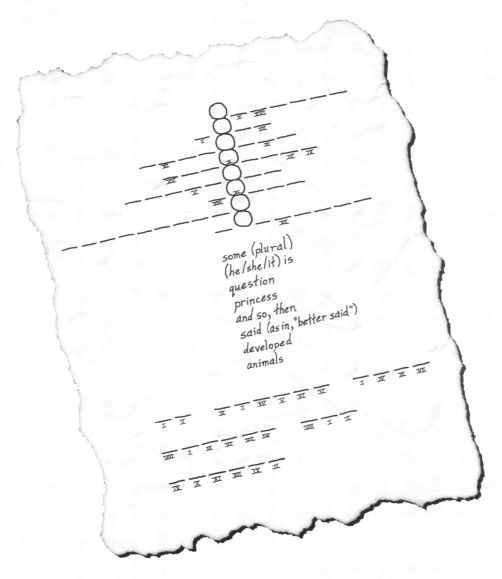

some (plural)
(he/she/it) is
question
princess
and so, then
said (as in, "better said")
developed
animals

INSTRUCTIONS Follow the clues to fill in the puzzle with the correct words. The circled letters will spell out your next adventure destination. Under some of the letters in the puzzle, Roman numerals are written. These numerals correspond to blanks at the bottom of the page. Fill in the blanks with the appropriate letters to receive a piece of the clue you will need to solve the adventure's climax.

After working the puzzle out yourself, check the answers in Appendix A, on page 332.

Dream of a Little Girl

In this activity you will:

→ Build fluency in past tense.

Disc **3**   Track **2**

Venezuela Culture Overview

Venezuela is rich in both oil and natural beauty, but since much of its material wealth remains concentrated in the hands of a few, its people remain deeply divided. A land of contrasts, Venezuela offers steamy jungles and snow-capped mountains, the world's highest waterfall and white sand Caribbean beaches. Old and new can be found side by side, in its capital city and elsewhere. The people of Venezuela are known for their good humor and their patriotism, though recently they have made the news more often for attempted coups and clashes with guerilla fighters near the Colombian border. Simón Bolívar, who liberated much of South America from Spanish control, was Venezuelan.

INSTRUCTIONS   Listen to and read this story. Use it to learn Spanish vocabulary and sentence patterns. In this story, you will build your fluency with the past tense.

English	Spanish
This I saw in a dream:	*Esto es lo que vi en un sueño:*
a little girl, walking down the street came to my house.	*una niñita, que caminaba por la calle vino a mi casa.*
She came up to the door, opened it, and went in.	*Vino a mi puerta, la abrió, y entró.*
She entered the kitchen,	*Entró a la cocina,*
went up to the table,	*fue a la mesa,*
sat on a chair,	*se sentó en una silla,*
put her hands on the table,	*puso sus manos sobre la mesa,*
laid her head in her hands,	*apoyó su cabecita en sus manos,*
and cried and cried.	*y lloró y lloró.*
And as I looked at her,	*Y mientras yo la miraba,*
I cried also.	*también lloré.*
Then she stood up,	*Después se puso de pie,*
wiped her tears,	*secó sus lágrimas,*
went to the door,	*fue a la puerta,*
opened it, and went out.	*la abrió, y salió.*
I watched her go down the street.	*Yo la miré ir por la calle.*

English *(cont.)*	Spanish
Why was she crying? I'd like to know.	*Me gustaría saber por qué lloraba.*
Perhaps she had lost a kitten?	*¿Habrá perdido un gatito?*
Perhaps she had lost a friend?	*¿Habrá perdido un amigo?*
Only she knows.	*Sólo ella sabe.*
I think that I'll never find out.	*Pienso que nunca lo sabré.*

Performance Challenge

Individual   This short story gave you several examples of past tense verbs. Go through the story again and make a written list of the past tense verbs you find.

....

....

....

....

....

....

....

....

....

....

Performance Challenge

Group   Have the students take all of the nouns out of the story. Using the list of nouns, have them write a new story in Spanish.

The Story of the Three Billy Goats

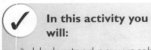

Disc **3** Track **3**

INSTRUCTIONS Listen to and read this story. Use it to learn vocabulary and sentence patterns. In this story, you will build on your comprehension and fluency with the past and present tenses.

Los Tres Cabritos

🔊

Habían tres cabritos que vivían en las montañas. Eran hermanos. Había un cabrito grande, un cabrito mediano, y un cabrito chiquito. A los cabritos les gustaba mucho comer zacate verde en las montañas, y nunca bajaron al valle. Nunca habían cruzado el puente.

Un día el cabrito chiquito observó que al otro lado del puente había mucho zacate verde. Entonces el cabrito chiquito pensó en cruzar el puente y bajar al valle para comer de aquel zacate verde. No sabía que abajo del puente vivía un enano muy feo y muy feroz. Bueno, el cabrito chiquito se acercó al puente y pronto comenzó a cruzarlo. Pero cuando iba cruzando el puente, se oían sus pisadas: Trip, trip, trip, trip... Al oír las pisadas del cabrito pequeño, el enano feo brincó del agua y gritó con voz feroz:

"¿Quién va cruzando mi puente?"

"Soy yo, el cabrito chiquito."

"¿Y a qué vienes aquí?"

"Voy a bajar al valle para comer el zacate verde que está allá."

"¡Fuera de mi puente! Si no, te como."

"Oh, por favor, no me coma a mí. Yo soy muy chiquito. Espérese mejor hasta que pase mi hermano por aquí. El es más grande y más gordo que yo."

"Bueno, entonces pasa esta vez."

Poco tiempo después, el cabrito mediano vio que su hermanito estaba en el valle abajo y estaba feliz allí comiendo zacate verde. Ahora él pensó en cruzar el puente para bajar al valle donde había mucho zacate verde. Se acercó al puente y comenzó a cruzar sin saber del enano feo que vive abajo. Pero cuando iba cruzando el puente, se oyeron sus pisadas: Trap, trap, trap, trap... Al oír las pisadas del cabrito mediano en el puente, el enano feo brincó del agua y grita con voz feroz:

"¿Quién va cruzando mi puente?"

"Soy yo, el cabrito mediano."

"¿Y a qué vienes aquí?"

"Voy a bajar al valle para comer del zacate verde que está allí con mi hermano."

"¡Fuera de mi puente! Si no, te voy a comer."

"Oh, por favor, no me coma a mí. Yo soy muy chico todavía. Espérese mejor hasta que pase por aquí mi hermano mayor. El es más grande y más gordo que yo."

"Bueno, entonces pasa esta vez."

Poco tiempo después el cabrito grande (el hermano mayor) ve que sus hermanitos están en el valle abajo comiendo felices zacate verde. Ahora él piensa cruzar el puente y bajar al valle para comer del zacate. Se acerca al puente y comienza a cruzar sin saber del enano feo. Pero cuando iba cruzando el puente, se oyeron sus pisadas: Trop, trop, trop, trop… y el puente se mecía de tanto peso. Al oír las pisadas y sentir que el puente se mecía, el enano feo brincó del agua y gritó con una voz feroz:

"¿Quién va cruzando mi puente?"

"Soy yo, el cabrito grande."

"¿Y a qué viniste aquí?"

"Voy a bajar al valle para comer del zacate verde allá con mis hermanitos."

"¡Fuera de mi puente! Si no, te voy a comer."

"Muy bien, adelante."

El enano feo se acercó, pero el cabrito grande bajó la cabeza, y con sus cuernos le dió un golpe tremendo al enano feo. Éste se cayó en el agua y se hundió. Y desde ese día en adelante, el enano feo no ha molestado a los cabritos. Los cabritos pueden cruzar el puente cuando quieren y pueden comer zacate en el valle así como en las montañas.

Performance Challenge

Individual Using as much Spanish as you can, write briefly about something that you and your brother or sister did together. If you don't have a brother or sister, write about something you did with a parent, classmate, or friend.

....

....

....

....

....

....

....

....

....

....

Performance Challenge

Group   Split the group into teams. Have each team rewrite the ending and then perform it for the group. Have the group vote on the best ending and award the winning team with some goat cheese to taste.

Vincent and Isabel

INSTRUCTIONS   Listen to this conversation and learn its vocabulary. Listen to it a second time in Spanish only.

English	Spanish
V: Hi.	*Hola.*
I: Hello.	*Hola.*
V: How are things?	*¿Cómo va todo?*
I: Very well, thanks.	*Muy bien, gracias.*
V: We met at the concert last week, remember?	*Nos conocimos en el concierto en la semana pasada, ¿se acuerda?*
I: Yes, I remember. Of course I remember. Nice to see you again.	*Si, me acuerdo, por supuesto que me acuerdo. ¡Qué bueno verlo otra vez!*
V: Forgive me, I forgot your name.	*Perdóneme, me he olvidado su nombre.*
I: My name is Isabel. And yours is Vincent, right?	*Me llamo Isabel. Y su nombre es Vicente, ¿no?*
V: Yes. Tell me, what's that?	*Sí. Dígame, ¿qué es eso?*
I: That's my dog!	*¡Es mi perro!*
V: Your dog?! He looks like a wolf.	*¿Su perro? Pero parece lobo.*
I: Yes. Actually his father was a wolf.	*Sí. En verdad su padre era lobo.*
V: By the way, where is your home?	*A propósito, ¿dónde está su casa?*
I: On the other side of the park. And yours?	*Al otro lado del parque. ¿Y la suya?*
V: On this side of the park.	*En este lado del parque.*
I: By the university?	*¿Por la universidad?*

In this activity you will:

→ Expand comprehension, fluency, and use of past and present tense.
→ Follow a conversation and understand its meaning.

Disc **3**   Track **4**

Facts and Figures on Venezuela

- The nation's full name is *República Bolivariana de Venezuela*.
- Venezuela's population is around 23.5 million.
- The capital city of Venezuela is Caracas.
- Spanish is Venezuela's official language, but English is a required course in many schools, and more than 30 Native American languages also survive.
- Venezuela's most popular sport is baseball.
- Venezuela's main industries include petroleum, iron ore, cereals, fruit, coffee, and sugar.
- Venezuela's government is a federal republic, with a president and a bicameral legislature.

English (cont.)	Spanish
V: Exactly. I was told that you are a pianist.	Exactamente. Se me ha dicho que Ud. es pianista.
I: No, I'm not a pianist. I'm a Russian spy.	No, yo no soy pianista. Soy una espía Rusa.
V: Hmm, how interesting! And I'm an American secret agent.	Hmm, ¡Qué interesante! Y yo soy un agente secreto Americano.
I: I know that.	Lo sé.
V: How did you find out?	¿Cómo lo supo?
I: My husband is also a secret agent. He told me that.	Mi esposo también es un agente secreto. Él me lo dijo.
V: How about that!	¡Qué cosa!
I: Well, I've got to go.	Bueno, tengo que irme.
V: Wait a second, I've got one last question.	Espere un segundo, tengo una pregunta final.
I: What is it?	¿Sí?
V: Tell me, what's your dog's name?	¿Cómo se llama su perro?
I: Napo. His name is Napo.	Napo. Su nombre es Napo.
V: Why do you call him Napo?	¿Por qué lo llamas Napo?
I: Hard to say. Napoleon…	Es difícil decir. Napoleón…
V: Well, got to go. Good-bye, Napo. Good-bye Isabel.	Bueno, tengo que ir. Adiós Napo. Adiós Isabel.
I: Good luck!	¡Buena suerte!

Performance Challenge

Individual   Using the vocabulary and grammar you've learned up to now, write a conversation of your own. It should be at least four lines long. Once you have written it, perform it with a friend, sibling, or classmate.

....

....

....

....

....

....

....

....

....

....

....

....

....

Performance Challenge

Group   Research and write about a Spanish pianist or musician. Listen to a musical composition of the artist you choose and write in Spanish how it makes you feel as you listen to it.

ACTIVITY

33

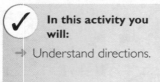

In this activity you will:

➡ Understand directions.

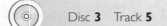

Disc **3**   Track **5**

A Geography Lesson

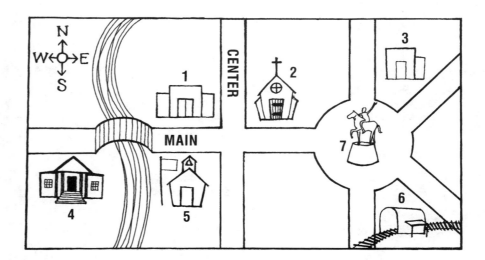

INSTRUCTIONS Learn more geography-related vocabulary. You will learn to give and receive directions.

English	Spanish
Today we are going to look at a different map.	*Hoy vamos a mirar un mapa diferente.*
It isn't a map of continents, countries, oceans, and seas but a simple city map.	*No es un mapa de continentes, países, océanos, y mares, sino un simple mapa de una ciudad.*
A city map can be very useful when you travel and can prevent you from getting lost if you know how to read one.	*El mapa de una ciudad puede ser muy útil cuando uno viaja y puede ayudarlo a uno a no perderse si sabe leerlo.*
Like all maps, the north is at the top and the south at the bottom.	*Como en todos los mapas, el norte está en la parte de arriba y el sur en la parte de abajo.*

English *(cont.)*	Spanish
Once you orient yourself, the rest is easy.	*Una vez que uno se orienta, el resto es fácil.*
Let's look at the map we have right here.	*Miremos el mapa que tenemos aquí.*
At the center of the map, you can see two wide streets crossing.	*Al centro del mapa, puedes ver dos calles anchas que se cruzan.*
The street that runs north and south is called Center Street.	*La calle que va de norte a sur se llama Center Street.*
The street that runs east and west is called Main Street.	*La calle que va de este a oeste se llama Main Street.*
At the northwest corner of this intersection is a department store (1), and right across the street from the department store there is an old church (2).	*En la esquina noroeste de esta intersección hay un negocio (1), y justo al frente del negocio, al otro lado de la calle, hay una iglesia antigua (2).*
So the old church is at the northeast corner of the intersection, right?	*Entonces la iglesia está en la esquina noreste de la intersección, ¿no?*
Across the street directly south of the department store is the city library (5).	*Al otro lado de la calle, directamente al sur del negocio está la biblioteca de la ciudad (5).*
What is this? Yes, it is a river.	*¿Qué es esto? Sí, es un río.*
It is a wide river that crosses the city from north to south.	*Un río ancho que cruza la ciudad de norte a sur.*
There is a bridge on the map.	*Hay un puente en el mapa.*
On the west side of the bridge is the city hall.	*Al lado oeste del puente está la municipalidad.*
What number is it?	*¿Qué número es?*
On the east side (the right side) of the map, we have a roundabout with a big statue in the center (7) and a couple of buildings on either side (3, 6).	*Al lado este (lado derecho) del mapa, verá una rotonda con una gran estatua en el centro (7) con un edificio a cada lado (3, 6).*
How do you go from the department store (1) to the city library (5)?	*¿Cómo se va del negocio (1) a la biblioteca (5)?*
It is simple. Go down Center Street straight through the intersection.	*Simple. Vaya por Center Street derecho por la intersección.*
The library is on your right.	*La biblioteca estará a su derecha.*

English *(cont.)*	Spanish
Tell me, how do you go from the old church to the train station (6)?	*Dígame, ¿Cómo se va desde la iglesia a la estación de trenes (6)?*
First, cross Main Street and turn left.	*Primero, cruce Main Street y doble a la izquierda.*
Walk until you see the roundabout with the statue in the middle.	*Camine hasta que vea la rotonda con la estatua en el centro.*
Take the second street on your right and continue to walk until you see a long blue building.	*Tome la segunda calle de la derecha y siga caminando hasta que vea un edificio azul largo.*
That's the train station.	*Esa es la estación de trenes.*
How do you go from the train station to city hall?	*¿Cómo se va de la estación de trenes a la municipalidad?*
Go back through the roundabout and take Main Street.	*Vuelva a la rotonda y tome Main Street.*
Go straight past the church and the department store.	*Vaya derecho pasando la iglesia y el negocio.*
You'll come to a bridge. Cross it, and you'll see the city hall on your left.	*Va a llegar a un puente. Crúcelo y verá la municipalidad a su izquierda.*

Performance Challenge

Individual   This activity focused on how to give directions in Spanish. Find or draw a map of your neighborhood. Then explain, in Spanish, where different places are located on the map.

Performance Challenge

Group 1   Set up a maze out of desks, chairs, or other objects. Have each student choose a partner. Blindfold one of the partners and have the other give them directions in Spanish on how to move through the maze. The pair that completes the maze in the least amount of time wins.

Performance Challenge

Group 2   Have the students draw a map of their town. In Spanish, have them write directions from three places in town to their house using at least 10 different words from this activity.

The Arab and His Camel

ACTIVITY 34

In this activity you will:

→ Follow a story line with full comprehension.

Disc **3**   Track **6**

INSTRUCTIONS   Read and listen to the following story. Work toward full comprehension.

Una Fábula de la Grecia del Antiguo

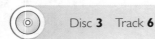

En una fría noche de invierno se encontraba un árabe durmiendo en su tienda. De repente su camello metió su nariz en la tienda y dijo:

"Amo, ¿podría entrar para calentarme?"

Después de dudar por un momento el árabe dijo:

"Está bien."

Luego el camello estiró su cuello dentro de la tienda y dijo:

"Todavía siento frío. ¿Podría meter mi cuello?"

"Sí, está bien," dijo el árabe. Luego el camello dijo:

"Todavía siento mucho frío. ¿Podría meter mis patas delanteras?"

"Está bien," dijo el árabe.

Ahora el árabe tenía que retroceder para hacer más lugar. El camello habló otra vez:

"En esta posición mantengo la tienda abierta, y ambos sentimos frío. Déjame entrar y cerrar la cortina. Así ambos podemos calentarnos."

"Bueno," dijo el árabe.

Y el camello entró y cerró la cortina. Pero ya no había suficiente espacio para ambos. La tienda era demasiada pequeña. Después de un momento el camello dijo:

"No hay suficiente espacio para ambos. Tú eres más pequeño que yo. Sería mejor que tú salieras. Entonces habrá espacio para mí. Por lo menos uno de nosotros estará cómodo."

Después el camello sacó a su amo de la tienda de un empujón. El árabe se dijo a sí mismo:

"Estaba equivocado. En primer lugar, no lo hubiera dejado meter la cabeza."

Performance Challenge

Individual   Using as much Spanish as you can, briefly write about what lesson you think the story is teaching.

....

....

....

....

....

....

....

....

....

....

....

....

....

....

Geography of Venezuela

Venezuela borders the Caribbean Sea on the north, Guyana on the east, Brazil on the south, and Colombia on the west. In the southeast of Venezuela are the Guyana Highlands. The central grassland plain, called the *Llanos*, dominates fully 30% of the country and is drained by South America's third largest river, the *Río Orinoco*. In the northwest of Venezuela, surrounded by marshy, fertile lowlands, is South America's largest inland lake, *Lago Maracaibo*. The *Cordillera de los Andes* rises south of the lake, with the highest peak, *Pico Bolívar*, towering 16,423 feet above sea level. Venezuela is home to an amazing variety of flora and fauna, with some of its native species including the anteater, armadillo, jaguar, ocelot, tapir, and anaconda. Venezuela's environment is primarily tropical, with a warm temperate zone along the coast. Temperatures seldom vary by more than a few degrees, so climate zones are determined by rainfall rather than temperature. The northern coastlands are relatively dry, but rainfall increases inland and at higher elevations. Venezuela's dry season, called *verano*, stretches from December to April, and the wet season, called *invierno*, covers the rest of the year. The Amazon area of Venezuela, though, has no distinct seasons and receives more than 78 inches of rainfall per year.

Performance Challenge

Group   Have each student write about a time when they went camping with their family or friends, in Spanish. Invite them to share what they have written with their family or friends, teaching them at least 10 new words in Spanish as they do.

You have completed all the activities for

**Section 1.3.1
Day Two, 12:00 Hours**

and are now ready to take the section quiz. Before continuing, be sure you have learned the objectives for each activity in this section.

Section Quiz

INSTRUCTIONS   Select the most correct answer for the following questions. Check your answers in Appendix D, on page 346.

1. **¿Por qué lloró la niña en el sueño?**

   A. *Perdió su gato.*

   B. *Perdió su amigo.*

   C. *No se sabe.*

   D. *Vino a la casa.*

2. **¿Quién vive abajo del puente?**

   A. *los tres cabritos*

   B. *un enano muy feo y muy feroz*

   C. *Caperucita Roja*

   D. *Vicente*

3. **¿Por qué entró el camello en la tienda del árabe?**

   A. *Porque tenía hambre.*

   B. *Porque tenía frío.*

   C. *Porque quería hablar con su amo.*

   D. *Para estar más cómodo.*

INSTRUCTIONS   For the following questions, choose the correct Spanish translation for the underlined English word or set of words.

4. *Cuando llegó a mi casa, la niña* <u>sat</u> *a la mesa.*

   A. *se sienta*

   B. *se sientó*

   C. *se sentó*

   D. *se senta*

5. *Había un hombre viejo que* <u>used to live</u> *en la calle.*

   A. *vive*

   B. *vivía*

   C. *vivió*

   D. *viva*

6. *Las chicas* <u>used to go</u> *a la escuela todos los días.*

   A. *van*

   B. *fueron*

   C. *iban*

   D. *vayan*

7. *Felipe y María* <u>met</u> *en un concierto la semana pasada.*

   A. *se conocieron*

   B. *nos conocimos*

   C. *se conocen*

   D. *nos conocieron*

8. *¿Dónde está tu casa?* <u>My</u> *casa está en la calle Revolución.*

   A. *La*

   B. *Mi*

   C. *Su*

   D. *Nuestra*

9. *La farmacia está en* <u>the corner</u> *de las calles Central y Avenida Juarez.*

   A. *el río*

   B. *el edificio*

   C. *el puente*

   D. *la esquina*

10. **Para ir a la iglesia: <u>Go</u> hasta el puente. Doble a la derecha.**

   A. *Van*

   B. *Va*

   C. *Vaya*

   D. *Ir*

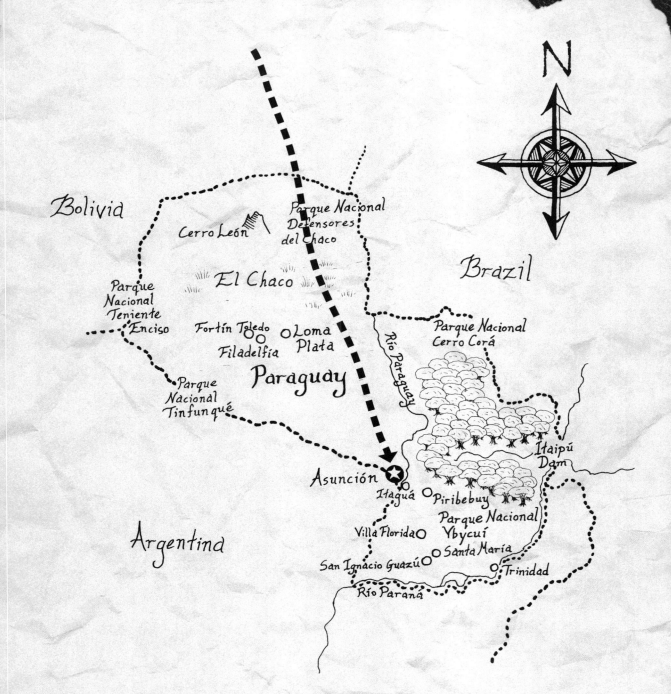

Netherlands
Antilles

ST. VINCENT AND
THE GRENADINES

N

Bolivia

Brazil

Cerro León

Parque Nacional
Defensores
del Chaco

Parque
Nacional
Teniente
Enciso

El Chaco

Parque Nacional
Cerro Corá

Fortín Toledo
Filadelfia

Loma
Plata

Paraguay

Parque
Nacional
Tinfunqué

Itaipú
Dam

Asunción

Itauá

Piribebuy

Parque Nacional
Ybycuí

Argentina

Villa Florida

Santa María

San Ignacio Guazú

Trinidad

Río Paraná

Paraguay

Day Two, 17:00 Hours

Viajando hacia Asunción

You and *Araña* finish the puzzle. "Definitely not *una receta*," *Araña* comments.

"It looks like we're bound for *Asunción*," you say.

"*¿Dónde está Asunción?*" *Araña* asks.

"Capital city of Paraguay," you answer absently, filling in the letters at the bottom of the puzzle. "This is interesting…look what this spells out! *El tesoro*…the treasure. I wonder what the rest of the sentence says."

"I guess we'll have to find the next puzzle, *el próximo rompecabezas*," says *Araña*. He gets up and goes to the phone to arrange passage to Paraguay.

Within *dos horas*, you board a commercial flight to Asunción. You and *Araña* pass the flight poring over the map and studying more *español*. It's after dark by the time you've landed, passed through customs, and found your way out of the airport.

At a nearby hotel, you check local news for anything that might be related to your case. *Nada*. No missing person reports, no museums robbed, not even a mention on the international report of the missing *Señor* Espinoza. Wearily, you turn off the news, study some more *español*, and get some rest.

✓ **In this section you will:**

→ Understand new vocabulary in a conversation.

→ Use repetition to gain full comprehension.

→ Master new vocabulary.

→ Use imperfect, perfect, and past participle verb endings.

→ Perform in aspects of past tense.

→ Use the simple verb tenses without an auxiliary verb.

⊚ Disc **3**   Track **7**

SECTION **1.3.2**

ACTIVITY

35

 In this activity you will:

→ Understand new vocabulary in a conversation.

 Disc **3** Track **8**

The Critical Mother

INSTRUCTIONS Listen to and read this short story. Learn as much vocabulary as you can.

🔊

English	Spanish
Reynaldo's mother sent him a gift for Christmas:	*La mamá de Reynaldo le mandó un regalo de navidad:*
she sent two silk ties, one red and one green.	*dos corbatas de seda, una roja y una verde.*
And she wrote him that she was coming to see him next Sunday and asked him to please come to the airport to meet her.	*Entonces ella le mandó una carta diciendo que va a visitar el próximo domingo y que por favor venga al aeropuerto a recibirla.*
Reynaldo knows that his mother is very critical.	*Reynaldo sabe que su madre es muy criticadora.*
He decides to wear the red tie.	*El decide ponerse la corbata roja.*

English (cont.)	Spanish
Arriving at the airport, he receives his mother with an embrace.	*Al llegar al aeropuerto, él recibe a su madre con un abrazo.*
She says: "So you didn't like the green tie, eh?"	*Ella le dice: "No te gustó la corbata verde, ¿no es cierto?"*

Performance Challenge

Individual   This activity presented a joke in Spanish. Think of your favorite joke, then try to tell it in Spanish. Use a dictionary, or ask a parent or instructor if you need help with some of the words! Rough out some ideas below.

....

....

....

....

....

....

....

....

....

....

Performance Challenge

Group   Ask students to write about a gift that has been in their families for several generations. Be sure they include who it belonged to originally, its history, and why it is so important. Have them give an oral presentation in Spanish about the gift.

History of Venezuela

Columbus was the first European to walk upon what is now Venezuela, though its name was given a year later by explorer Alonso de Ojeda. Some 500,000 indigenous peoples lived in Venezuela when the first Spanish settlement was built at Cumaná in 1521, but fighting against those settlers and the depredations of European disease cut those numbers by at least two thirds. Venezuela was not a source for gold or any other easily removed wealth at the time of its colonization, though, so it quickly fell into neglect, which in turn bred resentment among the American-born Spanish elites. This resentment grew more widespread and erupted into revolution, led by Simón Bolívar, "*El Libertador.*" Venezuela achieved its independence in 1821 with a decisive victory at Campo Carabobo. Bolívar had already liberated Colombia and went on later to liberate Ecuador, Peru, and Bolivia. Ecuador, Venezuela, and Colombia were united under Bolívar but divided after his death in 1830. Venezuela soon declared full independence under its own new constitution. This independence was marred by a succession of military dictators, political coups, poverty, and economic instability. Some economic stability arrived when oil was discovered in the Maracaibo basin in the late 1910s. By the late 1920s, Venezuela had become the world's largest exporter of petroleum. However, little of this wealth reached the common people. Widespread poverty, coupled with poor educational facilities and health care, led to a series of popular uprisings, which in turn led to the nation's first democratic elections in 1947. Political and economic instabilities continue to plague Venezuela, but its people still keep their goals in sight.

Chicken Little

ACTIVITY
36

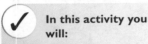

✓ In this activity you will:

→ Use repetition to gain full comprehension.

  Disc **3** Track **9**

INSTRUCTIONS Listen to and read this story. Use the repetition in this story to learn the new vocabulary and work toward full comprehension.

Pollito Chico

Esta es la historia de Pollito Chico, un pollito que se alarmó y se puso a creer que el cielo se estaba cayendo. Un día este pollito estaba comiendo en el jardín cuando una hoja, una hoja muy grande, le cayó en la cabeza.

El pobre pollito se asustó y se puso a creer que el cielo se estaba cayendo. Se puso a correr, gritando:

"Pío, pío, Mami, ¿dónde estás Mami?"

"Clo, clo, aquí estoy, Pollito. ¿Qué pasa?"

"¡El cielo se está cayendo! ¡El cielo se está cayendo!"

"¿Cómo lo sabes, Pollito?"

"Lo vi con mis propios ojos, y un pedazo del cielo cayó ¡BUM! sobre mi cabeza. Te digo la verdad."

"¡Huyamos!" gritó la gallina. "¡Huyamos, corre! Pato, Pato, ¿dónde estás, Pato?"

"Cuac, cuac, aquí estoy. ¿Qué pasó? ¿Qué pasó?"

"¡El cielo se está cayendo! ¡El cielo se está cayendo!"

"¿Cómo lo sabes, Gallina?"

"Me lo dijo el pollito."

"¿Cómo lo sabes, Pollito?"

"Lo vi con mis propios ojos, y un pedazo del cielo cayó ¡BUM! sobre mi cabeza. Les digo la verdad."

"¡Huyamos!" gritó el pato. "¡Huyamos, corran!"

"Ganso, Ganso, ¿dónde estás, Ganso?"

"Uank, uank, aquí estoy, Pato. ¿Qué pasó?"

"¡El cielo se está cayendo! ¡El cielo se está cayendo!"

"¿Cómo lo sabes, Pato?"

"Me lo dijo la gallina."

"¿Cómo lo sabes, Gallina?"

"Me lo dijo el pollito."

"¿Cómo lo sabes, Pollito?"

"Lo vi con mis propios ojos, y un pedazo del cielo cayó ¡BUM! sobre mi cabeza. Les estoy diciendo la verdad."

"¡Huyamos!" gritó el ganso. "¡Huyamos, corran!"

"Pavo, Pavo, ¿dónde estás, Pavo?"

"Gabul, gabul. Aquí estoy, Ganso.

¿Qué pasó? ¿Qué pasó?"

"¡El cielo se está cayendo! ¡El cielo se está cayendo!"

"¿Cómo lo sabes, Ganso?"

"Me lo dijo el pato."

"¿Cómo lo sabes, Pato?"

"Me lo dijo la gallina."

"¿Cómo lo sabes, Gallina?"

"Me lo dijo el pollito."

"¿Cómo lo sabes, Pollito?"

"Lo vi con mis propios ojos, y un pedazo del cielo cayó ¡BUM! sobre mi cabeza. Les estoy diciendo la verdad."

"¡Huyamos!" gritó el pavo. "¡Huyamos, corran!"

"Zorra, Zorra, ¿dónde estás, Zorra?"

"Yif, yif. Aquí estoy. ¿Qué pasa?"

"¡El cielo se está cayendo! ¡El cielo se está cayendo!"

"¿Cómo lo sabes, Pavo?"

"Me lo dijo el ganso."

"¿Cómo lo sabes, ganso?"

"Me lo dijo el pato."

"¿Cómo lo sabes, Pato?"

"Me lo dijo la gallina."

"¿Cómo lo sabes, Gallina?"

"Me lo dijo el pollito."

"¿Cómo lo sabes, Pollito?"

"Lo vi con mis propios ojos, y un pedazo del cielo cayó ¡BUM! sobre mi cabeza. Les estoy diciendo la verdad."

La zorra pensaba un poco y dijo:

"No tengan miedo. Yo les salvaré. Vengan conmigo a mi cueva."

Y todos los animales se fueron con la zorra a la cueva. Pobres animales!

Performance Challenge

Individual   This activity told a familiar story in Spanish. Using as much Spanish as you can, briefly write what you think happened to the animals in the fox's den. Did she eat them? Did she invite them to sit down for a spot of tea? Be creative!

....

....

....

....

....

....

....

....

....

....

....

....

Performance Challenge

Group 1   Using stuffed animals and any other props you can find, retell the story to a group of small children in Spanish as a Diglot-Weave. See how much of the story they're able to understand just by listening.

Performance Challenge

Group 2   Take the group to visit a local farm or petting zoo. Write about the animals you saw during your visit, in Spanish.

A Spanish Lesson

INSTRUCTIONS Use these sentences to master new vocabulary.

🔊

English	Spanish
Mine. My pencil. My pencil.	*Mío. El lápiz mío. Mi lápiz.*
Yours. Your pencil. Your pencil.	*(El) suyo. El lápiz suyo. Su lápiz.*
I have a yellow pencil.	*Tengo un lápiz amarillo.*
This is my yellow pencil.	*Este es mi lápiz amarillo.*
Do you have a pencil too?	*¿Tiene usted también un lápiz?*
Yes, you have a red pencil.	*Sí, Ud. tiene un lápiz rojo.*
This is my pencil.	*Este es el lápiz mío.*
Is this your pencil?	*¿Es éste el lápiz suyo?*
I have yellow paper.	*Tengo papel amarillo.*
Do you have white paper?	*¿Tiene usted papel blanco?*
Yes, this is your paper.	*Sí, éste es el papel suyo.*
This is my paper.	*Éste es el papel mío.*
To give. To give me. To give it to me.	*Dar. Darme. Dármelo.*
You want. You don't want.	*Ud. quiere. Ud. no quiere.*
Is this pencil yours or mine?	*¿Este lápiz es suyo o mío?*
I believe it's yours.	*Creo que es suyo.*
This sheet of paper isn't yours.	*Esta hoja de papel no es suyo.*
It's mine, right?	*Es mío, ¿verdad?*
Yes, I believe it's mine.	*Sí, creo que es mío.*
You want to give me your paper.	*Ud. quiere darme el papel suyo.*
Oh, you don't want to give me it.	*Oh, Ud. no quiere dármelo.*
Do you want to give me a pencil?	*¿Quiere darme un lápiz?*
Thank you. You're very kind.	*Gracias. Ud. es muy amable.*

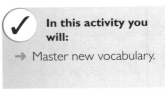

In this activity you will:

➡ Master new vocabulary.

◎ Disc **3** Track **10**

Sites to See in Venezuela

The capital city of Caracas boasts an abundance of impressive modern architecture but also holds sizable expanses of sprawling slums. Sites to visit include the *Plaza Bolívar* with its 17th century cathedral; the *Casa Natal de Bolívar*, birthplace of *El Libertador*; *Santa Capilla*, a church modeled after Paris' *Sainte Chapelle*; and the magnificent *Palacio de Miraflores*. The Río Orinoco also makes a splendid sight, with tours available along its southern stretches into the Amazon jungle. Along its lowland reaches lies Ciudad Bolívar (formerly Angostura), which still sports many examples of its colonial heritage. Not far from Ciudad Bolívar is Canaima, the town near which is located Salto Angel, the highest waterfall in the world. In the northwestern part of the country, Mérida makes a good starting point to treks up Pico Bolívar, one of Venezuela's most popular tourist destinations. Venezuela's Caribbean coast is the place to go for water activities and lounging in the sun. It's also the place to visit Coro, a town where some of the best colonial architecture in the country is preserved. Other attractions include its cathedral and art museum.

English (cont.)	Spanish
That pencil. That paper.	*Ese lápiz. Ese papel.*
This pencil is mine.	*Este lápiz es mío.*
That one is yours.	*Ese es suyo.*
That paper is yours.	*Ese papel es suyo.*
Your paper is here.	*El papel suyo está aquí.*
My paper is here.	*El papel mío está aquí.*
Is it clear? I hope so.	*¿Está claro? Espero que sí.*
There. Where?	*Allí. ¿Dónde?*
It's here. It's there.	*Está aquí. Está allí.*
The white paper is here.	*El papel blanco está aquí.*
Where is the yellow paper?	*¿Dónde está el papel amarillo?*
It's there.	*Está allí.*
The yellow pencil is there.	*El lápiz amarillo está allí.*
Where is the white pencil?	*¿Dónde está el lápiz blanco?*
It's here.	*Está aquí.*
Will you give me it?	*¿Quiere dármelo?*
With pleasure.	*Con mucho gusto.*
Many thanks.	*Muchas gracias.*
Your pencil. Your paper.	*Su lápiz. Su papel.*
Big or small?	*¿Grande o pequeño?*
Short or long?	*¿Corto o largo?*
Your pencil is long.	*Su lápiz es largo.*
Your paper is long too.	*Su papel es largo también.*
This pencil is short.	*Este lápiz es corto.*
Is it yours?	*¿Es suyo?*
That paper is small.	*Ese papel es pequeño.*
Is it mine?	*¿Es mío?*
Your paper is long.	*Su papel es largo.*
Is your pencil long?	*¿Es largo su lápiz?*
My yellow pencil is long.	*Mi lápiz amarillo es largo.*

English *(cont.)*	Spanish
Is my black pencil long too?	*¿Es largo también mi lápiz negro?*
Longer than. The longest.	*Más largo que. El más largo.*
I have three pencils: a red one, a black one, and a yellow one.	*Yo tengo tres lápices: uno rojo, uno negro, y uno amarillo.*
The black pencil is longer than the red one.	*El lápiz negro es más largo que el rojo.*
The yellow pencil is longer than the black one.	*El lápiz amarillo es más largo que el negro.*
So the yellow pencil is the longest, and the red one is the shortest.	*Entonces el lápiz amarillo es el más largo, y el rojo es el más corto.*
Is it clear? I hope so.	*¿Está claro? Espero que sí.*
You have three sheets of paper: a white one, a black one, and a red one.	*Usted tiene tres hojas de papel: una blanca, una negra, y una roja.*
The black paper is longer than the red, and the white is longer than the black.	*El papel negro es más largo que el rojo, y el blanco es más largo que el negro.*
So the white paper is the longest, and the red is the shortest.	*Entonces el papel blanco es el más largo, y el rojo es el más corto.*
Is it clear? I think so.	*¿Está claro? Creo que sí.*
Your red paper is shorter than my red pencil.	*Su papel rojo es más corto que mi lápiz rojo.*
My black pencil is longer than your black paper.	*Mi lápiz negro es más largo que su papel negro.*
My yellow pencil is longer than your white paper.	*Mi lápiz amarillo es más largo que su papel blanco.*
So my things are longer than yours.	*Entonces las cosas mías son más largas que las suyas.*
Do you understand? I hope so.	*¿Entiende? Espero que sí.*

Performance Challenge

Individual   This activity reviewed different vocabulary words, verbs, and ways of expressing ownership. Look at the things on your desk and describe what they look like and whose they are. If possible, repeat the challenge with a classmate's desk.

Performance Challenge

Group   Assign students to research the Rail Europe and travel in Spanish-speaking countries. Have each of them choose a route and then plan as if they were going to purchase tickets and take a trip. Make sure they look for hotels, car rentals, and tourist attractions along their route.

The Spanish Endings: *-aba*, *-ó*, and *-ado*

ACTIVITY **38**

 In this activity you will:

→ Use imperfect, perfect, and past participle verb endings.

The Imperfect, Perfect, and Past Participle

INSTRUCTIONS   Use these exercises to help you understand Spanish verb endings.

You are going to learn how to talk about things that happened in the past. To reap the benefits of this section, pay close attention now and come back and review it later. As you are aware, each of the following forms of the verb *viajar* has its own distinct meaning, yet each can be translated into English as "traveled." In other words, each of the endings *-aba*, *-ó* and *-ado* can be rendered as *-ed* in English.

Technical Term	Spanish	Explanation
Imperfect	*viaj-aba*	Viewed not as a single, unbounded event: traveled (not at specified time to given place).
Preterite (or Perfect)	*viaj-ó*	Viewed as a single, bounded event: traveled (at specified time(s) to given place).
Past Participle	*viaj-ado*	Viewed as a resultant state: has traveled.

Since all three endings are translated into English generally by the ending *-ed*, but since each signals a different meaning, it will be useful to indicate each in a distinctive way when we reference Spanish to English.

We will do this as follows:

- -ed* Imperfect
- -ed** Preterite
- -ed*** Past Participle

Ending	Spanish	English
Travel-ed*	Juan viaj-aba en México.	Juan traveled in Mexico.
Travel-ed**	Juan viaj-ó a México.	Juan traveled to Mexico (referring to a single trip).
Travel-ed***	Juan ha viaj-ado mucho.	Juan has traveled a lot.
	Juan ha viaj-ado a México.	Juan has traveled (made a trip) to Mexico.

The "past tense marker" of an English verb such as travel-ed contains more information than just placing the action in the past. By itself, the -ed marker does not reveal whether that action is to be viewed "generically" or as a particular instance. Only when an -ed verb is used in actual context can its meaning be known. For example, the statement

A. John traveled in Mexico.

we would think refers not to just a single act of traveling from one place to another, but rather as something which John did repeatedly over a period of time. But the statement

B. John traveled to Mexico.

most likely refers to one particular instance of travel—a single act viewed and presented by the speaker as bounded by both a beginning and end. Note that the past-tense marker -ed occurs in both (A) and (B) even though the meaning "completed, particular, one-time occurrence" (sentence B) contrasts sharply with the meaning "non-particular, non-one-time occurrence" (sentence A). If the context of a verb marked with -ed is too unclear, we have different ways to clarify it. For example, to clarify sentence (A), we could say

C. John traveled repeatedly in Mexico.
D. John used to travel in Mexico.
E. John was traveling in Mexico.
F. John went about traveling in Mexico.

Now look at some Spanish sentences and see how these meanings are handled.

English		Spanish
I. A. John used to travel in Mexico.		Juan viaj-aba en México.
B. John used to teach English.		Juan enseñ-aba inglés.

Here, the Spanish ending *-aba* corresponds to the English ending *-ed* in designating what the action was and in placing it in the past. But beyond that *-aba* contains certain information that *-ed* does not contain: it presents a view of that action NOT as a particular instance, NOT as something the speaker wants you to see as a single bounded action, carried through from beginning to end, but as an unbounded action.

Contrast (1A) and (1B) above with (2A) and (2B) below.

English	Spanish
2. A. John traveled to Mexico.	*Juan viaj-ó a México.*
B. John taught a lesson.	*Juan enseñ-ó una lección.*

Here, the stressed ending *-o* corresponds to the ending *-ed* in placing the action in the past, but beyond that it contains certain information that the *-ed* does not contain. It presents a view of a particular instance of an action, something the speaker wants you to see as a bounded action, carried through from beginning to end.

You should see from the above that in talking about someone else's action in the past, a Spanish speaker must present to his audience how he wishes them to view the action: he may present it as a single particular act carried through from start to finish, or designate the act without this particular aspect of meaning. To do this with *-ar* verbs ("*viaj-ar*," "*enseñ-ar*," etc.) the speaker MUST choose either *-aba* or *-ó*: *viajaba* or *viajó*. (With *-er* and *-ir* verbs such as *comer* and *dormir* the same contrast in aspect is signaled by *-ía* and *-ió*.)

Look closely. What would the following mean?

- *Juan viaj-aba a México.*
- *Juan enseñ-aba una lección.*
- *Eva com-ía y comía.*
- *Eva se com-ió un limón.*

Construct the proper form of the Spanish verb *visitar* to fit the following situations:

- Manuel visited with his friend often.
- He was visiting his friend when lightning struck him.
- He visited his friend once when it was winter.

Performance Challenge

Individual This activity helped you practice three important verb endings in Spanish. After reviewing how each ending is used, write several sentences of your own, using the verb forms in this activity.

....

....

....

....

....

....

....

....

....

....

....

....

....

....

....

....

....

....

....

....

....

☆

Performance Challenge

Group   Have the students write a story about something they did as a child, using the Spanish endings ~aba, ~o, and ~ado. Have them illustrate their stories with at least two pictures and then share them with a younger child.

Aspects of Past Time

INSTRUCTIONS   Use these explanations and self quizzes to gain a more thorough understanding of Spanish past tenses.

Things that happened in the past can be spoken of from different perspectives or different points of view. For example: *lo comía* "he ate it (from time to time)" vs. *lo comió* "he ate it (on a given occasion)." The former simply names a customary or unbounded action, the latter refers to a specific act, a bounded event carried through to completion. This is a crucial distinction that speakers of Spanish must make every time they refer to action in the past.

 In this activity you will:

→ Perform in aspects of past tense.

A closer look at what is meant by *cantaba* vs. *cantó*

In English there are several ways of referring to customary, recurring, or ongoing behavior in the past. For example:

When he was young...

A. he sang a lot.

B. he used to sing a lot.

C. he would sing a lot.

D. he did a lot of singing.

The one Spanish equivalent of these is:

Cuando él era joven...

A. *cantaba mucho.*

When Spanish speakers use the form *cantaba*, they are not indicating a single, completed act of singing; rather they are viewing the singing as a customary, recurring or ongoing action in the past. If they wish to indicate a single completed act of singing, as in: "She sang a song," (or specifically numerable completed acts of singing, as in: "She sang five songs," then they will use the form *cantó*: *Ella cantó un canto. Ella cantó cinco cantos.*

Él cantaba un canto is how to say "He was singing a chant." Note that this freezes the action, looks at its middle rather than its end, views it as ongoing. This in

Venezuelan Peppers with Shrimp

❦ 3 pounds shrimp, veined but not peeled

❦ 2 cups olive oil

❦ 4 large red bell peppers

❦ 6 cloves garlic, peeled and diced

❦ 1 chili pepper, seeded and finely chopped

❦ 1 loaf French bread, cut into 1" slices

❦ feta cheese (optional)

Directions

Remove seeds from red bell peppers and cut into strips. In a deep skillet, combine 1 cup of olive oil and the red pepper strips. Heat slowly and cook gently until peppers are tender but not browned. Set aside. Combine remaining cup of olive oil with diced garlic. Heat slowly and cook for 4 to 5 minutes, until garlic is tender and golden. Remove garlic with strainer and add to red bell peppers. Heat garlic oil until surface of oil ripples. Add chili pepper and shrimp. Saute until shrimp are pink and cooked through. Remove from oil and set aside. Stir together garlic, red bell peppers, and oil in which peppers were cooked. To serve, spoon red bell pepper mix onto a serving dish. Surround with shrimp. Serve with bread and cheese. To eat, put pepper mix onto bread, with cheese (if desired) and shrimp on top.

contrast to *Él cantó un canto*, in which the speaker views a given action as carried through to completion.

These contrasting views of the action as completed or not completed we will call the "aspectual" meaning. A marker of "aspectual" meaning always accompanies the designation of an action in the past. Verbal "aspect" is different from verbal "tense." Grammarians refer to the form *cantó* (and analogous forms of all other Spanish verbs) as the perfect or preterite—which indicates both past tense and completive aspect. They refer to the form *cantaba* (and analogous forms of all other Spanish verbs) as the imperfect—which indicates both past tense and incompletive aspect.

English	Imperfect	Preterite
he sang	*él cantaba*	*él cantó*

Performance Self Quiz 1

INSTRUCTIONS   Identify the meaning of the following forms by marking imperfect or preterite. Check your answers in Appendix A, on page 332.

			Imperfect	Preterite
1.	ate	*comió*		
2.	ate	*comía*		
3.	did	*hacía*		
4.	did	*hizo*		
5.	directed	*dirigió*		
6.	directed	*dirigía*		
7.	knew	*conocía*		
8.	lived	*vivió*		
9.	lived	*vivía*		
10.	met	*conocía*		
11.	spoke	*hablaba*		
12.	spoke	*habló*		
13.	wrote	*escribió*		
14.	wrote	*escribía*		

Performance Self Quiz 2

INSTRUCTIONS   Write the ending that gives the meaning indicated in the parentheses. Check your answers in Appendix A, on page 332.

	Ending	
1.	*llor-*	(preterite)
2.	*llor-*	(imperfect)
3.	*cant-*	(preterite)
4.	*cant-*	(imperfect)
5.	*sufri-*	(preterite)
6.	*sufr-*	(imperfect)
7.	*habl-*	(imperfect)
8.	*habl-*	(preterite)
9.	*vivi-*	(preterite)
10.	*viv-*	(imperfect)

Note that the simple past tense in English (he traveled, he ate) is ambiguous: to the Spanish mind it could refer to either preterite or imperfect.

A closer look at what is meant by *ha cantado* vs. *cantó* or *cantaba*

In English we make an important distinction between "has sung" and "sang." We use "sang" to indicate a past action not specified as relevant or connected to the present state of affairs. One might look back on the London Blitz of 1940 and say: "Hitler ordered air raids on London." To say: "Hitler has ordered air raids on London," indicates that the statement has some present moment. Similarly to say "Beethoven has composed a tenth symphony" makes our mind suppose that he must still be alive, or that in some odd way this statement has relevance to the present moment. Here are three views of past action:

English	Spanish
1. He has sung.	*El ha cantado.*
2. He sang (at times in the past).	*El cantaba.*
3. He sang (a song through to completion at a given time).	*El cantó.*

Ha cantado shows present relevance, so we can depict it in the same way as its English equivalent. Consider then these three ways of viewing past action: (1)

particularly relevant to the present state of affairs: *ha cantado*; or (2) not particularly relevant to the present state of affairs, but viewed as (a) completed (*cantó*) or (b) not completed (*cantaba*).

Practice

INSTRUCTIONS   Using the three views of past action, identify which view each verb form depicts.

-ar verbs	-er / -ir verbs
tomaba	comió
tomó	comía
ha tomado	ha comido
lloraba	tenía
lloró	tuvo
ha llorado	ha tenido
jugaba	sufría
jugó	sufrió
ha jugado	ha sufrido

Review

INSTRUCTIONS   Go back now over the sentences used to describe things that happened in the past. Make sure you understand each verb form and its meaning.

Performance Challenge

Individual   This activity compared different verb tenses that are used to describe things that happened in the past. Make sure you understand the differences, then write sentences of your own, using the verb tenses from this activity.

Performance Challenge

Group   Divide the students into groups. Have each group research and write about one aspect of the life of Beethoven. Then listen to several of his musical compositions as a class. Have each group share with the rest of the class what they have learned about his life.

Simple Verb Tenses

Verb Tenses Explained

Five "Indicative" Forms

Name		Form	Example
Simple present	(Pres)	[verb]s	He speaks English.
Imperfect past	(Imp)	[verb]ED*	As a child, she spoke {unbounded} a lot.
Preterite past	(Pret)	[verb]ED**	I spoke {bounded} with him yesterday.
Future	(Fut)	will [verb]	She will speak at the conference tomorrow.
Conditional	(Cond)	would [verb]	If he weren't shy, he would speak more.

Two "Subjunctive" Forms

Name		Form	Example
Present Subjunctive	(Pres Sub)	that he [verb]	I insist that he speak.
Past Subjunctive	(Past Sub)	that he [verb]ED***	I insisted that he spoke.
			I insisted that he speak.

✓ **In this activity you will:**
→ Use the simple verb tenses without an auxiliary verb.

Examples

INSTRUCTIONS   As you read through the examples, note that the subjunctive tense only affects the verb in the dependent clause. Note also that in English, the verb in the dependent clause is different depending on the nature of the verb in the independent clause. That difference, however, doesn't exist in Spanish.

Indicative Modes

Form	-ar	Spanish	English
Pres	-a	*Sé que el niño habl-a.*	I know the child speaks.
		Insisto que el niño habl-e.	I insist that the child speaks.
Imp	-a	*Sé que el niño habl-a.*	I know the child spoke (at times).
Pret	-ó	*Sé que el niño habl-ó.*	I know the child spoke (on a given occasion).
Fut	-ará	*Sé que el niño habl-ará.*	I know the child will speak.
Cond	-aría	*Sé que el niño habl-aría.*	I know the child would speak.

Form	-er / -ir	Spanish	English
Pres	-e	*Sé que el niño com-e.*	I know the child eats.
		Insisto que el niño com-a.	I insist that the child eats.
Imp	-ía	*Sé que el niño com-ía.*	I know the child ate (at times).
Pret	-ió	*Sé que el niño com-ió.*	I know the child ate (on a given occasion).
Fut	-erá	*Sé que el niño com-erá.*	I know the child will eat.
Cond	-ería	*Sé que el niño com-ería.*	I know the child would eat.

Subjunctive Modes

Subjunctive (Irrealis) is signaled by switching the thematic vowels from A to E and E/I to A:

Form	-ar	Spanish	English
Pres Sub	-e	*Insisto en que el niño habl-e.*	I insist that the child speak.
		Dudo que el niño habl-e.	I doubt the child speaks.
Past Sub	-ara	*Insistía en que el niño habl-ara.*	I insisted that the child speak.
	-ase	or *Insistía que el niño habl-ase.*	I insisted that the child speak.

Form (cont.) -ar	Spanish	English
	Dudaba que el niño habl-ara.	I doubted the child spoke.
	or *Dudaba que el niño habl-ase.*	I doubted the child spoke.

Form	-er / -ir	Spanish	English
Pres Sub	-a	*Insisto en que el niño com-a.*	I insist that the child eat.
		Dudo que el niño com-a.	I doubt the child eats.
Past Sub	-iera	*Insistía en que el niño com-iera.*	I insisted that the child eat.
	-iese	or *Insistía que el niño com-iese.*	I insisted that the child eat.
		Dudaba que el niño com-iera.	I doubted the child ate.
		or *Dudaba que el niño com-iese.*	I doubted the child ate.

There are two types of verbs in the independent clause: those that are affirmative (like insist) or negative (like doubt). Some examples of those verb types are listed below.

Affirmative Verbs	Negative Verbs
insisto…	*dudo que…*
digo que…	*no creo que…*
quiero que…	*no pienso que…*
es necesario que…	*tengo dudas que…*
es importante que…	etc.

Performance Challenge

Individual   This activity presented seven different verb tenses and showed how they work in both English and Spanish. Using what you have learned so far, write at least one Spanish sentence for each verb tense that is taught in this activity.

Performance Challenge

Group   Students can write either a poem or a song in Spanish using only simple verb tenses. Have them perform or read their work to the group.

You have completed all the activities for

**Section 1.3.2
Day Two, 17:00 Hours**

and are now ready to take the section quiz. Before continuing, be sure you have learned the objectives for each activity in this section.

Section Quiz

INSTRUCTIONS   Choose the correct Spanish word that fits in the blank. Check your answers in Appendix D, on page 346.

1. *¿De quién es … varilla?*
   - A. *ésa*
   - B. *está*
   - C. *esta*
   - D. *ésta*

2. *Las varillas son muy ….*
   - A. *largo*
   - B. *grande*
   - C. *largos*
   - D. *grandes*

3. *¿… es la clase de matemáticas?*
   - A. *A qué hora*
   - B. *Cuánto*
   - C. *Por qué*
   - D. *De dónde*

INSTRUCTIONS   Choose the correct Spanish translation for the following phrases or sentences.

4. **It is important to study.**

   A. *Hay que estudia.*

   B. *Es importante estudia.*

   C. *Hay que estudian.*

   D. *Es importante estudiar.*

5. **mission impossible**

   A. *mission impossible*

   B. *mission imposible*

   C. *misión imposible*

   D. *misión impossible*

6. **It's necessary to eat in order to live.**

   A. *Hay que come vivir.*

   B. *Hay que comer para vivir.*

   C. *Es tonto comer para vivir.*

   D. *Es importante come a vivir.*

7. **I don't like to sing either.**

   A. *No me gusta cantar también.*

   B. *No me gusta cantar ya no.*

   C. *No me gusta cantar tampoco.*

   D. *No me gusta cantar todavía.*

INSTRUCTIONS   Choose the most correct response.

8. **What is the predominant religion in both El Salvador and Guatemala?**

   A. Presbyterian

   B. Roman Catholic

   C. Native Indian religions

   D. Islam

INSTRUCTIONS   For the following questions, choose the correct Spanish translation for the underlined English word or set of words.

9. *El rey y la reina* <u>are playing</u> *el piano.*

    A. *tocan*

    B. *estar tocando*

    C. *están tocando*

    D. *tocaban*

10. *El príncipe* <u>used to sing.</u>

    A. *cantaba*

    B. *cantar*

    C. *está cantando*

    D. *canta*

You have completed all the sections for

Module 1.3

and are now ready to take the module test. Before continuing, be sure you have learned the objectives for each activity in this module.

Module Test

INSTRUCTIONS   Choose the correct English translation of the Spanish word or sentence. Check your answers in Appendix D, on page 345.

1. *ese lápiz*
   A. this pencil
   B. this pen
   C. that pencil
   D. that pen

2. *ese papel*
   A. that paper
   B. this paper
   C. that book
   D. this page

3. *Este lápiz es mío.*
   A. That pencil is mine.
   B. This pen is mine.
   C. This pencil is mine.
   D. That pen is mine.

4. *Ése es suyo.*
   A. That one is small.
   B. That one is yours.
   C. This one is large.
   D. This one is yours.

5. *Ese papel es suyo.*

   A. This paper is yours.

   B. That page is yours.

   C. This book is yours.

   D. That paper is yours.

6. *El papel suyo está aquí.*

   A. Your paper is here.

   B. Your book is here.

   C. Your paper is there.

   D. Your paper is gone.

7. *El papel mío está aquí.*

   A. My book is here.

   B. My paper is there.

   C. My paper is here.

   D. Your paper is here.

8. *¿Está claro?*

   A. Are you clear?

   B. Is it clear?

   C. Is he clear?

   D. Are we clear?

9. *Espero que sí.*

   A. I hope not.

   B. I think so.

   C. I don't know.

   D. I hope so.

10. *Ud. es muy amable.*

    A. You are very honest.

    B. You are very kind

    C. He is very smart.

    D. You are very mean.

INSTRUCTIONS   True or False: The following phrases or sentences are translated correctly.

11. *¿Qué le ha pasado a la reina?* = Where is the queen?

   A. True

   B. False

12. *¿Qué le ha pasado a la princesa?* = What has happened to the princess?

   A. True

   B. False

13. *¿Qué le ha pasado a ella?* = What has happened to him?

   A. True

   B. False

14. *¿Qué le ha pasado al rey?* = What happened to her?

   A. True

   B. False

15. *¿Qué le ha pasado al príncipe?* = What has happened to the principal?

   A. True

   B. False

16. *La princesa ha sufrido mucho.* = The princess has suffered a lot.

   A. True

   B. False

17. *Ahora ella ha comido los chocolates.* = Now she has eaten the chocolates.

   A. True

   B. False

18. *Ella ya ha comido los chocolates.* = She has eaten all the chocolates.

   A. True

   B. False

19. *Pero ha llorado mucho.* = But she has cried a lot.

   A. True

   B. False

20. **Y la reina ha llorado con ella.** = **And the queen has laughed with her.**

 A. True

 B. False

....

INSTRUCTIONS   For the following questions, choose the correct English translation of the Spanish word or phrase.

21. **dió**

 A. day

 B. he gave

 C. he said

 D. today

22. **un regalo**

 A. a gift

 B. a crown

 C. a box

 D. a horse

23. **corbatas**

 A. shoes

 B. gloves

 C. hats

 D. ties

24. **domingo**

 A. flamingo

 B. Sunday

 C. domino

 D. ping-pong

25. **aeropuerto**

 A. airplane

 B. astronaut

 C. airport

 D. door

You have completed all the modules for

Semester 1

Review any material in this semester that you feel needs extra attention. When you're ready, move on to Semester 2.

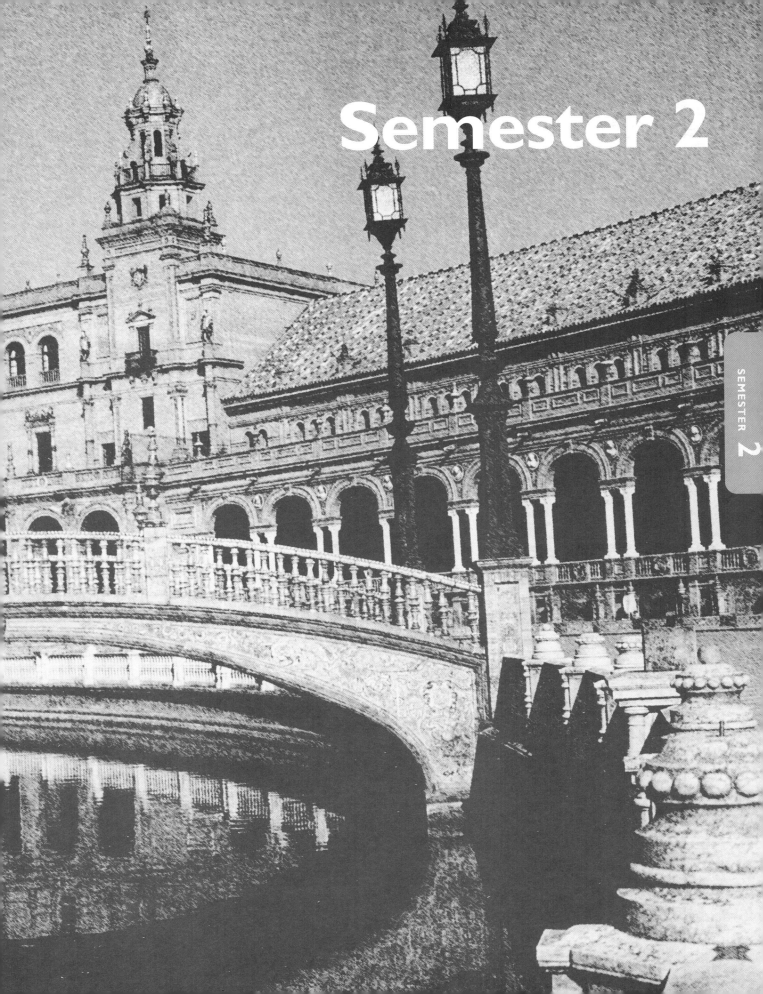

Semester 2

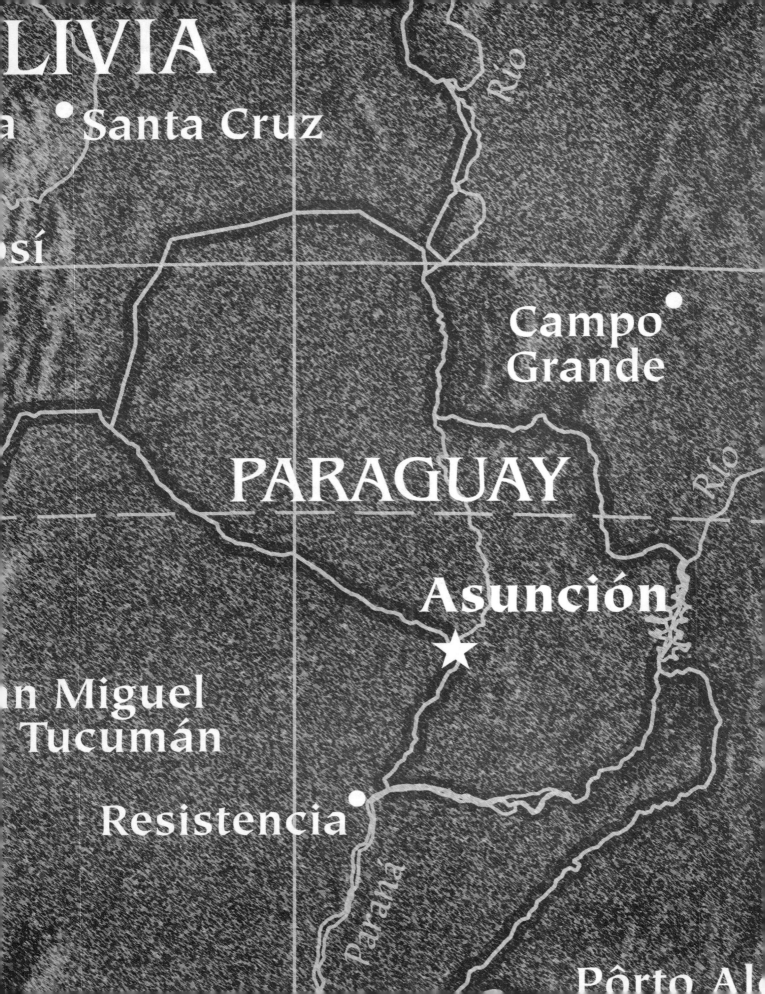

Module 2.1

Throughout this module we'll be learning about the culture of Paraguay.

Keep these tips in mind as you progress through this module:

1. Read instructions carefully.
2. Repeat aloud all the Spanish words you hear on the audio CDs.
3. Learn at your own pace.
4. Have fun with the activities and practice your new language skills with others.
5. Record yourself speaking Spanish on tape so you can evaluate your own speaking progress.

BOLIVIA

N

Bolivia

Cerro León

Parque Nacional
Defensores
del Chaco

Brazil

El Chaco

Parque
Nacional
Teniente
Enciso

Fortín Toledo

Loma
Plata

Parque Nacional
Cerro Corá

Filadelfia

Paraguay

Río Paraguay

Parque
Nacional
Tinfunqué

Itaipú
Dam

Asunción

Itaguá

Piribebuy

Argentina

Villa Florida

Parque Nacional
Ybycuí

San Ignacio Guazú

Santa María

Trinidad

Río Paraná

Paraguay

Day Three, 08:00 Hours

Una vista inesperada

You check *el mapa* in the morning, reading the hint written on the edge of *el mapa*. "Casa Viola," *Araña* reads aloud. "I wonder what that is."

An hour of researching local sightseeing spots reveals that *Casa Viola* is an old colonial *casa* that has been remodeled into a *museo*. It's not that far away. You and *Araña* catch a cab across town and pull to a stop in front of the elegant old building.

After tipping the driver, you enter the popular *museo*. There appear to be several school groups coming through *el museo* today—it's packed with *niños*, *profesoras*, and guides. You and *Araña* split up to cover ground more quickly. You scan each exhibit carefully, not sure exactly what to expect. Suddenly, through a glass case, you catch sight of someone you didn't expect to see—a slim older man with salt-and-pepper hair and a bushy mustache. You double-check the picture in your case-file to make sure. Yes, it's him! Firmly escorted between two large, muscular men, *Señor* Espinoza just entered the building! You make eye contact with him, motion for him to stay where he is, and start working your way towards him.

Unfortunately, *Señor* Espinoza doesn't appear to be as skilled at reading your hand gestures as he is with words—he immediately starts shouting for help and trying to escape his escorts. The duo escorting him take a firmer grip and quickly start dragging him back out. Abandoning subtlety, you push through the crowds after them, trying to reach *Señor* Espinoza.

It's no use. By the time you reach the spot where *Señor* Espinoza had stood, he and two of his captors are gone. You hear a car starting outside and tires squealing on the pavement, but by the time you can make your way to a window, all you can see is a large black sedan that turns the corner several blocks away and vanishes from sight. You've lost them.

You make your way back toward where *Señor* Espinoza was standing, hoping that he at least managed to leave you a clue. Sure enough, near the exhibit where *Señor* Espinoza and his captors had stood, you find a crumpled piece of paper which unfolds to reveal another *rompecabezas*.

In this section you will:

→ Increase reading and listening comprehension, and vocabulary usage.

→ Read a dialogue for comprehension and then repeat it.

→ Recognize your ability to understand Spanish.

→ Increase reading and listening comprehension, and vocabulary usage.

→ Recognize your ability to understand Spanish.

Disc **4**   Track **1**

As you're smoothing it out, *Araña* hurries up. *"¿Qué pasó?"* he asks. "I heard shouting."

You summarize quickly and show *Araña* the new puzzle. "We know now that we've made up the lag time," you explain, "but things get even more dangerous now, for *Señor* Espinoza and for us. The kidnappers know my face, and they know someone's trying to rescue Espinoza. We have to move quickly and can't afford mistakes."

"Let's get right to work, then," *Araña* replies. You give local and airport authorities a description of the two men you saw and of *Señor* Espinoza and ask to be notified at once if any of the three are sighted. Then you and *Araña* start work on the activities you'll need to solve *este nuevo rompecabezas.*

Puzzle

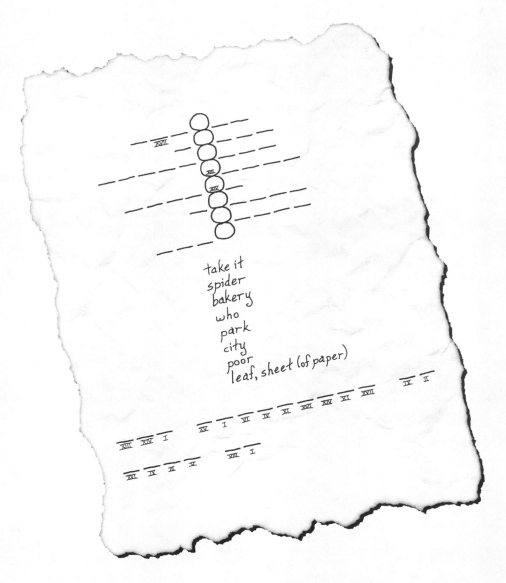

take it
spider
bakery
who
park
city
poor
leaf, sheet (of paper)

INSTRUCTIONS   Follow the clues to fill in the puzzle with the correct words. The circled letters will spell out your next adventure destination. Under some of the letters in the puzzle, Roman numerals are written. These numerals correspond to blanks at the bottom of the page. Fill in the blanks with the appropriate letters to receive a piece of the clue you will need to solve the adventure's climax.

After working the puzzle out yourself, check the answers in Appendix A, on page 333.

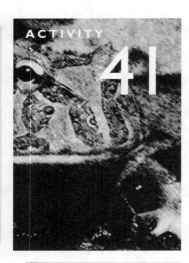

A Little Boy and a Flower

In this activity you will:

→ Increase reading and listening comprehension, and vocabulary usage.

Disc **4**   Track **2**

INSTRUCTIONS   Read and listen to this story. Use it to increase your vocabulary.

English	Spanish
A little boy found a pretty flower.	*Un niñito halló una bonita flor.*
"Because this is such a pretty flower, and because I love my sister, I'll pick it and give it to her."	*"Porque ésta es una flor tan bonita, y porque yo amo a mi hermana, la voy a tomar y dársela."*
So he picked the flower and took it to his sister.	*Entonces el levantó la flor y se la llevó a su hermana.*
"Here," he said, "take it.	*"Aquí," dijo, "tómala.*
This flower is for you from me.	*Esta flor es para tí de parte de mí.*
It says I love you."	*Dice que te amo."*
The sister took the flower and said,	*La hermana tomó la flor y dijo:*
"Then we love each other.	*"Entonces nos amamos el uno al otro.*
Thank you, dear brother."	*Gracias, querido hermano."*
The sister took the flower to her father, gave it to him, and said,	*La hermana llevó la flor a su padre, se la dió, y dijo:*
"Here, take it!	*"¡Aquí, tómala!*
This flower is for you from me.	*Esta flor es para tí de parte de mí.*
It says I love you."	*Dice que te amo."*
The father took the flower and said,	*El padre tomó la flor y dijo:*
"Then we love each other.	*"Entonces nos amamos el uno al otro.*
Thank you, dear daughter."	*Gracias, querida hija."*
The father took the flower to his wife, gave it to her, and said,	*El padre llevó la flor a su esposa, se la dió a ella, y dijo:*

English *(cont.)*	Spanish
"Here, take it!	"¡Aquí, tómala!
This flower is for you from me.	Esta flor es para tí de parte de mí.
It says I love you."	Dice que te amo."
The wife took the flower and said,	La esposa tomó la flor y dijo:
"Then we love each other.	"Entonces nos amamos el uno al otro.
Thank you, dear husband."	Gracias, querido esposo."

Performance Challenge

Individual   Look at a picture of your own family and then describe them, using as much Spanish as possible.

Performance Challenge

Group   Have the students write an essay on five people they love, explaining why they love them. Ask each student to write those five people a letter telling them five things they like about them and teaching them at least five new Spanish words.

ACTIVITY 42

The Three Little Pigs

 In this activity you will:

→ Read a dialogue for comprehension and then repeat it.

Paraguay Culture Overview

For many years, little was known about Paraguay, even by neighboring South American nations. Nowadays, though, as the nation has taken steps to overcome its economic and political isolation, people are discovering what a charming place it is. The people of Paraguay are proud of their heritage and fond of conversation. They are generally courteous and expect the same of visitors. Western dress is standard in Paraguay, but regional traditional costumes do still exist. From its relaxed riverside capital, Asunción, to its impressive national parks, visitors can see the source of the Paraguayan's national pride.

INSTRUCTIONS   Cover the English and read the Spanish account of this popular story. See how much you can understand without looking at the English. Then compare the English and the Spanish.

English	Spanish
Three little pigs.	*Tres cochinitos.*
Brothers.	*Hermanos.*
Three houses.	*Tres casas.*
One house of straw.	*Una casa de paja.*
One house of sticks.	*Una casa de leños.*
One house of bricks.	*Una casa de ladrillos.*
A wolf.	*Un lobo.*
He is hungry.	*Viene con hambre.*
He comes to the house of straw.	*Viene a la casa de paja.*

English (cont.)	Spanish
He blows.	*Sopla.*
The house of straw falls.	*La casa de paja se cae.*
But the little pig escapes.	*Pero el cochinito se escapa.*
The wolf comes another time.	*El lobo viene otra vez.*
He comes to the house of sticks.	*Viene a la casa de leños.*
He is very hungry.	*Viene con mucha hambre.*
He blows.	*Sopla.*
The house of sticks falls.	*La casa de leños se cae.*
But the little pig escapes.	*Pero el cochinito se escapa.*
The wolf comes another time.	*El lobo viene otra vez.*
He comes to the house of bricks.	*Viene a la casa de ladrillos.*
He is VERY hungry.	*Viene con MUCHA hambre.*
He blows.	*Sopla.*
He blows another time.	*Sopla otra vez.*
But the house of bricks	*Pero la casa de ladrillos*
doesn't fall.	*no se cae.*
And the wolf leaves	*Y el lobo sale*
VERY, VERY, hungry.	*con MUCHA, MUCHA hambre.*

Performance Challenge

Individual   This activity presented a familiar story in simple Spanish. Using this activity as a model, choose another familiar story and tell it to a teacher or parent, using as much Spanish as you can.

Performance Challenge

Group   Have the students write and illustrate a story in Spanish about what happens to either the pigs or the wolf after the end of the story. Have the class vote on the best story and illustration.

A Spanish Lesson

ACTIVITY 43

In this activity you will:

→ Recognize your ability to understand Spanish.

Disc **4**   Track **3**

INSTRUCTIONS   Read and listen to these sentences. Use them to learn new vocabulary from context.

English	Spanish
Take your pencil and draw a line.	*Toma tu lápiz y dibuja una línea.*
Draw another line, a long line.	*Dibuja otra línea, una larga.*
Draw a line, a straight line.	*Dibuja una línea, una línea derecha.*
Draw a longer line.	*Dibuja una línea más larga.*
Draw a still longer line.	*Dibuja una línea aún más larga.*
Draw a vertical line.	*Dibuja una línea vertical.*
Draw a taller vertical line.	*Dibuja una línea vertical más larga.*
Draw a long horizontal line.	*Dibuja una línea horizontal larga.*
Draw two parallel horizontal lines.	*Dibuja dos líneas horizontales paralelas.*
Draw a vertical line in the middle of the page.	*Dibuja una línea vertical en el centro de la página.*
Draw a line from left to right in the middle of the page.	*Dibuja una línea de izquierda a derecha en el centro de la página.*
Draw a vertical line from top to bottom in the middle of the page.	*Dibuja una línea vertical de arriba hacia abajo en el centro de la página.*
Make a dot.	*Haz un punto.*
Draw a string of dots.	*Dibuja una línea de puntos.*
Draw a long curved line.	*Dibuja una larga línea curva.*
Draw a square, a large one.	*Dibuja un cuadrado, uno grande.*
Draw a rectangle, a small one.	*Dibuja un rectángulo, uno pequeño.*
Draw a face, the face of a girl.	*Dibuja una cara, la cara de una niña.*
Draw another face, that of a man.	*Dibuja otra cara, la cara de un hombre.*
Draw a stairway (some steps).	*Dibuja unas escaleras.*

English (cont.)	Spanish
Draw a line from left to right.	*Dibuja una línea de izquierda a derecha.*
Compare these two lines.	*Compara estas dos líneas.*
In what way are they similar?	*¿De qué manera son similares?*
Both are long, thin lines, aren't they?	*Ambas son líneas largas y finas, ¿no?*
Now contrast these similar lines.	*Ahora contrasta estas líneas similares.*
What kind of line is this?	*¿Qué tipo de línea es ésta?*
Straight or curved?	*¿Derecha o curva?*
It's straight. It's a straight line.	*Es derecha. Es una línea derecha.*
With your finger draw a straight line.	*Con tu dedo dibuja una línea derecha.*
Below it draw a curved line.	*Debajo de esta dibuja una línea curva.*
On top draw another curved line.	*Encima dibuja otra línea curva.*

Performance Challenge

Individual   Get some paper and a pencil. Listen to the activity again and follow the directions as they are given.

Performance Challenge

Group   Split into two or three teams. Have each team stand in a line. Read a sentence in English and ask the first student in each line to translate it into Spanish. If translated and pronounced correctly, the student can sit down. The team with all students sitting first, wins.

The Crocodile

In this activity you will:

→ Increase reading and listening comprehension, and vocabulary usage.

Disc **4**   Track **4**

Facts and Figures on Paraguay

- Paraguay's full name is *República del Paraguay.*
- Paraguay's population stays around 5.6 million.
- Asunción is the nation's capital, with about one tenth of the population living there.
- Paraguay has two official languages: Spanish and Guaraní.
- Soccer, basketball, volleyball, and swimming are popular sports in Paraguay.
- Corn and rice are staples of the Paraguayan diet.
- Paraguay's main industries include brewing, milling, cotton, textiles, soybeans, timber, hides and skins, meat packing, and sugarcane.
- Paraguay's federal government is a republic, with a president, a bicameral legislature, and an independent judicial branch.

INSTRUCTIONS   Read and listen to this vocabulary-building story.

English	Spanish
A pale, nervous man came into the office of a psychiatrist who was a personal friend.	*Un hombre pálido y nervioso entró en la oficina de un psiquiatra, de quien era amigo.*
The doctor said: "Paulo, my friend, I see you are under great stress. Tell me what your problem is."	*El doctor dijo: "Paulo, mi amigo, veo que estás bajo mucha presión. Dime ¿cuál es tu problema.?"*
"Oh doctor, please help me. I am extremely frightened."	*"Oh, doctor, por favor ayúdeme. Me siento extremadamente asustado."*
"What is it that's frightening you?"	*"¿Qué es lo que te asusta?"*
"There's a crocodile under my bed."	*"Hay un cocodrilo debajo de mi cama."*
"A crocodile under your bed?"	*"¿Un cocodrilo debajo de tu cama?"*
"Yes, there's a crocodile under my bed one meter long.	*"Sí, hay un cocodrilo debajo de mi cama, de un metro de largo.*
I'm afraid it's going to eat me."	*Tengo miedo que me va a devorar."*
"Don't worry, Paulo," said the doctor.	*"No te preocupes, Paulo," dijo el doctor.*
"It's only an illusion.	*"Es sólo una ilusión.*
I have many patients who have a similar problem.	*Tengo muchos pacientes que tienen problemas similares.*
It's really nothing serious.	*En verdad no es muy serio.*
I have some pills that will cure your ailment in a short time.	*Tengo unas píldoras que te van a curar la enfermedad en poco tiempo.*
Here, take three of these little pills three times a day: three in the morning, three at noon, and three at night before going to bed.	*Mira, toma tres de estas píldoritas tres veces al día: tres en la mañana, tres al mediodía, y tres en la noche antes de acostarte.*
I can assure you, you'll soon be well again.	*Te aseguro que te mejorarás muy pronto.*

English (cont.)	Spanish
Come back and see me in three weeks, will you?"	Regresa a verme de nuevo en tres semanas."
"Thank you doctor, thank you very much."	"Muchas gracias, doctor, muchas gracias."
In three weeks the man came again to the office.	En tres semanas el hombre regresó de nuevo a la oficina.
He was even paler and thinner than before.	Estaba aún más pálido y delgado que antes.
He said: "Oh doctor, I still have the same problem.	Dijo: "Oh doctor, todavía tengo el mismo problema.
And it's getting worse.	Y está empeorando.
The crocodile is still under my bed, only now it is one-and-a-half meters long.	El cocodrilo todavía está debajo de mi cama, sólo que ahora mide metro y medio.
I'm sure it's going to eat me.	Estoy seguro que va a devorarme.
Oh, what will I do? You've got to help me."	Oh, ¿Qué hago? Tiene que ayudarme."
"Have you taken the three pills three times a day as I prescribed?"	"¿Has tomado las tres píldoras tres veces al día, tal como te lo prescribí?"
"Yes, yes, of course. Three in the morning, three at noon, and three at night before going to bed."	"Sí, sí, claro. Tres en la mañana, tres al mediodía, y tres en la noche antes de acostarme."
"Well then, I'll give you these other pills.	"Bueno entonces, te daré otras píldoras.
They are more powerful than the others.	Estas son más fuertes que las otras.
Take six of them, three times a day: six in the morning, six at noon, and six at night before going to bed.	Toma seis de estas tres veces al día: seis en la mañana, seis al mediodía, y seis en la noche antes de acostarte.
I can assure you, you'll soon be well again.	Te aseguro que te mejorarás muy pronto.
Come back and see me in six weeks, will you?"	Regresa a verme de nuevo en seis semanas."
"Thank you doctor, thank you very much."	"Gracias, doctor, muchas gracias."

English (cont.)	Spanish
In six weeks the man came again to the office.	En seis semanas el hombre regresó de nuevo a la oficina.
He was even thinner, paler, and more nervous than before.	Estaba aún más delgado, pálido, y nervioso que antes.
He said: "Oh doctor, I still have the same problem, and it's getting worse.	Dijo: "Ay, doctor, todavía tengo el mismo problema, y se está empeorando.
The crocodile is still under my bed, only now it is two meters long.	El cocodrilo está todavía debajo de mi cama, sólo que ahora mide dos metros.
I know it's going to eat me.	Sé que va a devorarme.
Oh, what shall I do? You've got to help me."	Oh, ¿Qué haré? Tiene que ayudarme."
"Have you taken the six pills three times a day as I prescribed?"	"¿Has tomado las seis píldoras tres veces al día como te lo prescribí?"
"Yes, yes, of course. Six in the morning, six at noon, and six at night before going to bed."	"Sí, sí, claro. Seis en la mañana, seis en la tarde, y seis en la noche antes de acostarme."
"Well then, I'll give you these new pills.	"Bueno, entonces te daré otras píldoras.
They are extremely powerful. I want you to take nine of them three times a day: nine in the morning, nine at noon, and nine at night before going to bed.	Son bastante fuertes. Quiero que te tomes nueve tres veces al día: nueve en la mañana, nueve al mediodía, y nueve en la noche antes de acostarte.
I can assure you you'll be well soon.	Te puedo asegurar que pronto te mejorarás.
Come back and see me in nine weeks, will you?"	Regresa a verme en nueve semanas."
Nine weeks went by but the man didn't come.	Nueve semanas pasaron, pero el hombre no regresó.
Ten weeks, eleven weeks, twelve weeks.	Diez semanas, once semanas, y doce semanas.
After twelve weeks, the doctor by chance was walking along a street, and he passed the house of his sick friend.	Después de doce semanas, por casualidad el doctor caminaba por la calle, y pasó por la casa de su amigo enfermo.
He decided to stop and call on him.	Entonces decidió visitarlo.

English *(cont.)*	Spanish
He knocked on the door, and his friend's wife answered the door. She was crying.	*Golpeó la puerta, y la esposa de su amigo salió llorando.*
"Good evening, Mrs. Lopez, I came to see how Paulo is doing."	*"Buenas noches, señora López. Vengo para ver cómo está Paulo."*
"Oh doctor, haven't you heard?"	*"Ay, doctor, ¿acaso no se enteró?"*
"What?"	*"¿Qué?"*
"Paulo is dead."	*"Paulo está muerto."*
"Dead?"	*"¿Muerto?"*
"Yes, he was eaten by the crocodile."	*"Sí, se lo comió un cocodrilo."*

Performance Challenge

Individual   In Spanish, briefly summarize the doctor's orders to his patient in this story.

Performance Challenge

Group   Have students share stories about what they thought lived under the bed when they were children. Have them write and illustrate their stories, and share them, in Spanish, with younger students.

ACTIVITY

45

Mini-Dialogues

In this activity you will:

→ Increase reading and listening comprehension, and vocabulary usage.

Disc **4** Track **5**

INSTRUCTIONS Read and listen to the following dialogues. Then see if you can repeat them in Spanish.

English	Spanish
I'm very proud of my son.	*Estoy muy orgulloso de mi hijo.*
Why?	*¿Por qué?*
He can spell his name backwards and forwards.	*El sabe escribir su nombre al derecho y al revés.*
What's his name?	*¿Cómo se llama él?*
Bob.	*Bob.*
I'm going to leave you.	*Te voy a dejar.*
Oh!	*¡Oh!*
I'm never coming back.	*Jamás volveré.*
Oh!	*¡Oh!*
Good luck.	*Buena suerte.*
Farewell!	*¡Que te vaya bien!*
How many cars do you have?	*¿Cuántos autos tiene usted?*
Cars? In America? Three. One big one and two small ones.	*¿Autos? ¿En América? Tres. Uno grande y dos pequeños.*
All are new?	*¿Son nuevos ellos?*
No. One new one and two old ones.	*No. Uno nuevo y dos viejos.*
How much does a new car cost in America?	*¿Cuánto cuesta un auto nuevo en América?*
About $20,000, $30,000.	*Alrededor de 20, 30,000 dólares.*
For this one I paid $20,000.	*Por éste pagué 20,000 dólares.*
You must be very rich.	*Usted debe ser muy rico.*
Not really.	*En verdad no.*

English (cont.)	Spanish
Nonsense!	¡No puede ser!
No, it's absolutely true.	No, es absolutamente verdad.
I don't believe it.	No lo creo.
I'm telling the truth.	Digo la verdad.
You're lying.	Está mintiendo.
Believe me! I'm not lying to you.	¡Créame! No le miento.
Impossible!	¡Imposible!
I can prove it.	Lo puedo comprobar.
It means I won the prize?	¿Quiere decir que gané el premio?
That's right.	Es correcto.
Heavens! I can't believe it.	¡Cielos! No lo puedo creer.
I have a headache.	Me duele la cabeza.
And I have a toothache.	Me duele un diente.
Where do we have aspirin?	¿Dónde tenemos aspirina?
Where is the dentist?	¿Dónde está el dentista?
We're proud of you.	Estamos orgullosos de usted.
No reason to be. I didn't do anything special.	Sin razón. No hice nada en particular.
There is reason. You're our hero (f).	Hay una razón. Usted es nuestra heroína.
Get out of bed! You're so lazy!	¡Quítate de la cama! ¡Eres tan perezoso!
I'm sick. I can't budge!	Estoy enfermo. ¡No me puedo mover!
Lazy! Lazy! Lazy!	¡Perezoso! ¡Perezoso! ¡Perezoso!
Where's your daddy?	¿Dónde está su papá?
He is working today.	Está trabajando hoy.
And your mother?	¿Y tu mamá?
She's in town today.	Está en el centro hoy.
Ha ha ha ha!	¡Ha ha ha ha!
Don't make fun of me!	¡No te burles de mí!
But you're so funny!	¡Pero eres tan cómico!

English (cont.)	Spanish
Are you married?	¿Es casada?
No, I'm single. Are you married?	No, soy soltera. ¿Es usted casado?
No, I'm single too.	No, soy soltero también.
There's a letter on the table for you.	Hay una carta en la mesa para usted.
Oh, I hadn't noticed.	Oh, no me había fijado.
What do you want from me?	¿Qué desea usted de mí?
Respect. Nothing more.	Respeto. Nada más.
That shouldn't be too hard.	Esto no debe ser tan difícil.

Performance Challenge

Individual   This activity presented a series of mini-conversations. Go back and practice at least ten lines from the different conversations until you can say them fluently without looking at your book. Look for chances to use the lines you have practiced in everyday conversations.

Performance Challenge

Group   Divide students into groups and give each group a Spanish newspaper. Have them choose an article and translate as much of it as they can into English. Invite them to share what they think the article says with the group.

The Little Red Hen

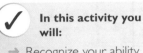

ACTIVITY
46

INSTRUCTIONS   Read and listen to this familiar story. See how much Spanish you can understand.

In this activity you will:
→ Recognize your ability to understand Spanish.

Disc **4**   Track **6**

English	Spanish
A hen found a grain of wheat.	*Una gallina encontró un granito de trigo.*
"Let's plant it," she said.	*"Vamos a sembrarlo," dijo.*
"Who is going to help me?"	*"¿Quién me va a ayudar?"*
"Quack, quack. Not I," said the duck.	*"Cuaac, cuaac. Yo no," dijo el pato.*
"Honk, Honk. Not I," said the goose.	*"Uank, uank. Yo no," dijo la gansa.*
"Gobble, gobble. Not I," said the turkey.	*"Gabul, gabul. Yo no," dijo el pavo.*
"Then I'll plant it myself," said the hen.	*"Entonces yo lo haré sola," dijo la gallina.*
And she planted it.	*Y lo sembró.*
The wheat ripened.	*El trigo se maduró.*
"Who is going to help me harvest it?" said the hen.	*"¿Quién me va a ayudar a cosecharlo?" dijo la gallina.*
"Not I," said the duck.	*"Yo no," dijo el pato.*
"Not I," said the goose.	*"Yo no," dijo la gansa.*
"Not I," said the turkey.	*"Yo no," dijo el pavo.*
"Then I'll do it myself," said the hen.	*"Entonces yo lo haré sola," dijo la gallina.*
And she did.	*Y lo hizo.*

Geography of Paraguay

Landlocked Paraguay borders Bolivia to the north, Brazil to the east, and Argentina to the south and west. *El Río Paraguay* unevenly divides the country in half. The western half, called *El Chaco*, is dry and very sparsely populated. Almost all of Paraguay's 5.6 million citizens live east of the river, on the well-watered, elevated grasslands. Pockets of subtropical forest also crop up on this side of the river, mostly near the Brazilian and Argentinian borders. Paraguay's diverse wildlife includes birds such as parrots, parakeets, wood storks, and hyacinth macaws; large reptiles such as caimans, anacondas, and boa constrictors; and rarer mammals such as the giant anteater, maned wolf, and jaguar. Paraguay's climate is humid in the east and drier in the west. Temperatures are hot in summer but can get fairly cold in winter. Frost is not uncommon, though snow rarely falls.

English (cont.)	Spanish
"Who is going to help me take it to the mill?"	"¿Quién me va a ayudar a llevarlo al molino?"
"Not I," said the duck.	"Yo no," dijo el pato.
"Not I," said the goose.	"Yo no," dijo la gansa.
"Not I," said the turkey.	"Yo no," dijo el pavo.
"Then I'll take it myself," said the hen.	"Entonces yo lo haré sola," dijo la gallina.
And she did.	Y lo hizo.
"Now who is going to help me make bread?"	"Ahora ¿quién me va a ayudar a hacer el pan?"
"Not I," said the duck.	"Yo no," dijo el pato.
"Not I," said the goose.	"Yo no," dijo la gansa.
"Not I," said the turkey.	"Yo no," dijo el pavo.
"Then I'll make it myself," said the hen.	"Entonces yo lo haré sola," dijo la gallina.
And she did.	Y lo hizo.
"Now," said the hen, "who wants to eat bread?"	"Ahora," dijo la gallina, "¿quién quiere comer pan?"
"Me," said the duck.	"Yo," dijo el pato.
"Me," said the goose.	"Yo," dijo la gansa.
"Me," said the turkey.	"Yo," dijo el pavo.
"Oh no," said the hen.	"Ah no," dijo la gallina.
"You didn't help me plant.	"Ustedes no me ayudaron a sembrar.
You didn't help me harvest.	No me ayudaron a cosechar.
You didn't help me carry it to the mill.	No me ayudaron a llevarlo al molino.
And you didn't help me make the bread."	Y no me ayudaron a hacer el pan."
Then the hen and her chicks ate all the bread.	Entonces la gallina y sus pollitos se comieron todo el pan.

Performance Challenge

Individual   Review the story one more time. Make a list in Spanish of what animals appear in the story. Make another list of what everyone but *la gallina* refuses to do.

....

....

....

....

....

....

....

....

....

....

....

....

....

....

....

Performance Challenge

Group   Set up a mock courtroom with the Little Red Hen as the plaintiff and her friends as the defendants. Are her friends true friends? In Spanish, present the case from the point of view of each character. Assign one student, or the teacher, to be the judge and the jury.

You have completed all the activities for

Section 2.1.1
Day Three, 08:00 Hours

and are now ready to take the section quiz. Before continuing, be sure you have learned the objectives for each activity in this section.

Section Quiz

INSTRUCTIONS   Choose the correct Spanish translation for the underlined English word or set of words. Check your answers in Appendix D, on page 346.

1. *Un chico compró una flor y* <u>gave it</u> *a su hermana.*
   A. *la dió*
   B. *se la dió*
   C. *diósela*
   D. *dióse*

2. *El regalo es para* <u>you</u> *de parte de* <u>me</u>.
   A. *tú / yo*
   B. *ti / mi*
   C. *tí / mí*
   D. *Ud. / mi*

3. *Los cochinitos se escapan* <u>again</u>.
   A. *mucho*
   B. *otra vez*
   C. *entonces*
   D. *antes*

4. <u>Take</u> *tu lápiz y* <u>make</u> *tres puntos.*
   A. *Dibuja / toma*
   B. *Hace / dibuja*
   C. *Toma / haz*
   D. *Compara / hace*

5. **No soy casada** (married) *sino que soy* <u>single</u>.

   A. *soltero*

   B. *soltera*

   C. *enfermo*

   D. *enferma*

- -

INSTRUCTIONS   For the following questions, choose the most correct answer.

6. **En el cuento "El Cocodrilo," ¿Había un cocodrilo debajo de la cama de Paulo?**

   A. *Sí*

   B. *No*

7. **¿Porqué el doctor le dio muchas píldoras a Paulo?**

   A. *cree que el cocodrilo es una ilusión*

   B. *para dar al cocodrilo*

   C. *para asustarlo*

   D. *porque el cocodrilo es muy grande*

8. **¿Cómo se dice 'lazy' en español?**

   A. *grande*

   B. *perezoso*

   C. *orgulloso*

   D. *cómico*

9. **¿Quién le ayuda a la gallina sembrar y cosechar el trigo?**

   A. *el pato*

   B. *la gansa*

   C. *el pavo*

   D. *nadie* (nobody)

10. **¿Quién come el pan?**

   A. *el pato*

   B. *la gansa*

   C. *el pavo*

   D. *la gallina y sus pollitos*

Bolivia

Cerro León

Parque Nacional
Defensores
del Chaco

El Chaco

Brazil

Parque
Nacional
Teniente
Enciso

Fortín Toledo
Filadelfia

Loma
Plata

Parque Nacional
Cerro Corá

Río Paraguay

Parque
Nacional
Tinfunqué

Paraguay

Asunción

Itaipú
Dam

Itaguá

Piribebuy

Parque Nacional
Ybycuí

Villa Florida

Santa María

Argentina

San Ignacio Guazú

Trinidad

Río Paraná

Paraguay

Day Three, 13:00 Hours

El mapa desgarrado

You pause your studies for a chat with the museum curator, who wants to know what the shouting was about and heard from one of the guides that you were trying to reach the fellow doing the shouting. You quickly summarize your current assignment and ask if she has any idea what *Señor* Espinoza's kidnappers might have wanted badly enough for them to bring their captive to such a public place. She hesitates, then tells you, *"Vengan conmigo, por favor."*

She leads you out of the display area, down a flight of worn steps, into the museum's musty-smelling storage area. "The name Alonso Hernández rang a bell," she tells you, sifting through a pile of old books. "Ah, here we go." She pulls out a pile of old maps, *mapas viejos*, each signed with the name Alonso Hernández. "It would seem that your scholar was a decent cartographer as well," she says, handing you the maps. "They are quite *viejos*, so please be careful with them—there's already one in the collection that's ripped. *Sí, está desgarrado.*"

With a growing feeling of excitement, you sift through the pile for *el mapa desgarrado*. It matches the half-map you already have perfectly. There's no tiny writing around the edges of this half. Looking closely, the curator informs you that the tiny writing on your half was added long after the map was made, probably using a ball-point pen.

The other half of the map, being ripped, is worthless to the museum, especially since they have other much nicer specimens from the same time period, so the curator agrees to let you take both halves with you.

Feeling quite satisfied that, here in Asunción at least, you have foiled the kidnappers, you return upstairs, where *Araña* has moved work on *el rompecabezas* to the museum *café*.

✓ In this section you will:

→ Tell a joke in Spanish.

→ Understand and use geometry vocabulary.

→ Read and understand a story in Spanish.

→ Increase the number of useful phrases you can say.

→ Follow a story line with full comprehension.

→ Increase vocabulary through poems and ditties.

 Disc **4** Track **7**

ACTIVITY 47

Nobody Cares About Me

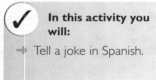

✓ In this activity you will:

→ Tell a joke in Spanish.

Disc **4**   Track **8**

INSTRUCTIONS   Listen to this joke in Spanish. Repeat it until you can tell it yourself.

	English	Spanish
	(M: Medical doctor, P: Patient)	(M: *Médico*, P: *Paciente*)
M:	Please come in. Sit down.	*Entre por favor. Siéntese.*
P:	Thank you, doctor.	*Gracias, doctor.*
M:	Tell me, what is your problem?	*Dígame, ¿cuál es su problema?*
P:	Oh, doctor. Please help me.	*Oh, doctor, por favor ayúdeme.*
	Tell me what to do.	*Dígame que puedo hacer.*
	I feel I am worthless.	*Siento que no valgo nada.*
	I feel no one cares about me.	*Siento que a nadie le importo.*
	No one pays attention to me.	*Nadie me presta atención.*
	Everyone treats me as if I didn't matter.	*Todos me tratan como si yo no valiera nada.*
	Everyone treats me as if I didn't even exist.	*Todos me tratan como si yo no existiera.*
M:	Next!	*¡El siguiente!*

Performance Challenge

Individual   This activity presented a joke in Spanish. Think of a good joke that you know. Try to tell that joke in Spanish. If you're not sure of all the words, check a dictionary, or ask a parent or instructor for help.

Performance Challenge

Group   Have each student in the group write and perform their own joke in Spanish. Then have the entire group vote on the best joke. Give out awards.

ACTIVITY

48

A Geometry Lesson

✓ **In this activity you will:**

→ Understand and use geometry vocabulary.

 Disc **4** Track **9**

INSTRUCTIONS Listen to and read this lesson. Use it to learn geometry-related vocabulary.

English	Spanish
A rectangle, like a square has four straight lines and four right angles, is that not so?	*Un rectángulo, como un cuadrado, tiene cuatro líneas y cuatro ángulos rectos, ¿no?*
Then what is the difference between a rectangle and a square?	*Entonces, ¿cuál es la diferencia entre un rectángulo y un cuadrado?*
Listen. I will explain it to you.	*Escucha. Yo te lo voy a explicar.*
A square is one kind of rectangle.	*Un cuadrado es un tipo de rectángulo.*
Like any rectangle, a square has four sides.	*Como todo rectángulo, un cuadrado tiene cuatro lados.*
But different from other rectangles, the four sides of a square are equal in length.	*Pero a diferencia de otros rectángulos, los cuatro lados de un cuadrado son del mismo largo.*
Each side is parallel with the opposite side.	*Cada lado es paralelo al lado opuesto.*
This is a rectangle.	*Este es un rectángulo.*
This is one side.	*Este es un lado.*
This is the opposite side.	*Este es el lado opuesto.*
This side and the opposite side are parallel.	*Este lado y el lado opuesto son paralelos.*
Also the top side and the bottom side are parallel.	*También el lado de arriba y el de abajo son paralelos.*
What's the difference between a circle and an oval?	*¿Cuál es la diferencia entre un círculo y un óvalo?*

English (cont.)	Spanish
In what way are a circle and an oval alike?	¿En qué manera son similares el círculo y el óvalo?
Can you explain?	¿Puedes explicar?

Performance Challenge

Individual   Take a few minutes to answer the question at the end of this activity. Use as much Spanish as you can in your answer.

Performance Challenge

Group   Find a box of multi-shaped blocks. Divide students into pairs. Blindfold one of the students and lay some blocks in front of them. They must then describe each shape in Spanish to their partner who tries to correctly identify the shape. Have the learners trade places.

History of Paraguay

In 1524, Alejo García was the first European to arrive in Paraguay. When he arrived, a semi-nomadic people called the Guaraní occupied Paraguay's eastern half, and the Chaco was home to hunter-gatherers called the *Guaycurú*. Alejo García crossed Paraguay with the help of Guaraní guides but never built any settlements. That task was left to Pedro de Mendoza, whose expedition founded Asunción. Asunción grew into the springboard for Spanish settlement of southeastern South America and acquired a fascinating blend of the local and Spanish cultures. Paraguay declared independence from Spain in 1811, and as Spain made no objections, that independence took effect at once. It was not long-lived, however. Within a few years, the country fell under the control of xenophobic José Gaspar Rodríguez de Francia, who did his best to cut the country off completely from the rest of the world. When he died in 1840, his successor, Carlos Antonio López, reopened Paraguay's borders and began efforts to modernize the country. His efforts, unfortunately, were undone by his son, Francisco Solano López, who came to power and nearly destroyed the country by waging the War of the Triple Alliance (1864-70) against Uruguay, Brazil, and Argentina—all at once. By the time the war ended, Paraguay had lost 58,500 square miles of territory and almost a quarter of its population, including its misguided leader. After the war, new waves of immigration from Europe and neighboring Argentina replenished Paraguay's population, but its political situation continued to be chaotic, with a war with Bolivia in 1932, a small civil war in 1949, and a string of dictators, followed by a string of corrupt presidents. Relative stability has reigned since Luis Gonzalez Macchi was sworn in as president in 1999.

Unity

In this activity you will:

→ Read and understand a story in Spanish.

Disc **4**   Track **10**

Sites to See in Paraguay

Inside Asunción, visitors can view el *Palacio de Gobierno* (not safe during the rule of Rodriguez de Francia, as he ordered anyone caught gazing at it to be shot). Nearby are *Casa Viola*, one of Asunción's few surviving colonial buildings; *la Casa de Cultura Paraguaya*; *la Casa de Independencia*, the city's oldest building (completed 1772) and site of its declaration of independence; and *el Jardín Botánico*, an excellent park. Not far from the capital city are Itaguá, a town famous for its weaving and lace-making; lakeside resort towns of Areguá and San Bernadino; and tranquil *Parque Nacional Ybycuí*, a preserved area of rainforest. Itaipú Dam, the world's largest hydroelectric project, is also well worth a visit. Near the Bolivian border in *el Chaco* lies el *Parque Nacional Defensores del Chaco*, where you can find some of the country's most endangered wildlife, including its big cats, such as jaguars, pumas, and ocelots.

INSTRUCTIONS   Read and listen to this story, and learn its vocabulary.

English	Spanish
"Unity is Strength"	*"La Unidad Hace la Fuerza"*
A man had several sons who often quarreled with each other.	*Un hombre tenía varios hijos, los cuales se peleaban mucho entre sí.*
The father tried to teach them to live in peace, but they would not listen.	*El padre trató de enseñarles a vivir en paz, pero no le hacían caso.*
Finally he hit on an idea: he gathered several sticks and tied them together in a bundle.	*Finalmente se le ocurrió un idea: juntó varios palillos y los ató.*
Then he called his sons to him and said:	*Entonces llamó a sus hijos y les dijo:*
"Let's see if you can break this bundle of sticks."	*"Veamos si pueden romper este atado de palillos."*
Each of the sons took the bundle of sticks and tried with all his might to break it, but they could not.	*Cada uno de los hijos tomó el atado de palillos e intentó con todas sus fuerzas romperlo, pero no pudieron.*
After they had tried and given up, the father said:	*Después de que habían tratado y se habían dado por vencidos, el padre les dijo:*
"Now I'll untie the bundle, and each of you take one stick and see if you can't break it."	*"Ahora desataré los palillos y cada uno de ustedes va a tomar uno para ver si lo puede romper."*
This they did without difficulty.	*Lo cual hicieron sin ninguna dificultad.*
Then the father said: "When the sticks were bound together you saw that they were strong.	*Entonces les dijo el padre: "Cuando los palillos estaban unidos, se dieron cuenta que eran muy fuertes.*
You couldn't break them.	*No los pudieron romper.*
But one stick at a time you could break easily.	*Sin embargo, a un solo palillo lo pudieron romper fácilmente.*

English *(cont.)*	Spanish
If you stop quarreling and live in peace with each other you'll be like the bundle of sticks.	*Si dejan de pelear y viven en paz el uno con el otro serán fuertes como este atado de palillos.*
But if you quarrel with each other and live in disunity you will be as weak as one of the sticks all by itself."	*Pero si pelean el uno con el otro y viven en desunión, serán tan débiles como un solo palillo."*
Unity is strength.	*La unidad hace la fuerza.*

Performance Challenge

Individual   Read the story out loud a few times to familiarize yourself with the words used in it. Then, in your own words, summarize the story for a teacher, parent, or friend.

Performance Challenge

Group   Split into small groups. Assign each group to represent a sports team from a Spanish-speaking country. Keep track of the team's performance throughout the semester. Reward the group representing the team that performs the best at the end of the semester.

Openers and Rejoinders

In this activity you will:

➡ Increase the number of useful phrases you can say.

Disc **4**   Track **11**

INSTRUCTIONS   Listen to and learn these useful phrases and sentences.

🔊

English	Spanish
Give me an example.	*Déme un ejemplo.*
Well, for example…	*Bueno, por ejemplo…*
Tomorrow is Saturday.	*Mañana es sábado.*
Thank the Lord!	*¡Gracias al Señor!*
Please. After you.	*Por favor, después de usted.*
You're very kind.	*Ud. es muy amable.*
Let's take a walk in the park.	*Vamos a dar una vuelta en el parque.*
Why not?	*¿Por qué no?*
We'll arrive at the meeting late.	*Llegaremos tarde a la reunión.*
Better late than never.	*Mejor tarde que nunca.*
Edy Gorme was a very popular singer.	*Edy Gorme era una cantante muy popular.*
And now she's hardly known. How can it be?	*Y ahora casi no se conoce. ¿Cómo puede ser?*
We did it ourselves.	*Lo hicimos nosotros mismos.*
You've done well.	*Lo han hecho bien.*
Try not to move so much.	*Procure no moverse tanto.*
But it hurts so much.	*Pero me duele mucho.*
He should not complain.	*Él no debe quejarse.*
That's just what I told him.	*Eso mismo le dije yo.*
So, you're from Barcelona.	*De modo que Ud. es de Barcelona.*

English (cont.)	Spanish
It's true.	Es cierto.
I can't! I can't!	¡No puedo! ¡No puedo!
Yes you can. Try!	Sí, puedes. ¡Esfuérzate!
Good news for you.	Buenas noticias para tí.
Well tell me!	¡Dígame pues!
We reached the top.	Alcanzamos la cumbre.
Well now let's rest a bit.	Pues ahora descansemos un poco.
I can't leave until Friday.	No puedo salir hasta el viernes.
Me neither.	Yo tampoco.
They say a cow jumped over the moon.	Dicen que una vaca saltó sobre la luna.
Incredible!	¡Increíble!
These papers are worthless. Throw them out.	Estos papeles no valen nada. ¡Tíralos!
As you say.	Como Ud. diga.
I have lived here five months.	Hace cinco meses que vivo aquí.
A very short time.	Muy poco tiempo.
I'm mistaken. Excuse me.	Me equivoqué. Disculpe Ud.
No reason.	No hay por qué.
I'd like to talk with Mr. Perez.	Quisiera hablar con el Señor Perez.
Who is calling?	¿De parte de quién?
Stay with me.	Quédate conmigo.
I can't. I have to go.	No puedo. Tengo que irme.

Performance Challenge

Individual   This activity taught you a new series of openers and rejoinders. Focus on three of them and look for opportunities to use those three in your regular conversations this week.

Performance Challenge

Group   Have the students choose their favorite nursery rhyme and translate it into Spanish. Then, have them perform their nursery rhymes for the class.

The Silent Fisherman

INSTRUCTIONS Read and listen to this vocabulary-building story.

🔊

English	Spanish
Early one Saturday morning a fisherman and his son went out fishing.	*Temprano un sábado por la mañana, un pescador y su hijo salieron a pescar.*
Because fishermen don't like to talk a lot, the men in our story were quiet as fish.	*Puesto que a los pescadores no les gusta hablar mucho, los hombres en nuestro cuento estaban tan callados como los peces.*
Only at noon, when clouds appeared on the horizon, did the son say to his father:	*Solamente al mediodía, cuando las nubes aparecieron en el horizonte, el hijo le dijo al padre:*
"Looks like it's going to rain."	*"Parece que va a llover."*
The father looked up for a while and nodded to the son.	*El padre levantó la vista hacia el cielo y movió la cabeza en señal de aprobación.*
But he did not say a word.	*Pero no dijo ni una palabra.*
A day went by like that.	*Un día pasó de esa manera.*
On Sunday they took a rest.	*El domingo tomaron un descanso.*
But as usual, they said nothing to each other.	*Pero como de costumbre, no se dijeron nada.*
On Monday they went fishing again.	*El lunes fueron de nuevo a pescar.*
But they were still in silence.	*Pero todavía en silencio.*
Tuesday, Wednesday, Thursday, Friday, all passed in the same way.	*Así pasaron el martes, el miércoles, el jueves, y el viernes, todos pasaron de la misma manera.*

✔ **In this activity you will:**

→ Follow a story line with full comprehension.

◎ Disc **4** Track **12**

Dulce de Miel y Maní: A Recipe of Paraguay

🥄 2 cups honey

🥄 1 pound toasted peanuts

Directions

In a medium saucepan, heat the honey to boiling, stirring constantly until very clear. Add peanuts a heaping tablespoon at a time. Continue cooking about 5 minutes more. Pour mixture into a shallow, water-moistened pan or mold. Cool before removing.

ACTIVITY 51

English *(cont.)*	Spanish
It was only on Friday evening when it was raining hard, the father wiped his forehead with his hand and said:	*No fue sino hasta el viernes por la noche, cuando empezó a llover fuerte, que el padre se secó la frente con su mano y dijo:*
"Yes, you're right."	*"Sí, tienes razón."*

Performance Challenge

Individual   This activity presented a humorous short story. Think of an amusing short story you know, or make up one of your own. Then, using as much Spanish as you can, share that story with a teacher, parent, or friend.

Performance Challenge

Group   Set up a fishing pond. Write the words from the story in Spanish on the fish. Have each student take turns fishing out words. If they can pronounce the word, award them a point. The student with the most points at the end of the game, wins.

Poems and Ditties

INSTRUCTIONS   Here are some more poems and ditties for you to enjoy. Use these ditties to practice sentence structures and vocabulary.

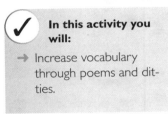

In this activity you will:

→ Increase vocabulary through poems and ditties.

Disc **4**   Track **13**

English	Spanish
I don't know…	*No sé…(que te diera)*
For a glance…the world.	*Por una mirada…el mundo.*
For a smile…the sky.	*Por una sonrisa…el cielo.*
For a kiss…	*Por un beso…*
I don't know what I'd give thee for a kiss!	*¡Ay, no sé que te diera por un beso!*
I see the moon,	*Veo la luna,*
and the moon sees me.	*y la luna ve a mi.*
God bless the moon, and also bless me!	*¡Que Dios bendiga la luna, y bendiga también a mi!*
Hi there, Johnny.	*Hola Johnny.*
Gringo boy.	*Gringo boy.*
What are you doing?	*¿Qué estás haciendo?*
I'm just leaving.	*Ya me voy.*
I am hungry,	*Tengo hambre,*
what is there to eat?	*¿qué hay de comer?*
Sandwiches and soup.	*Sandwiches y sopa.*
Well, let me see.	*Pues, a ver.*
I am thirsty,	*Tengo sed,*
what drinks are there?	*¿qué bebidas hay?*

English *(cont.)*	Spanish
Coffee, tea, and Pepsi.	*Té, café, y Pepsi.*
Ay ay ay!	*¡Ay ay ay!*
I am sleepy,	*Tengo sueño,*
I'm going to go to sleep,	*voy a dormir,*
Don't say anything to me,	*No me digas nada,*
I want to go now.	*ahora quiero ir.*
Let's go, Bertha.	*Vamos Berta.*
Where to then?	*¿A dónde, pues?*
Let's go to the moon,	*Vamos a la luna,*
this time.	*esta vez.*
How's it going, Carlos?	*¿Qué tal Carlos?*
Where are you going?	*¿Adónde va?*
I'm going to my banker.	*Voy con mi banquero.*
I hope so!	*¡Ojalá!*
I am cold,	*Tengo frío,*
blankets.	*sábanas.*
Otherwise I'll die soon.	*Si no, me muero pronto.*
Bring them to me.	*Tráemelas.*
Give me ice,	*Dame hielo,*
it's hot (weather)	*hace calor*
here in this house.	*aquí en esta casa.*
What pain! Yes, sir.	*¡Qué dolor! Sí, señor.*

Ditties can teach you useful words and sentences in a context that makes them very easy to remember.

Performance Challenge

Individual Think of some of the useful words and sentences you've learned elsewhere in this course. Then, using the tune from this activity, or a different activity, turn those words and sentences into a ditty of your own.

Performance Challenge

Group   Have the students write a poem in Spanish about one the things mentioned in this activity. Have them share their poems with the class.

You have completed all the activities for

**Section 2.1.2
Day Three, 13:00 Hours**

and are now ready to take the section quiz. Before continuing, be sure you have learned the objectives for each activity in this section.

Section Quiz

INSTRUCTIONS   Select the most correct answer for the following questions. Check your answers in Appendix D, on page 346.

1. *El médico le presta mucha atención al paciente.*
   A. *Sí*
   B. *No*

2. *El paciente siente como que no le importa a nadie.*
   A. *Sí*
   B. *No*

3. *¿Cuál es la diferencia entre los cuadrados y los rectángulos?*
   A. *Los 4 lados de un cuadrado son del mismo largo.*
   B. *Los rectángulos no tienen 4 ángulos rectos.*
   C. *Los cuadrados tienen 4 lados.*
   D. *Los rectángulos tienen lados opuestos que son paralelos.*

4. *¿Por qué los hijos no pueden romper el atado de palillos?*
   A. *Porque pelean mucho.*
   B. *Porque los palillos unidos son fuertes.*
   C. *Porque los hijos son débiles (weak).*
   D. *Porque el papá dice que no.*

5. *¿Qué es la lección que el papá les enseña a sus niños?*
   A. *Los palillos solos son fuertes.*
   B. *La unidad hace la fuerza.*
   C. *Es difícil romper palillos solos.*
   D. *Es fácil romper palillos atados.*

SECTION 2.1.2

6. **¿Cómo se dice 'better late than never' en español?**

   A. *Lo han hecho bien.*

   B. *Es cierto.*

   C. *Mejor tarde que nunca.*

   D. *Llegaremos tarde a la reunión.*

7. **¿Cómo se dice 'for example' en español?**

   A. *buenas noticias*

   B. *por ejemplo*

   C. *esfuérzate*

   D. *dar vuelta*

INSTRUCTIONS   For the following questions, choose the correct Spanish translation for the underlined English word or set of words.

8. **Un <u>fisherman</u> es una persona que trabaja en un barco.**

   A. *cocinero*

   B. *pescador*

   C. *bailador*

   D. *bombero*

9. **Cuando <u>I am hungry</u> me gusta comer chocolate.**

   A. *tengo sed*

   B. *tengo calor*

   C. *tengo sueño*

   D. *tengo hambre*

10. **Cuando <u>you are hot</u> quieres hielo.**

    A. *tienes frío*

    B. *tienes hambre*

    C. *tienes calor*

    D. *tienes sed*

You have completed all the sections for

Module 2.1

and are now ready to take the module test. Before continuing, be sure you have learned the objectives for each activity in this module.

Module Test

INSTRUCTIONS   Choose the correct English translation of the Spanish word, phrase, or sentence. Check your answers in Appendix D, on page 345.

1. *tres cochinitos*

   A. three little cars

   B. very little wolves

   C. three little pigs

   D. three pigs

2. *hermanos*

   A. brothers

   B. hermits

   C. sisters

   D. manners

3. *tres casas*

   A. three boxes

   B. three houses

   C. small houses

   D. small boxes

4. *una casa de paja*

   A. a house on straw

   B. a box of straw

   C. a house of straw

   D. a roof of straw

5. *una casa de leños*

   A. a house of sticks

   B. a pile of sticks

   C. a roof of sticks

   D. a house of straw

6. *una casa de ladrillos*

   A. a house of straw

   B. a house of sticks

   C. a house of bricks

   D. a pile of bricks

7. *un lobo*

   A. a ball

   B. a wolf

   C. a pig

   D. a chimney

8. *Viene con hambre.*

   A. He comes with a man.

   B. He wants a hamburger.

   C. He wants to eat.

   D. He comes with hunger.

9. *Viene a la casa de paja.*

   A. He comes to the house of straw.

   B. He comes to the house of bricks.

   C. He comes to the house of sticks.

   D. He comes to the pig's house.

10. *Y sopla.*

   A. And he falls.

   B. And he eats.

   C. And he blows.

   D. And he sleeps.

INSTRUCTIONS   True or False: The following phrases or sentences are translated correctly.

11. **I am very proud of my son.** = *Estoy muy orgulloso de mi hija.*

    A. True

    B. False

12. **He can spell his name backward and forward.** = *El sabe escribir su nombre al derecho y al revés.*

    A. True

    B. False

13. **What's his name?** = *¿Cómo se llama él?*

    A. True

    B. False

14. **I'm going to leave you.** = *Me voy a dejar.*

    A. True

    B. False

15. **I'm never coming back.** = *Nunca volveré.*

    A. True

    B. False

16. **How many cars do you have?** = *¿Cuántos autos tiene usted?*

    A. True

    B. False

17. **How much does a new car cost in America?** = *¿Cuánto cuesta un auto viejo en América?*

    A. True

    B. False

18. **You much be very rich.** = *Usted debe ser muy rico.*

    A. True

    B. False

19. **Nonsense!** = *¡No puede ser!*

    A. True

    B. False

20. **No, it's absolutely true. = No, *es absolutamente falso.***

    A. True

    B. False

INSTRUCTIONS   For the following questions, choose the correct English translation of the Spanish word or phrase.

21. *un pescador*

    A. a pilot

    B. a fighter

    C. a fisherman

    D. a speaker

22. *hijo*

    A. boy

    B. son

    C. daughter

    D. child

23. *mucho*

    A. a lot

    B. big

    C. tall

    D. some

24. *los hombres*

    A. the legs

    B. the hands

    C. the women

    D. the men

25. *solamente*

    A. only

    B. sometimes

    C. often

    D. softly

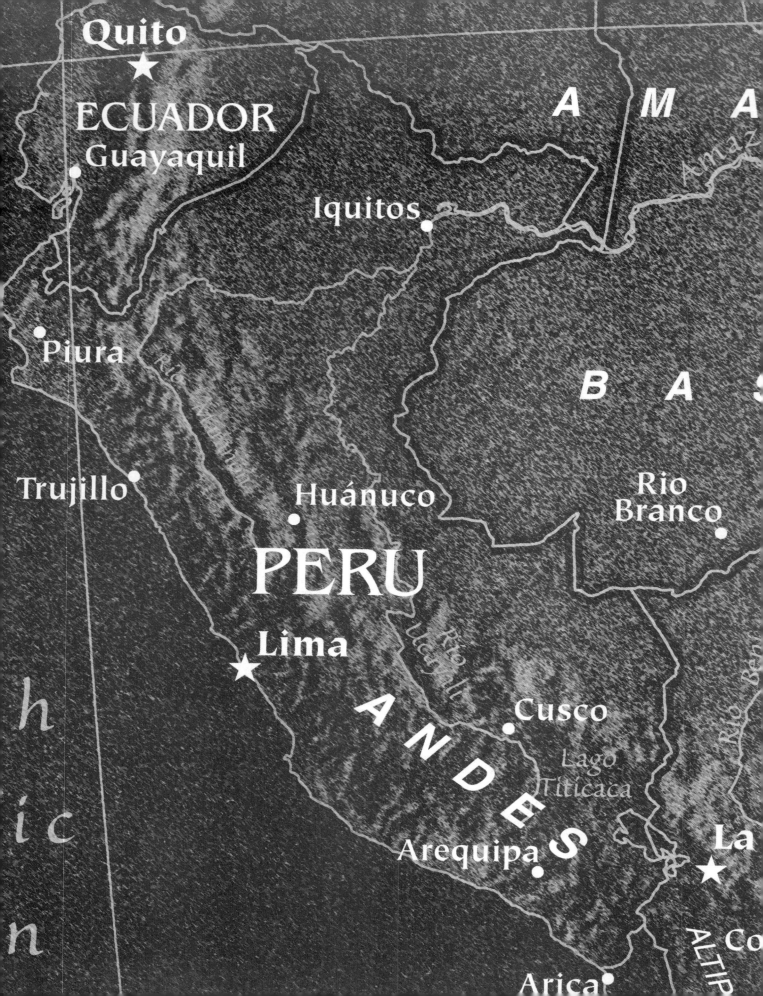

Module 2.2

Throughout this module we'll be learning about the culture of Perú.

Keep these tips in mind as you progress through this module:

1. Read instructions carefully.
2. Repeat aloud all the Spanish words you hear on the audio CDs.
3. Learn at your own pace.
4. Have fun with the activities and practice your new language skills with others.
5. Record yourself speaking Spanish on tape so you can evaluate your own speaking progress.

Quito

Bolivia

N

A

Parque Nacional
Defensores
del Chaco

Cerro León

Brazil

El Chaco

Parque
Nacional
Teniente
Enciso

Parque Nacional
Cerro Corá

Fortín Toledo
Loma
Plata

Río Paraguay

Filadelfia

Paraguay

Parque
Nacional
Tinfunqué

T

Itaipú
Dam

Asunción

Itauguá
Piribebuy

Parque Nacional
Ybycuí

Argentina

Villa Florida

San Ignacio Guazú
Santa María

Trinidad

Río Paraná

Paraguay

Arica

Day Three, 19:00 Hours

Una incursión de noche

You and *Araña* finish *el rompecabezas* just as the museum is closing for the night. With that and the full map (carefully taped together) in hand, you thank the curator and leave the museum. It's too late to fly out of Asunción tonight, so you head back to your hotel and spend the rest of the evening studying *español* and learning more about the next country marked on the map—Peru.

Day Four, 03:45 hours

Well before dawn, you wake to the sound of your *teléfono* ringing. You answer it. It's the authorities at *el aeropuerto*. A small group broke onto the airport runway a couple of hours ago and stole a small airplane, *un avión pequeño*, before the authorities could stop them. They're calling you because, according to the authority who got closest to the stolen plane, the man piloting it closely resembles the description you gave of one of *Señor* Espinoza's kidnappers.

You wake *Araña* in the next room, and both of you rush to *el aeropuerto*. You learn the kidnappers were last seen flying northwest, toward Bolivia.

"You know, just northwest of Bolivia is Peru," *Araña* says quietly.

"I know," you reply, "and I'll bet that's where they're going." You quickly arrange legal rental of another small *avión* and, thankful that you maintain a current piloting license, you guide the plane up into the grey pre-dawn sky.

As you race the small plane toward Peru, *Araña* examines the map and tries to learn what he can about your next clue. "Arequipa is surrounded with mountains," he says. "It looks like at least one of them is a volcano—it's called *El Misti*."

"Mountains?" you repeat. You check the small plane's fuel gauge. "That will make for some tricky flying. Call ahead on the radio, will you, *Araña*? We're going to be running on fumes by the time we get there."

In this section you will:

→ Listen to a Spanish story and maintain comprehension without a text.

→ Read a story in Spanish and understand new vocabulary from context.

→ Increase geometry vocabulary.

→ Read to increase all skill levels of language learning.

→ Learn and use important phrases.

Disc **5**   Track **1**

The Story of the Three Bears

In this activity you will:

→ Listen to a Spanish story and maintain comprehension without a text.

Disc **5**   Track **2**

Culture Overview of Peru

Peruvians tend to be strong-willed and fond of their homeland. It's easy to see why. Peru's layers of civilizations and its natural beauty make it one of the most fascinating places in the world to visit. Despite sizable dangers from drug barons and Shining Path guerillas (to say nothing of smaller dangers like rampant pickpocketing), visitors continue to pour into this amazing corner of the world. Peru's many artists and authors have gained fame for their skillful blending of native and Spanish cultural elements.

INSTRUCTIONS   Listen carefully and try to understand the Spanish. If you have difficulty with the story, go back and review it in Activity 9.

Performance Challenge

Individual   This activity tested your listening comprehension skills. You had to listen closely since you weren't able to follow along with the text. Now, go back to an earlier story and listen to it without reading the text. See how much of the story you can still remember and understand.

Performance Challenge

Group   Divide Spanish-speaking countries among students. Have each student write an essay, in Spanish, on the wildlife in their assigned country.

Openers and Rejoinders

INSTRUCTIONS Listen to and learn these useful phrases and sentences.

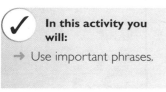

In this activity you will:
→ Use important phrases.

Disc **5**   Track **3**

English	Spanish
Juan Gonzalez is an acquaintance of mine.	*Juan González es un conocido mío.*
I don't know him.	*Yo no lo conozco.*
I'm sorry, but I have to go now.	*Lo siento, pero tengo que salir ahora.*
Come and see me soon.	*Venga a verme pronto.*
It was nice talking with you.	*Ha sido un placer hablar con Ud.*
Same here.	*Igualmente.*
Thank you for helping me.	*Gracias por haberme ayudado.*
Thank you.	*Gracias a usted.*
You remind me of my brother.	*Usted me hace acordar de mi hermano.*
How can that be?	*¿Cómo puede ser eso?*
I have something special I want to give you.	*Tengo una cosa especial que quiero presentarle.*
Thanks, but you don't owe me anything.	*Gracias, pero Ud. no me debe nada.*
Come at once.	*Venga pronto.*
Right away. I'm coming.	*Ahorita. Ya vengo.*
Evidently I was mistaken.	*Evidentemente yo me equivoqué.*
You should have known.	*Debería de haber sabido.*
You're driving me crazy.	*Me vas a volver loco.*
But you don't give me what I want.	*Pero tú no me das lo que quiero.*

ACTIVITY 54

English *(cont.)*	Spanish
I know you're busy with the exams.	*Sé que Ud. está ocupada con los exámenes.*
Yes, and in view of this, I can't see you.	*Sí, y en vista de esto, no puedo verle hoy.*
Perhaps we can see each other tomorrow.	*Tal vez mañana podamos vernos.*
I hope so.	*Espero que sí.*
It's been a long time since we've seen each other.	*Hace mucho tiempo que no nos vemos.*
Too long.	*Demasiado tiempo.*
Everybody is contributing but the rich.	*Todos contribuyen menos los ricos.*
That I don't understand.	*No comprendo eso.*
I'm sorry for having run over you!	*¡Siento mucho que la pisé!*
It's nothing. Such things happen.	*No es nada. Tales cosas suceden.*
Point out the way.	*Muéstrame el camino.*
I don't know the way myself.	*Ni yo misma sé el camino.*
I was ashamed of you.	*Yo estaba avergonzada de tí.*
I'm ashamed of myself.	*Yo estaba avergonzado de mí mismo.*
This time it's my turn to pay the bill.	*Esta vez me toca a mí pagar la cuenta.*
Don't even think of it!	*¡Ni pensar!*
I noticed a mistake here.	*Me di cuenta de un error aquí.*
Yes, I'm aware of it.	*Sí, estoy enterado.*
I must go now.	*Ahora me tengo que ir.*
I'm going to miss you a lot.	*Te voy a extrañar mucho.*
If today is Monday, this must be Madrid.	*Si hoy es lunes, ésta ha de ser Madrid.*
It must be.	*Ha de ser.*
It turns out they're going to kick you out of here.	*Resulta que te van a echar de aquí.*
That doesn't matter. It's nothing.	*Eso no importa. No es nada.*
I'm going to the beach.	*Voy a la playa.*

English (cont.)	Spanish
Look out for the sharks.	*Cuidado con los tiburones.*

Performance Challenge

Individual   This activity taught you a new series of openers and rejoinders. Focus on three of them and look for opportunities to use those three in your regular conversations this week.

Performance Challenge

Group   Have each student create a three-generation family pedigree chart. Once completed, have each student describe, in Spanish, the characteristics they have in common with one of their family members.

The House of Chuchurumbel

In this activity you will:

→ Read a story in Spanish and understand new vocabulary from context.

Disc **5** Track **4**

Facts and Figures on Peru

- Peru's full name is *República de Perú*
- Peru's population is over 27 million.
- Lima is Peru's capital city, with a population of 8 million.
- Spanish and Quechua are Peru's official languages, though Aymara is also widely spoken and understood.
- In Peru, Sunday is the favorite day for family outings.
- Peru's federal government is now a democracy, with a president, prime minister, and legislature.
- Peru's major industries include paper, fishmeal, steel, chemicals, oil, cement, auto assembly, and shipbuilding.

INSTRUCTIONS Listen to this story in Spanish. Read along and see how much you can understand. This activity will give you practice with dependent verb clauses (for example, "the dog that chased the cat" or "cat that killed the rat").

English	Spanish
This is the house of Chuchurumbel.	*Ésta es la casa de Chuchurumbel.*
This is the door of the house of Chuchurumbel.	*Ésta es la puerta de la casa de Chuchurumbel.*
This is the key of the door of the house of Chuchurumbel.	*Ésta es la llave de la puerta de la casa de Chuchurumbel.*
This is the cord of the key of the door of the house of Chuchurumbel.	*Éste es el cordón de la llave de la casa de Chuchurumbel.*
This is the rat that ate the cord of the key of the door of the house of Chuchurumbel.	*Éste es el ratón que se comió el cordón de la llave de la puerta de la casa de Chuchurumbel.*
This is the cat that killed the rat that ate the cord of the key of the door of the house of Chuchurumbel.	*Éste es el gato que mató al ratón que se comió el cordón de la llave de la puerta de la casa de Chuchurumbel.*
This is the dog that chased the cat that killed the rat that ate the cord of the key of the door of the house of Chuchurumbel.	*Éste es el perro que persiguió al gato que mató al ratón que se comió el cordón de la llave de la puerta de la casa de Chuchurumbel.*

Performance Challenge

Individual   Using vocabulary you've learned so far, write a sentence in Spanish that has at least two dependent verb clauses. For an extra challenge, develop that sentence into a story like this one! Rough out some ideas below.

A Geometry Lesson

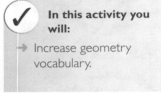

In this activity you will:

→ Increase geometry vocabulary.

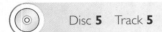

Disc **5**   Track **5**

INSTRUCTIONS   Listen to this geometry lesson in Spanish. Read along and try to pick up new vocabulary.

English	Spanish
There are lines that have no end.	Hay líneas que no tienen fin.
For example, the equator is a line that has no end.	Por ejemplo, el ecuador es una línea que no tiene fin.
Of course such lines also have no midpoint.	Claro que tales líneas tampoco tienen punto central.
That's logical, isn't it?	Eso es lógico, ¿verdad?
But if a line has one end, a beginning, then it must also have an end.	Pero si una línea tiene un extremo, un principio, entonces también debe tener otro extremo.
There is no line that has only one end.	No hay línea que tenga sólo un extremo.
Nor is there a line that has three ends.	Tampoco hay línea que tenga tres extremos.
Here is a line, a line with two ends.	Aquí hay una línea, una línea con dos extremos.
Therefore this line has a midpoint.	Luego esta línea tiene un punto central.
Here is the approximate midpoint.	Aquí está el punto central aproximado.
Locate the left end.	Localiza el extremo izquierdo.
Label it A.	Márquelo A.
Label the other end B.	Marque el otro extremo B.
This line can then be called AB.	Entonces esta línea puede llamarse AB.

Performance Challenge

Individual   Get a pencil and paper. Starting with the phrase "Here is a line, a line with two ends" begin drawing what is described in the activity. Label your drawing "Line AB" when you are finished.

Performance Challenge

Group   Have the students choose three homework problems from an algebra, geometry, trigonometry, or calculus book. Rewrite each problem in Spanish. Solve the problems and share the answers with the class.

ACTIVITY

57

Five Blind Men Describe an Elephant

In this activity you will:

→ Read to increase all skill levels of language learning.

Disc **5**   Track **6**

INSTRUCTIONS   Read and listen to this vocabulary-building story.

🔊

English	Spanish
One day five blind men were chatting and the subject turned to elephants.	*Un día cinco ciegos conversaban y el tema resultó ser los elefantes.*
One of them said: "I've grown this old, and I still don't know what an elephant looks like."	*Uno de ellos dijo: "Yo he llegado a esta edad y todavía no sé como es un elefante."*
"Neither do I."	*"Ni yo tampoco."*
"Me, I haven't seen one either."	*"Yo tampoco he visto uno."*
"Same here."	*"Ni yo tampoco."*
"What in fact does an elephant look like?"	*"En realidad, ¿cómo es un elefante?"*
All five had the same feeling, so they at once decided to ask someone to take them to an elephant so they could feel it.	*Los cinco tenían el mismo deseo, por lo que decidieron pedirle a alguien que los llevara cerca de un elefante para poder tocarlo.*
One day the group of blind men finally got the chance to "see" what an elephant was.	*Un día el grupo de ciegos logró ir a "ver" qué era un elefante.*
With great delight they went up to the elephant and attentively began to feel it.	*Con gran deleite se dirigieron hacia el elefante y atentamente empezaron a tocarlo.*
"Aha! Now I know, an elephant is the shape of a wall."	*"¡Ajá! Ya sé, un elefante es como una pared."*

English (cont.)	Spanish
"No! An elephant has the shape of a thick rope."	"¡No! Un elefante tiene la forma de una soga gruesa."
"No! No! An elephant looks like a big fan."	"¡No! ¡No! Un elefante se parece a un gran abanico."
"You are all wrong! An elephant looks like a pillar."	"¡Todos ustedes están equivocados! Un elefante se parece a una columna."
"All of you are wrong. An elephant looks like a snake."	"Todos ustedes están equivocados. Un elefante se parece a una serpiente."
Each thought only his own opinion was right.	Cada uno creía solamente en su propia opinión.
Since each thought the part he felt constituted the whole elephant, they would not listen to one another or accept one another's opinions.	Ya que cada uno de ellos pensaba que la parte que había tocado era el elefante entero, no escuchaban el uno al otro ni aceptaban las opiniones de los demás.
It finally ended in a quarrel.	Y todo terminó en una pelea.

Performance Challenge

Individual Using as much Spanish as you can, briefly describe the moral of this story.

Performance Challenge

Group Divide the group into teams and appoint a judge. Choose a subject that can be easily debated. Study as a team so that you can succinctly present your point of view. Debate with the other team about this subject. Try to keep the discussion completely in Spanish.

ACTIVITY 57

Geography of Peru

Peru borders Colombia to the north, Brazil and Bolivia to the east, Chile to the south, the Pacific Ocean to the west, and Ecuador to the northwest. Geographically, the country is divided into three major regions: the narrow coastal belt, the Andes mountains and highlands, and the Amazon Basin. Bird and marine life abound in the arid coastal region. Human life does as well, with most of Peru's cities concentrated in that region. The Andes highlands are home to birds such as the Andean condor, the puna ibis, and a variety of hummingbird, and also to the llama, alpaca, guanaco, and vicuña. The eastern slopes are home to jaguars, bears, and tapirs, and Peru's Amazon Basin is one of the top ten spots for biodiversity in the world. Peru's climate can be divided into two seasons—wet and dry—but when and how those seasons fall varies by region. On the coast and the western slopes of the Andes, the dry summer months fall between December and April, with the garúa (coastal fog) clouding the sun for much of the rest of the year. In the Andean highlands, the dry season stretches from May to September, with the rest of the year being rather wet. The area east of the Andes has dry months similar to the highlands but has a more distinct wet season running from January to April.

A Geometry Lesson

In this activity you will:

→ Learn and use important phrases.

 Disc **5**   Track **7**

INSTRUCTIONS   Read and listen to this geometry lesson in order to acquire more vocabulary.

English	Spanish
We've seen many kinds of lines.	*Hemos visto muchas clases de líneas.*
For example, vertical lines like this one.	*Por ejemplo, líneas verticales como ésta.*
Diagonal lines like this one.	*Líneas diagonales como ésta.*
Solid lines like this one.	*Líneas sólidas como ésta.*
Broken lines like this one.	*Líneas quebradas como ésta.*
What kind of line is this?	*¿Qué clase de línea es ésta?*
It's different from the lines already seen.	*Es diferente de las líneas ya vistas.*
It's different from line AB.	*Es diferente de la línea AB.*
This section, from point A to point B, is called a wave.	*Esta sección, del punto A al punto B, se llama onda.*
A wave has essentially three parts: the crest, the trough, and the slope.	*Una onda tiene tres partes esenciales: la cima, la artesa, y la inclinación.*
This is the crest of the wave.	*Esta es la cima de la onda.*
This is the trough of the wave.	*Esta es la artesa de la onda.*
This is the slope of the wave.	*Esta es la inclinación de la onda.*
This line resembles a snake, doesn't it?	*Esta línea parece una culebra, ¿verdad?*
So it can be called a "serpentine line."	*Así que puede llamarse una "línea serpentina."*
In what way are these lines alike?	*¿En qué se parecen estas líneas?*

English (cont.)	Spanish
Both are long, thick lines.	*Ambas son líneas largas y gruesas.*
Is either of them curved?	*¿Es alguna de ellas curva?*
Which is longer, the top one or the bottom one?	*¿Cuál es más larga, la de arriba o la de abajo?*
This line is different from those lines.	*Esta línea es diferente de ésas líneas.*
For one thing it's longer.	*Por una parte es más larga.*
Also it's thicker.	*También es mas gruesa.*
The other lines are all short and thin.	*Las otras líneas son cortas y delgadas.*

Performance Challenge

Individual   Look around your house and neighborhood for examples of the different kinds of lines described in this activity. How many can you find?

Performance Challenge

Group   Have the students create a geometrical shape or picture using the words taught in this lesson. Then, have them present their shapes or pictures to the class in Spanish.

You have completed all the activities for

**Section 2.2.1
Day Three, 19:00 Hours**

and are now ready to take the section quiz. Before continuing, be sure you have learned the objectives for each activity in this section.

Section Quiz

INSTRUCTIONS   Select the most correct answer for the following questions. Check your answers in Appendix D, on page 346.

1. *Tal vez mañana podamos vernos.*
   A. *Igualmente.*
   B. *Demasiado tarde.*
   C. *Sí, estoy enterado.*
   D. *Espero que sí.*

2. *Ahora me tengo que ir.*
   A. *Eso no importa.*
   B. *Te voy a extrañar mucho.*
   C. *Gracias a usted.*
   D. *Espero que sí.*

....

INSTRUCTIONS   For the following question, choose the correct conjugation of the past tense of the verb "comer" to fit in the blank.

3. *Este es el ratón que … el cordón de la llave de la puerta de la casa de Chuchurumbel.*
   A. *come*
   B. *comí*
   C. *como*
   D. *comió*

....

INSTRUCTIONS Choose the correct vocabulary word to fit in the blank.

4. *Este es el … que quemó el garrote que le pegó al perro que persiguió al gato que….*

   A. *ratón*

   B. *agua*

   C. *fuego*

   D. *cordón*

....

INSTRUCTIONS For the following questions, choose the most correct answer.

5. **¿Cuál es una línea que no tiene fin?**

   A. *una calle*

   B. *una línea vertical*

   C. *el Ecuador*

   D. *la línea en una cancha de tenis*

6. **Un punto central está en medio de los dos extremos.**

   A. True

   B. False

7. **Los hombres ciegos tocan la misma parte del elefante.**

   A. True

   B. False

8. **¿Qué parte del elefante toca el hombre que piensa que es una columna (pillar)?**

   A. *la pierna*

   B. *la cola*

   C. *la oreja*

   D. *el estómago*

9. **¿Cuál de los siguientes NO es una parte de una onda?**

   A. *la cima*

   B. *la curva*

   C. *la artesa*

   D. *la inclinación*

INSTRUCTIONS Choose the correct Spanish translation for the underlined English word.

10. *Esta línea es más <u>thick</u> que los demás.*

   A. *delgada*

   B. *gruesa*

   C. *larga*

   D. *corta*

Quito

4

N

Colombia

Río Napo

Ecuador

Iquitos O

Río Marañon

O Tumbes

Reserva Nacional Pacaya-Samiria

O Piura

Río Ucayali

Chiclayo O

Brazil

Trujillo O

Pucallpa O

Caraz O

Chimbote O   O Huascarán

Parque Nacional Manu

Sechin O   O Huaraz

Parque Nacional Huascarán

Perú

Lima ✪   O Huancayo   Machu

Océano   Ayacucho O   O Picchu

Pacífico   Pisco O O Ica   O Cuzco

Nazca O

Bolivia

Lago Titicaca

O Puno

El Misti   O Puno

Arequipa O

Perú

Chile

Arica

Day Four, 07:30 Hours

¡Hundiéndose!

Only halfway across Bolivia, the plane starts spluttering—its engine isn't designed for the altitudes you need to get over the Andean peaks standing between you and Arequipa. You encourage it along as best you can, while you have *Araña* scan the ground below for any signs of the other plane—it surely had the same problems you are having, and you wouldn't want to pass it unknowing.

Araña doesn't see anything except the alarmingly close faces of the surrounding mountains, along with the occasional city or village. A strong wind picks up, and despite your best efforts to stay on course, the plane drifts east of the course you want.

Far below, you see a narrow ribbon of a road that leads to a border crossing. You heave a sigh of relief. *¡Finalmente!* You may be a bit off course, but at least you're in the right country now.

The engines start spluttering again, even worse than before. In addition to the altitude problems, the fuel gauge just passed empty. You're running on fumes, and if the engine noises are any indication, even the fumes are running low. You're not going to make it to Arequipa. You need to find a good spot to land before you crash. Looking ahead, you see a huge lake nestled in between several mountain peaks. This has to be Lake Titicaca, the highest freshwater lake in the world. Along its shoreline, you spot a stretch of beach that's wide and flat enough to land a small plane like this. Quickly, you steer toward the beach and coast to a very rough landing as both engines finally die.

After a few moments to catch your breath, you and *Araña* climb out of the plane. The landing gear is in bad shape—*está en mal estado*—but other than that, both you and it are unharmed. *Araña* spots a village not far ahead—probably Puno, the town from which people hire boats to go out on the lake. Hopefully they'll have cars for rent as well.

By noon, you're frustrated. It seems that in the whole town, not one single wheeled vehicle is for rent. Right now, you'd even settle for *una bicicleta*. You pause for lunch at a local café, then notice what is unmistakably a taxi cab parked

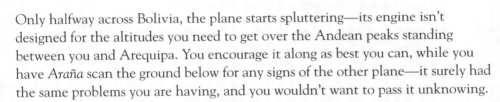

✓ **In this section you will:**

→ Read to increase all skill levels of language learning.

→ Learn and use important phrases.

→ Build comprehension and vocabulary through reading.

→ Ask and answer useful questions.

→ Gain a better understanding of verb forms.

◎ Disc **5**   Track **8**

261

just outside. The only other patron in the small *café* is sitting not far away—a short, middle-aged man with thinning curly hair and laugh lines crinkling the corners of his eyes. Could he be the cab driver? You decide to approach him.

"Perdóneme, señor, pero ¿es usted el dueño del auto que está afuera?" you ask.

"Sí, yo soy. ¿Por qué quiere saber?" the man replies.

You heave a great sigh of relief and smile. *"Nosotros queremos ir a Arequipa, pero no tenemos auto,"* you explain.

The man nods. *"Es difícil encontrar transporte en un pueblo tan pequeño,"* he says. He smiles back at you and slaps his hands on *la mesa*, making his drink glass shake. *"Bueno, yo los llevaré. Quieren ir a Arequipa, ¿no es cierto?"*

"Sí, a Arequipa," you answer. *"Vámonos después del almuerzo."*

The cab driver smiles. *"Sí, después del almuerzo."*

With a parting nod and wave, you return to your own table, just as your meal of tasty *ají de gallina* arrives. "Well?" asks *Araña*.

"That's the cab driver, all right," you reply. "He'll take us to Arequipa after lunch."

After a wonderful lunch, you and *Araña* try to while away the hair-raising cab ride through the mountains by learning more Spanish.

Recipe: *Ají de Gallina*

- 3 pounds chicken, cooked, boned, and cubed
- 1 loaf white bread, crusts removed
- 1 can evaporated milk
- 1 cup chicken broth
- 3 onions, chopped
- 2 tablespoons vegetable oil
- 1 green pepper, chopped
- 1 1/2 teaspoons garlic powder
- 1 teaspoon cumin
- 2-3 tablespoons chili powder
- salt and pepper to taste
- 1 can sliced olives, drained

Directions　In a medium bowl, soak bread in evaporated milk. Stir in chicken broth. Mix thoroughly and set aside.

In a large pan, sauté onions in oil. Stir in chicken, green pepper, garlic powder, cumin, chili powder, and bread mixture. Add salt and pepper to taste. Simmer about 20 minutes, until thick and bubbly. Just before serving, stir in sliced olives.

Serve warm over rice or potatoes. Makes 8 main dish servings.

The Shepherd Boy Who Cried Wolf!

In this activity you will:

→ Read to increase all skill levels of language learning.

 Disc **5**   Track **9**

INSTRUCTIONS Read and listen to this familiar story. Pay attention to any new words or phrases that will broaden your vocabulary base.

English	Spanish
There was once a shepherd boy who liked to play tricks on people.	*Había una vez un pastorcillo a quien le gustaba bromear con la gente.*
Every day he herded his sheep to the hillside to graze.	*Cada día llevaba sus ovejas a la ladera a pastar.*
One day with nothing to do he felt bored, so he decided to play a trick on the villagers.	*Un día que no tenía nada que hacer, se sentía aburrido, así que decidió bromear con los aldeanos.*
He cried out: "Wolf! Wolf! Help!"	*Gritó: "¡Lobo! ¡Lobo! ¡Socorro!"*
The villagers heard the cry and rushed up the mountain with stones and sickles.	*Los aldeanos oyeron los gritos y subieron con piedras y guadañas.*
But when they got there and looked around, there was simply no wolf to be seen.	*Pero cuando llegaron allá y miraron alrededor, simplemente no había ningún lobo a la vista.*
In anger the villagers scolded the boy:	*En su enojo los aldeanos reprendieron al niño:*
"Don't ever play such tricks again.	*"Nunca hagas esa clase de bromas.*
It's very dangerous. Do you understand?"	*Es muy peligroso. ¿Entiendes?"*
The boy said: "I'm sorry. I won't do it again."	*El niño dijo: "Lo siento. No lo volveré a hacer."*

English (cont.)	Spanish
A week went by. With nothing to do, the boy was bored, so he decided to play the trick again.	Una semana pasó. No teniendo nada que hacer, el muchacho estaba aburrido, entonces decidió jugar la broma nuevamente.
He cried: "Wolf! Wolf! Help!"	El gritó: "¡Lobo! ¡Lobo! ¡Socorro!"
Hearing the desperate cries of the shepherd boy, the villagers rushed up the mountain to save the sheep.	Escuchando los gritos desesperados del pastorcillo, los aldeanos corrieron subiendo la montaña a salvar las ovejas.
When they again found there was no wolf but only a laughing boy playing tricks, they were extremely angry.	Cuando encontraron una vez más que no había ningún lobo, sólo un niño riendo que le gustaba hacer bromas, estuvieron extremadamente enojados.
They severely scolded him again.	Le regañaron fuertemente una vez más.
Finally he said: "I'm sorry. I won't do it again."	Finalmente el niño dijo: "Lo siento. No lo volveré a hacer."
And the villagers returned home, shaking their heads.	Los aldeanos regresaron a sus casas, moviendo sus cabezas en señal de desaprobacíon.
Not long after this, wolves really did come and attack the sheep.	No pasó mucho tiempo y los lobos de verdad vinieron y atacaron las ovejas.
The shepherd boy was desperate. He shouted at the top of his voice: "Wolf! Wolf! Help!"	El pastorcillo estaba desesperado. Gritaba a toda voz: "¡Lobo! ¡Lobo! ¡Socorro!"
But the villagers only shook their heads and said: "The foolish chap is playing tricks again."	Pero los aldeanos, sólo movían sus cabezas y dijeron: "Ese chico tonto vuelve a hacer bromas."
So no one went to help the poor boy.	Así que nadie fue para ayudar al pobre pastorcillo.
No one trusted his word.	Nadie creyó en sus palabras.
So the wolves killed many, many sheep.	Así que los lobos mataron muchas muchas ovejas.

Performance Challenge

Individual   Using as much Spanish as you can, briefly describe the moral of this story.

....

....

....

....

....

....

....

....

....

....

....

....

....

....

....

....

Performance Challenge

Group   Have a word scramble. Divide the group into two teams. Write words from the story on pieces of paper. Pin a word on each child. Read a portion of the story in Spanish. The team that can line up the words in the correct order, and in the shortest amount of time, is the winner.

Useful Words and Phrases

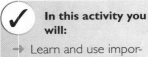

In this activity you will:

→ Learn and use important phrases.

Disc **5**   Track **10**

INSTRUCTIONS   Listen to and become familiar with these useful words and phrases.

English	Spanish
A bit faster.	*Un poco más rápido.*
A bit slower.	*Un poco más lento.*
A little bit.	*Un poquito.*
A long time ago.	*Hace mucho tiempo.*
A table for two.	*Una mesa para dos.*
About 100 pesetas.	*Más o menos 100 pesetas.*
About ten minutes ago.	*Hace como diez minutos.*
Above or below?	*¿Arriba o abajo?*
According to him, I made an error.	*Según él yo cometí un error.*
Accustomed. He's accustomed to it.	*Acostumbrado. Está acostumbrado.*
After breakfast.	*Después del desayuno.*
After they came, we left.	*Después que llegaron, salimos.*
After you, ma'am.	*Después de usted, señora.*
Again he spoke.	*Otra vez habló.*
Again you're late.	*Otra vez estás tarde.*
All at once.	*De una vez.*
All day and all night.	*Todo el día y toda la noche.*
All of the time.	*Todo el tiempo.*
All week long.	*Toda la semana.*
Already you speak well.	*Ya hablas bien.*

English (cont.)	Spanish
Although he doesn't have a car…	*Aunque él no tenga carro…*
Although he is sick…	*Aunque esté enfermo…*
I'll always help you.	*Yo siempre te ayudaré.*
And now what will she do? Do you know?	*Y ahora, ¿que hará ella? ¿Sabes?*
And so? (So what?)	*¿Y entonces?*
Another cup, please.	*Otra tasa, por favor.*
Anyone want my sandwich?	*¿Alguien quiere mi sandwich?*
Anything but this!	*¡Cualquier cosa menos esto!*
Anyway…	*De todos modos…*
Are you angry with me?	*¿Estás enojado conmigo?*
Are you comfortable?	*¿Estás cómodo?*
Are you hungry?	*¿Tienes hambre?*
Are you sleepy?	*¿Tienes sueño?*
Are you thirsty?	*¿Tienes sed?*
Are you tired?	*¿Está cansado?*
Are you upset?	*¿Estás agitado?*
As soon as possible.	*Lo antes posible.*
As you like.	*Cómo quieras.*
At first she wrote often.	*Al principio, ella me escribía a menudo.*
At what time does the party begin?	*¿A qué hora comienza la fiesta?*
Be careful not to fall.	*Cuidado con caerse.*
Be careful! Don't break the cups.	*¡Cuidado! No rompas las tazas.*
Be careful. Watch out!	*Ten cuidado. ¡Ojo!*
Before he left he was crying.	*Antes de salir estaba llorando.*
Before Christmas or after New Year's.	*Antes de navidad o después del Año nuevo.*
Before dinner.	*Antes de la cena.*
Before he comes, let's talk.	*Antes que venga, hablemos.*
Before leaving we'll have to…	*Antes de salir tendremos que…*

History of Peru

Advanced cultures such as the Chavín, Salinar, Nazca, Paracas Necropolis, Wari, and Inca prospered in Peru long before Francisco Pizarro arrived in 1526. From 1526-28, he explored the coastal regions, then, intrigued by rumors of Incan wealth, returned to Spain to raise money and recruit forces for another expedition. In 1533, he returned in a big way, conquering the Incan empire and ransoming and executing its emperor within the same year. Pizarro went on to found the modern-day capital of Lima but was assassinated just six years later. Rebellions from remnants of Incan civilization continued until the final Incan leader was killed in 1572.

The next two hundred years proved peaceful, though the treatment of Indians under their colonial masters led to an uprising in 1780. That rebellion, too, was crushed, and Peru remained loyal to Spain until it was liberated in 1824 by Simón Bolívar of Venezuela and José de San Martín of Argentina. After brief and mostly successful wars with Spain and Ecuador and a decidedly unsuccessful war with Chile, Peru entered the latter half of the twentieth century with Cuban-inspired guerilla uprisings in 1965. Nationwide strikes and particularly violent insurgencies led by the Shining Path (Sendero Luminoso) guerillas led to widespread instability throughout the 1980s. During the 1990s, the situation calmed somewhat under the rule of Alberto Fujimori, though problems of poverty and unemployment remained during and after his rule.

English (cont.)	Spanish
Believe me.	Créame.
Besides that.	Además de eso.
Besides that, I like to read.	Además de eso, me gusta leer.
Besides this one, also that one.	Además de eso, ése.
Better and better.	Mejor y mejor.
Bring anyone you'd like.	Traiga a quien quiera.

Performance Challenge

Individual   This activity presented a number of useful words and phrases. Choose at least five of them, and practice them until you can say them fluently without looking at the book. Then look for chances to use them in everyday conversations this week.

Performance Challenge

Group   Find a Spanish newspaper. Have the students circle as many of the words from this activity that they can find on one page of the newspaper. Then, ask them to use these words to write their own news story. Invite them to be as creative as they can!

Questions and Answers

INSTRUCTIONS Listen to and learn these useful questions and answers.

🔊

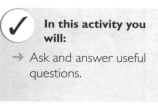

In this activity you will:
→ Ask and answer useful questions.

Disc **5** Track **11**

English	Spanish
Which of the two do you prefer?	*¿Cuál de los dos prefiere Ud.?*
I like this one better.	*Me gusta más éste.*
Can I drop by Saturday morning?	*¿Puedo pasar el sábado por la mañana?*
Please do.	*Con todo gusto.*
How was the film?	*¿Cómo fue la película?*
Marvelous! I loved it.	*¡Maravillosa! Me gustó muchísimo.*
Is today Saturday?	*¿Hoy es sábado?*
Yes, if I'm not mistaken.	*Sí, si no me equivoco.*
Then tomorrow is Sunday, right?	*Entonces mañana es domingo, ¿verdad?*
Right.	*Correcto.*
Who can do it?	*¿Quién puede hacerlo?*
I can do it.	*Yo puedo hacerlo.*
Can you take care of my dog?	*¿Puedes cuidar a mi perro?*
Trust me.	*Confía en mí.*
At what window do they sell stamps?	*¿En qué ventanilla venden sellos?*
At window five.	*En la ventanilla cinco.*
Whose turn is it now?	*¿A quién le toca ahora?*
Let's see. Seems like it's mine.	*A ver. Parece que me toca a mí.*
How does tomorrow seem to you?	*¿Qué le parece mañana?*
Sure, that's fine. Why not?	*Pues sí, está bien. ¿Por qué no?*

English *(cont.)*	Spanish
How can I be of service to you?	*¿En qué puedo servirle?*
Thanks, you're very kind, but there's no need.	*Gracias, muy amable, pero no hay necesidad.*
Did you understand what I told you?	*¿Entendió lo que le dije?*
Yes, I understood more or less.	*Sí, entendí más o menos.*
May I ask you some questions?	*¿Me permite hacerle unas preguntas?*
Oh yes. As you like.	*Pues sí, como quiera.*
Is this yours?	*¿Es suyo ésto?*
Yes, it's mine. And that is mine too.	*Sí, es mío. Y eso también es mío.*
Didn't you like it?	*¿No te gustó?*
Not that much.	*No tanto.*
Who is in charge here?	*¿Quién es la persona responsable aquí?*
It's me.	*Soy yo.*
Are you sure of that?	*¿Está segura de eso?*
Absolutely.	*Absolutamente.*
You're from California, right?	*Ud. es de California, ¿verdad?*
Yes, from Santa Barbara.	*Sí, de Santa Bárbara.*
Where were you born?	*¿Dónde nació Ud.?*
In Buenos Aires.	*En Buenos Aires.*
Can I eat some of your bread?	*¿Puedo comer un poco de tu pan?*
Go right ahead.	*Con toda confianza.*
How do you like the climate here?	*¿Le gusta el clima aquí?*
I like it very much. It's very nice.	*Me gusta muchísimo, muy agradable.*
Why isn't there any gas today?	*¿Por qué no hay gasolina hoy?*
It's all gone (used up).	*Ya se acabó.*
Do you remember I loaned you $1000?	*¿Se acuerda que yo le presté $1000?*
No sir, I don't remember. When was it?	*No, señor, no me acuerdo. ¿Cuándo fue eso?*
Have you paid the fine already?	*¿Ya has pagado la multa?*
Not yet. I'll pay it on Monday.	*Todavía no. La pagaré el lunes.*

English *(cont.)*	Spanish
Do you feel better now?	*¿Te sientes mejor ahora?*
Yes, a bit. But my head still aches.	*Sí, un poco. Pero todavía me duele la cabeza.*
How do you feel?	*¿Cómo te sientes?*
I'm hungry, thirsty, and sleepy.	*Tengo hambre, tengo sed, y tengo sueño.*
You'll win the prize, don't you think?	*Vas a ganar el premio, ¿no crees?*
I doubt it.	*Lo dudo.*
Are you going already?	*¿Ya te vas?*
I'll be right back.	*Ahorita vuelvo.*

Performance Challenge

Individual   This activity presented a number of useful questions and answers. Focus on three of them and look for opportunities to use those three in your regular conversations this week.

Performance Challenge

Group   Have the students write ten "Why" questions in Spanish. Then have them research the answers and share them with the rest of the class.

Sites to See in Peru

One of the best things about Lima is its generally friendly and hospitable populace. Other attractions include the *Museo de Arte*, the *Museo Nacional de Antropología y Arqueología*, churches *San Francisco* and *Santo Domingo*, and the popular market of *Polvos Azules*. Farther south along the coast, visitors can view wildlife on the Islas Ballestas and fly over the mysterious, immense Nazca lines. Scenic Arequipa with its buildings of white sillar stone is worth a visit and is also a good starting point for a trip to Lake Titicaca, the highest navigable lake in the world and the largest lake in South America. Boat trips on the lake are available. The ancient Incan capital of Cuzco is now a modern city and major travel hub. Its cathedral, Coricancha ruins, and *Museo de Arquelogía* all make excellent sightseeing spots, and just west of the city are the famed ruins of Machu Picchu. The largest city Peru has in the Amazon Basin, Iquitos is accessible only by river and by air. Though founded as an oil and rubber boomtown, Iquitos now sustains its economy with tourism, specifically with jungle excursions. Those in the mood for an exciting outdoor experience can visit the Auras Area, where climbing, trekking, and backpacking are all available in the area's beautiful, rugged mountains.

Afanti and the Clown

ACTIVITY

62

✓ **In this activity you will:**
→ Build comprehension and vocabulary through reading.

Disc **5**   Track **12**

INSTRUCTIONS   Read and listen to this vocabulary-building short story.

🔊

English	Spanish
Afanti had a dye shop.	Afanti tenía una tintorería.
One day a clown came in.	Un día entró un payaso.
In his hand was a cloth.	En su mano llevaba una tela.
"What can I do for you?" said Afanti.	"¿En qué puedo servirle?" dijo Afanti.
"I'd like to have you dye this cloth," said the clown.	"Me gustaría que tintieras esta tela," dijo el payaso.
"What color do you want?" Afanti asked.	"¿Qué color quiere?" Afanti preguntó.
"I want it a non-existent color."	"La quiero de un color no existente."
Obviously the clown was joking.	Obviamente el payaso estaba bromeando.
"And what is a non-existent color?" asked Afanti.	"Y ¿qué es un color no existente?" preguntó Afanti.
"It's one that's	"Es uno que
neither black nor gray	no es negro ni gris
nor red nor brown	ni rojo ni café
nor blue nor green	ni azul ni verde
nor purple nor white	ni púrpura ni blanco
nor yellow nor orange.	ni amarillo ni anaranjado.
Do you understand?"	¿Entiendes?"
"I understand. Okay, I'll do as you ask."	"Entiendo. Bueno, haré lo que pides."

English (cont.)	Spanish
"When shall I come to pick it up?" the clown asked.	"¿Cuándo vengo a buscarla?" preguntó el payaso.
"Come and get it on a non-existent day."	"Venga a buscarla en un día no existente."
"And what is a non-existent day?" the clown asked.	"¿Y qué es un día no existente?" preguntó el payaso.
"It is neither Monday,	"No es el lunes,
nor is it Tuesday,	ni es el martes,
nor is it Wednesday,	ni es el miércoles,
nor is it Thursday,	el jueves,
Friday, Saturday,	el viernes, el sábado,
or Sunday.	ni domingo.
Do you understand?"	¿Entiendes?"

Performance Challenge

Individual   This activity gave you practice with colors and days of the week. Listen to the activity one more time. Circle the colors and underline the days of the week in Spanish. Make a list of them in Spanish on a separate sheet of paper.

Performance Challenge

Group   Spain has 47 provinces, each with their own style of dance. Let the students choose one of the dances and research its history, the costumes, and the music. Have them give either an oral presentation or a demonstration to the class in Spanish.

ACTIVITY
63

✓ **In this activity you will:**

→ Learn and use important phrases.

Disc **5**   Track **13**

Useful Words and Phrases

INSTRUCTIONS   Study these words and phrases until they become familiar to you.

English	Spanish
Bring the boxes here.	*Traiga las cajas aquí.*
But of course.	*Pero por supuesto.*
By boat.	*Por barco.*
By plane or by train?	*¿Por avión o por tren?*
By the way.	*A propósito.*
Call me tomorrow.	*Llámeme mañana.*
Can you help me?	*¿Me puedes ayudar?*
Can you see the sign?	*¿Puede usted ver la señal?*
Can you tell me where the café is located?	*¿Me puede decir dónde está el café?*
Can't anything be done?	*¿No se puede hacer algo?*
Close the door.	*Cierre la puerta.*
Come and eat.	*Ven a comer.*

Performance Challenge

Individual   This activity presented several useful words and phrases. Choose at least five of them, and practice them until you can say them fluently without looking at the book. Then, look for chances to use them in everyday conversations this week.

Performance Challenge

Group   Find a local, authentic *mercado* or *panadería*. Take the students on a field trip and have them practice their Spanish as they order and pay for their purchases.

ACTIVITY
64

Past Participle

In this activity you will:

➜ Gain a better understanding of verb forms.

INSTRUCTIONS Read the following explanations to gain a better understanding of Spanish verb forms.

Infinitive ending -ar: -Ado

Tomar: tom-Ado; Fumar: fum-Ado; Cantar: cant-Ado

Practice

English	Spanish
1. (He) has sung.	*H-a cantado.*
2. I have drunk the water.	*H-e tomado el agua.*

Infinitive ending -er, -ir: -Ido

Vender: vend-Ido; Salir: sal-Ido; Leer: le-Ido; Dormir: dorm-Ido

Practice

English	Spanish
1. (He) has left.	*H-a salido.*
2. (He) has sold the house.	*H-a vendido la casa.*
3. I have read the book.	*H-e leído el libro.*
4. You have slept two hours.	*H-as dorm-ido dos horas.*

Irregular Past Participles

The following list shows irregular past participles that end in *-to* rather than *-do*.

Verb	Infinitive	1000 A.D.	Current	English
to die	*MORir*	*MORto*	*MUERto*	has died
to return*	*VOLVer*	*VOLto*	*VUELto*	has returned
to resolve	*reSOLVer*	*reSOLto*	*reSUELto*	has resolved

Papas a la Huancaina: A Recipe of Peru

- 10 medium potatoes, cooked, peeled, and quartered
- 1 pound feta cheese
- 2 small hot peppers, seeded
- 1 cup evaporated milk
- 1/2 cup vegetable oil
- 2 cloves garlic, peeled
- 8 saltine crackers
- 1 tablespoon prepared mustard
- salt and pepper to taste
- lettuce
- 3 hard boiled eggs, sliced
- black olives, sliced

Directions

In a blender, mix cheese, peppers, milk, oil, garlic, crackers, mustard, salt, and pepper until smooth. The mixture will be thick. Add more crackers to thicken it, or milk to thin it. Lay lettuce in the serving dish. Arrange potato quarters on top of lettuce. Pour on cheese sauce. Garnish with slices of egg and olives.

Verb (cont.)	Infinitive	1000 A.D.	Current	English
to open	*ABRir*	*ABIRto*	*ABIERto*	has opened
to cover	*CUBRir*	*CUBIRto*	*CUBIERto*	has covered
to write*	*eSCRIBir*	*eSCRIBto*	*eSCRIto*	has written
to position*	*PONer*	*POSto*	*PUESto*	has positioned
to see	*VEr*	*VESto*	*VISto*	has seen
to say	*DECir*	*DICto*	*DICHo*	has said
to do	*HACer*	*FACto /* *HACto*	*HECHo*	has done
to break	*ROMPer*	*ROMPto*	*ROto*	has broken

NOTE

* *deVOLVer* (return something), *reVOLVer* (revolve), *desenVOLVer* (develop)

* *deSCRIBir* (describe), *preSCRIBir* (prescribe), *proSCRIBir* (proscribe), *subSCRIBir* (subscribe)

* *dePONer* (deposit), *rePONer* (put back), *comPONer* (compose), *descomPONer* (decompose)

Performance Challenge

Individual   This activity gave you practice with the past participle verb tense. Carefully review the information presented in the activity, then use some of the verbs you've learned in other activities to write your own sentences in the past participle tense.

....

....

....

....

Performance Challenge

Group   Create a Diglot-Weave using a book written in English. Ask the students to underline the regular and irregular past participles in a chapter of the book. Have them translate the verbs into Spanish. Read the chapter to the class and see how many of the verbs they understand.

You have completed all the activities for

Section 2.2.2
Day Four, 07:30 Hours

and are now ready to take the section quiz. Before continuing, be sure you have learned the objectives for each activity in this section.

Section Quiz

INSTRUCTIONS   Select the most correct answer for the following questions. Check your answers in Appendix D, on page 346.

1. *¿Cuál de los siguientes puede ser la moraleja del cuento (moral of the story)* **El Muchacho Pastor Mentiroso?**

   A. *Hay que pedir ayuda cuando hay un problema.*

   B. *Es importante ayudar a los demás.*

   C. *No hagas bromas, porque el día que necesitas ayuda nadie te ayudará.*

   D. *A los lobos les gustan mucho a las ovejas.*

2. *¿Cómo se dice 'are you hungry' en español?*

   A. *¿Tienes sed?*

   B. *¿Tienes sueño?*

   C. *¿Tienes comida?*

   D. *¿Tienes hambre?*

3. *¿Cómo se dice 'before' en español?*

   A. *todo*

   B. *más*

   C. *después*

   D. *antes*

4. **How would you answer the question** *¿Cómo es tu español oral (spoken Spanish)?*

   A. *Mejor y mejor.*

   B. *Todo el tiempo.*

   C. *Lo antes posible.*

   D. *Cómo quieras.*

Choose the question that best corresponds with following answer.

5. **Me gustó mucho.**

   A. *¿Cuál de los dos prefiere Ud.?*

   B. *¿Cómo fue la película?*

   C. *¿Qué le parece mañana?*

   D. *¿Cómo te sientes?*

INSTRUCTIONS Choose the most correct response.

6. **Which is an appropriate answer to the question *¿Cómo te sientes?***

   A. *Me gusta mucho.*

   B. *No tanto.*

   C. *Soy yo.*

   D. *Tengo sed y tengo hambre.*

7. **En el cuento Afanti y el payaso, ¿qué color quiere el payaso su tela?**

   A. *rojo*

   B. *azul*

   C. *verde*

   D. *Ninguno* (none of the above).

8. **Which of the following verbs is not conjugated correctly in the past participle?**

   A. *vender: vendido*

   B. *comprar: comprado*

   C. *poner: puesto*

   D. *decir: decido*

INSTRUCTIONS For the following questions, choose the correct Spanish translation for the underlined English word or set of words.

9. **Vamos a viajar by avión o __by__ barco.**

   A. *para*

   B. *por*

   C. *con*

   D. *el*

10. **Mi *mamá* <u>has done</u> *muchas cosas interesantes*.**

   A. *he hacido*

   B. *ha hacido*

   C. *he hecho*

   D. *ha hecho*

You have completed all the sections for

Module 2.2

and are now ready to take the module test. Before continuing, be sure you have learned the objectives for each activity in this module.

Module Test

INSTRUCTIONS   Choose the correct Spanish translation of the English sentence. Check your answers in Appendix D, on page 345.

1. **I don't know him.**
   A. *Yo no lo conozco.*
   B. *Yo no la conozco.*
   C. *Yo no lo conoce.*
   D. *Yo no lo conozco a él.*

2. **I'm sorry, but I have to go now.**
   A. *Siento, pero tengo que salir ahora.*
   B. *Lo siento, pero tienes que salir ahora.*
   C. *Siento, pero tengo que ir ahora.*
   D. *Lo siento, pero tengo que salir ahora.*

3. **Come and see me soon.**
   A. *Venga a verme pronto.*
   B. *Vienes a verme pronto.*
   C. *Vengas y verme pronto.*
   D. *Vienes y ver a mí pronto.*

4. **It was nice talking to you.**
   A. *Había sido un placer hablar con Ud.*
   B. *Ha sido un placer hablar con Ud.*
   C. *Ha sido una placer hablar con Ud.*
   D. *Ha sido un placer a hablar con Ud.*

5. **Same here.**

   A. *Igualmente.*

   B. *Igual aquí.*

   C. *El mismo aquí.*

   D. *Sí.*

6. **Thank you for helping me.**

   A. *Gracias para me ayudando.*

   B. *Gracias a tí por ayudarme.*

   C. *Gracias por haberme ayudado.*

   D. *Gracias para haberme ayudando.*

7. **You remind me of my brother.**

   A. *Usted acordarme de mi hermano.*

   B. *Usted me hace acordar del hermano mío.*

   C. *Usted me hace acordar de mi hermano.*

   D. *Usted hacerme acordar de mi hermano.*

8. **How can that be?**

   A. *¿Cómo puede estar eso?*

   B. *¿Cómo puede ser eso?*

   C. *¿Cómo puso ser eso?*

   D. *¿Cómo poder es eso?*

9. **I have something special I want to give you.**

   A. *Tengo una cosa especial que quiero presentarle.*

   B. *Tengo un especial cosa que quiero presentarle.*

   C. *Tieno una cosa especial que quiero presentarle.*

   D. *Tengo una cosa especial que quiero presentarle.*

10. **Juan is an acquaintance of mine.**

   A. *Juan es una conocida mío.*

   B. *Juan es un conocido de mí.*

   C. *Juan es un conocido mío.*

   D. *Juan es conocido por mí.*

INSTRUCTIONS For the following questions, choose the correct English translation of the Spanish word or phrase.

11. *aproximado*
    A. close
    B. about
    C. near
    D. approximate

12. *un punto central*
    A. a main point
    B. a main thought
    C. a midpoint
    D. a central punt

13. *un principio*
    A. a principal
    B. a principle
    C. a beginning
    D. an end

14. *claro*
    A. Clara
    B. of course
    C. glassy
    D. especially

15. *lógico*
    A. logical
    B. logic
    C. logistics
    D. illogical

MODULE **2.2**

INSTRUCTIONS   True or False: The following phrases or sentences are translated correctly.

16. *Un poco más rápido.* = A bit faster.

    A. True

    B. False

17. *Un poco más lento.* = A bit slower.

    A. True

    B. False

18. *Un poquito.* = A pocket.

    A. True

    B. False

19. *Hace mucho tiempo.* = He made up a lot of time.

    A. True

    B. False

20. *Una mesa para dos.* = A table for two.

    A. True

    B. False

21. *Más o menos 100 pesetas.* = More than 100 pesetas.

    A. True

    B. False

22. *Hace como diez minutos.* = About ten minutes ago.

    A. True

    B. False

23. *¿Arriba o abajo?* = Above or below?

    A. True

    B. False

24. *Según él yo cometí un error.* = According to him, I made an error.

    A. True

    B. False

25. *Está acostumbrado.* = He is in costume.

   A. True
   B. False

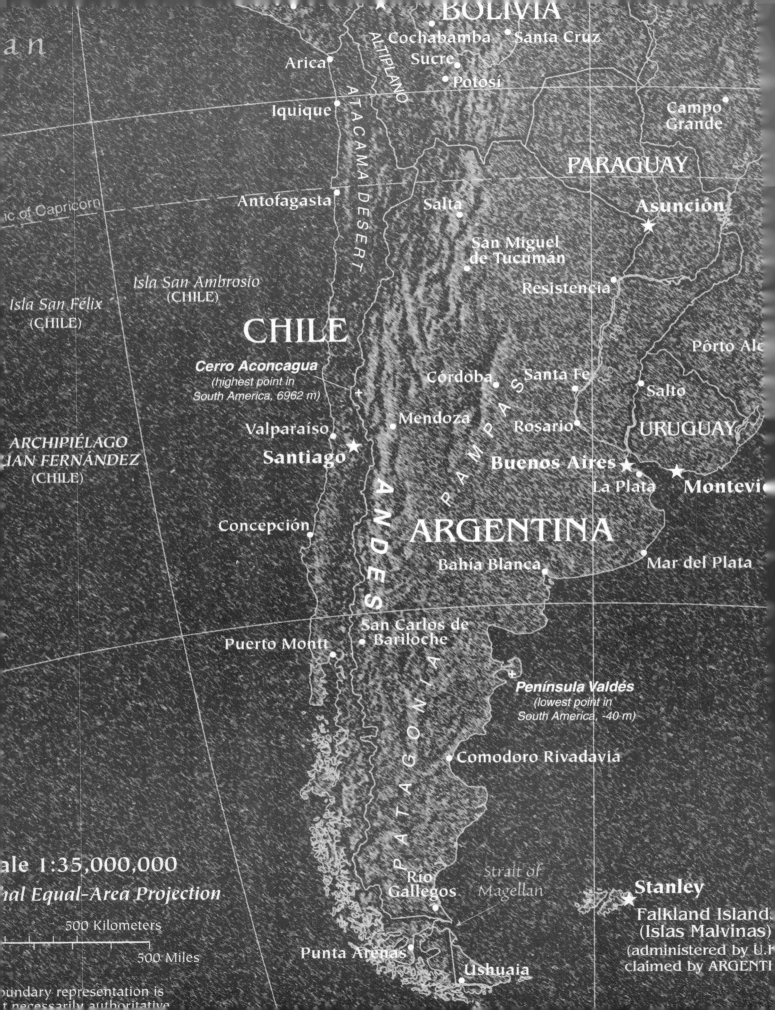

Module 2.3

Throughout this module we'll be learning about the culture of Chile.

Keep these tips in mind as you progress through this module:

1. Read instructions carefully.

2. Repeat aloud all the Spanish words you hear on the audio CDs.

3. Learn at your own pace.

4. Have fun with the activities and practice your new language skills with others.

5. Record yourself speaking Spanish on tape so you can evaluate your own speaking progress.

N

Colombia

Ecuador

Río Napo

Islв

Tumbes

Río Marañon

Iquitos

Río Ucayali

Piura

Reserva Nacional

Brazil

ARCH

IAN

Chiclayo

Pacaya-Samiria

Trujillo

Pucallpa

Caraz

Chimbote

Huascarán

Sechin

Huaraz

Parque Nacional Manu

Parque Nacional Huascarán

Perú

Lima

Huancayo

Machu Picchu

Océano Pacífico

Ayacucho

Cuzco

Pisco

Ica

Bolivia

Nazca

Lago Titicaca

El Misti

Puno

Arequipa

Chile

Perú

le 1

al E

Day Four, 15:45 Hours

La ciudad blanca

Finalmente, the taxi rounds the last hairpin turn, and you catch your first glimpse of Arequipa nestled in *el valle* below. Travel guides said *la ciudad* was nicknamed "the white city," and looking down on it in the bright mid afternoon sunlight, you can see why. Many of the buildings in Arequipa are built of *sillar*, a light-colored volcanic rock that catches and reflects the sunlight.

Another hour of driving places you in the heart of town. You generously tip the taxi driver for his time and trouble, then consider where to go from here. You take a closer look at the map. The hint for this location is only a scribble—it looks like *Señor* Espinoza was forcefully stopped in the middle of writing it. You can just make out the first word—*casa*—but that's as much of a hint as you're going to get this time. You look around. *La ciudad* is full of *casas*. Which one are you supposed to find? Entering the local government office, you find a pamphlet on sights to see here in Arequipa. You look through it, hoping one of these attractions will pertain to your clue.

There it is! *Casa* Ricketts, one of Arequipa's beautiful old colonial houses, is now home to a museum. This sounds like just the sort of place the kidnappers you're pursuing would investigate. It's not far away. You and *Araña* walk over and investigate.

The old building is beautiful, in a dignified, well-preserved sort of way. Inside, you find the elderly man running the museum, who offers you a tour. You accept and, toward the end of the tour, ask if he has any exhibits related to Alonso Hernández.

The old man answers that, yes, he does. He expresses *sorpresa* at hearing your question—just *esta mañana*, as *el museo* was opening, another group asked him that very same question. *"Ellos no fueron muy amables,"* he tells you, *"pero no podemos escoger quien viene a nuestro museo."* As he leads you toward the cabinet holding things that had belonged to the 17th century traveler, he tells you that Alonso Hernández spent several years in Peru, recording local histories and legends, before moving on.

In this section you will:

→ Build comprehension and vocabulary through reading.
→ Use important phrases.
→ Read and comprehend stories that are longer.
→ Understand and use compound tenses and conjugations.
→ Master geometry-related vocabulary.
→ Listen to a Spanish story and maintain comprehension without a text.

Disc **6**   Track **1**

Arriving in front of the cabinet, the elderly tour guide gasps. The glass in its front is broken. Though a thin layer of dust still marks where the items in the exhibit were, none of them are there now. *"¡Que horror!"* the man exclaims and wonders aloud who on earth could have done this.

Grimly, you inform him that you have a pretty good idea. You ask what the exhibit contained. He tells you that it held a portrait of Alonso Hernández—the only verifiable one in existence—as well as an example of the sort of travel book in which he kept his notes and a chronological map showing the different places Hernández visited before his death in southern Chile.

You then pull out a picture of Julio Roberto Espinoza, the missing author, ask the elderly fellow if he has seen him. The old man nods happily. *"Oh, sí—Señor Espinoza. Él es un autor muy famoso, y también tiene un gran interés en Alonso Hernández. Viene a mi museo por lo menos una vez cada dos años, y siempre le escribo cuando escucho de algo nuevo que tiene que ver con Alonso Hernández. Él es un buen hombre, Señor Espinoza. ¿Por qué quiere saber?"*

You inform *el hombre viejo* of *Señor* Espinoza's kidnapping and of your pursuit of his kidnappers. He shakes his head sadly and wishes you the very best of luck in bringing *Señor* Espinoza home safely. You thank him and ask if he heard where the kidnappers were going. He informs you that, while they didn't offer any specific destination, he did hear them mention the international airport in Cuzco.

"Cuzco…," *Araña* says thoughtfully. "That's hours away, though. They'll be long gone by the time we arrive."

"That's why we're going to take a shortcut," you tell him. "So far, all the places they've been are places this Alonso Hernández travelled through. There's only one more spot marked on the map. It has to be where he died—that's the most likely spot for him to have left the journal these crooks are after."

"Right," says *Araña*. "So, what sort of shortcut between here and southern Chile do you propose?"

"Another small plane," you reply, "this time with a full tank of fuel."

Leaving the museum, you spot *una hoja de papel* on the ground outside. At first mistaking it for trash, you pick it up and start back toward the museum's trash bin. Then you notice writing on it—very familiar writing. You smooth out the sheet of paper. On it is written, in *Señor* Espinoza's writing, a final *rompecabezas*.

It's past sunset by the time you finish arranging for a plane. Then, letting *Araña* pilot it toward southern Chile, you start studying the activities you will need to complete the final puzzle.

Puzzle

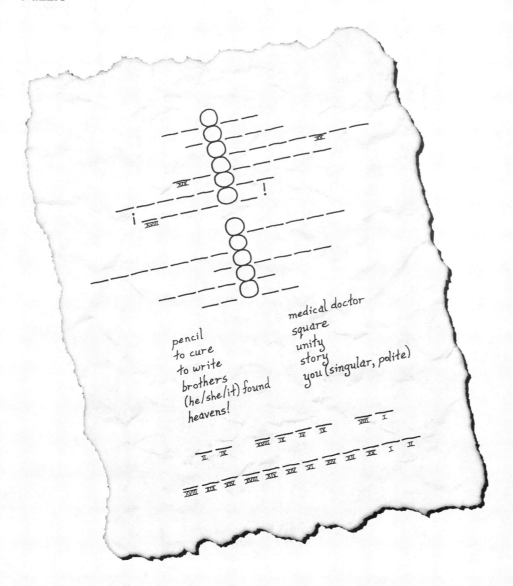

INSTRUCTIONS   Follow the clues to fill in the puzzle with the correct words. The circled letters will spell out your next adventure destination. Under some of the letters in the puzzle, Roman numerals are written. These numerals correspond to blanks at the bottom of the page. Fill in the blanks with the appropriate letters to receive a piece of the clue you will need to solve the adventure's climax.

After working the puzzle out yourself, check the answers in Appendix A, on page 333.

The Story of Little Red Riding Hood

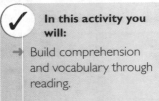

✓ **In this activity you will:**

→ Build comprehension and vocabulary through reading.

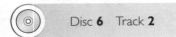

◎ Disc **6** Track **2**

Chile Culture Overview

The Chileans' cultural refinements and witty humor have earned them the nickname of "The British of South America." Chileans are also well-known for their warmth and resilience, traits that have served them well in their country's occasionally turbulent history. Greetings and titles are very important to the occupants of this country and are used to show respect or familiarity. While Chile is a grand place for shopping, relaxing, and sampling the spicy local cuisine, most travelers go to Chile for its spectacular and amazingly varied scenery and its opportunities for adventure sports.

INSTRUCTIONS   Listen to this familiar story in Spanish. Read along and see how much you can understand.

🔊

English	Spanish
Here is a little girl.	*Aquí está una niñita.*
She is called Red Riding Hood.	*Se llama Caperucita Roja.*
Here is her mother.	*Aquí está su mamacita.*
Here is her grandma.	*Aquí está su abuelita.*
Here is her mother's house.	*Aquí está la casa de su mamacita.*

English (cont.)	Spanish
Here is her grandma's house.	*Aquí está la casa de su abuelita.*
Here is the woods.	*Aquí está el bosque.*
Here is a wolf.	*Aquí está un lobo.*
Well.	*Bueno.*
The grandma is sick.	*La abuelita está enferma.*
Mother sends Red Riding Hood with a basket of cookies.	*La mamacita manda a Caperucita Roja con una canasta de galletas.*
In the woods the wolf asks her:	*En el bosque el lobo le pregunta:*
"Where are you going?	*"¿Adónde vas?*
What is your name?"	*¿Cómo te llamas?"*
Red Riding Hood tells him, and he goes away.	*Caperucita Roja le dice, y él se aleja.*
He runs to the grandma's house.	*Corre a la casa de la abuelita.*
He knocks on the door.	*Toca a la puerta.*
The grandma asks:	*La abuelita pregunta:*
"Who is it?"	*"¿Quién es?"*
The wolf answers:	*El lobo responde:*
"Red Riding Hood."	*"Caperucita Roja."*
"Come in."	*"Adelante."*
Grandma sees the wolf and runs from the house.	*La abuelita ve al lobo y corre de la casa.*
The wolf gets in bed.	*El lobo se mete en la cama.*
Red Riding Hood comes.	*Viene Caperucita Roja.*
She enters and sees the wolf.	*Entra y ve al lobo.*
She thinks it's her grandma.	*Piensa que es su abuelita.*
She asks: "Why do you have such big ears?"	*Pregunta: "¿Por qué tienes las orejas tan grandes?"*
The wolf answers: "To hear you better."	*El lobo responde: "Para oírte mejor."*
"Why do you have such big teeth?"	*"¿Por qué tienes los dientes tan grandes?"*
"To EAT YOU better."	*"Para COMERTE mejor."*

English (cont.)	Spanish
Red Riding Hood screams:	Caperucita Roja grita:
"Oh, it's the wolf!"	"¡Ay, es el lobo!"
At that moment the grandma enters with a dog.	En ese momento entra la abuelita con un perro.
The wolf runs out and escapes.	El lobo sale corriendo y se escapa.
Then Red Riding Hood and the grandma and the dog eat the cookies.	Entonces Caperucita Roja y la abuelita y el perro se comen las galletas.

Performance Challenge

Individual   This activity told a familiar story in simple Spanish. Choose a story that you like, and using the Spanish you've learned so far, retell the story in Spanish.

Performance Challenge

Group   Split students into two or three groups. Have each group rewrite the ending to "Little Red Riding Hood." Once complete, ask the groups to act out their version in Spanish.

More Openers and Rejoinders

INSTRUCTIONS   Listen to and learn the following sentences.

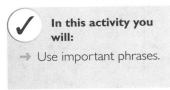

In this activity you will:
→ Use important phrases.

Disc **6**   Track **3**

English	Spanish
We lost the game.	*Perdimos el juego.*
How can that be?	*¿Cómo puede ser (eso)?*
I'm sorry for having run over you.	*Siento mucho haberle atropellado.*
Well, so it goes from time to time.	*Pues así sucede de vez en cuando.*
Life gets harder and harder.	*La vida está siempre más y más dura.*
Keep the faith, brother.	*Mantenga la fe, hermano.*
I'm looking for a person who knows how to draw.	*Yo busco a una persona que sepa dibujar.*
And I'm looking for someone who can read Chinese.	*Y yo busco a alguien que pueda leer chino.*
I'm looking for a Mr. Juan Gonzalez.	*Busco a un señor Juan González.*
There's no such person here.	*No hay tal persona aquí.*
You must be a millionaire.	*millonario*
On the contrary, I'm not even rich.	*Al contrario, ni siquiera soy rico.*
For sure you told me 2+2=5.	*Seguro que me dijiste que 2+2=5.*
Then I was mistaken.	*Entonces me equivoqué.*
I flunked the exam.	*Fallé en el examen.*
Don't worry. For sure the sun will come out tomorrow.	*No te preocupes. Seguro que el sol saldrá mañana.*
You collided with a tree.	*Chocaste con un árbol.*
I didn't realize it.	*No me di cuenta.*

Facts and Figures on Chile

- Chile's full name is *la República de Chile.*
- Chile's population is about 15 million.
- Santiago, the capital city, holds about 5 million of those 15 million.
- Spanish is Chile's native language, but a handful of native languages, including Aymara, Mapuche, and Rapa Nui, are also spoken.
- Rodeos are very popular in areas where cattle have been important.
- Chile is one of only two countries in South America that does not share a border with Brazil.
- Chile contains the driest desert in the world—the Atacama—as well as the southernmost permanent city in the world—Punta Arenas.
- Chile's major industries include copper, fishmeal, and wine.
- Chile's federal government is a republic and consists of a president and a bicameral congress.

English (cont.)	Spanish
This is a very important matter.	*Esto es un asunto muy importante.*
I'll do it as soon as possible.	*Lo haré cuanto antes.*
This is a robbery. Hands up!	*Este es un asalto. ¡Manos arriba!*
Get out of here.	*Fuera de aquí.*
The most important thing in the world is money.	*La cosa más importante en el mundo es el dinero.*
I doubt it. I don't believe that.	*Lo dudo. Yo no creo eso.*
A little piece of bread is better than none.	*Un pedacito de pan es mejor que nada.*
You're right.	*Tienes razón.*
I feel sad.	*Me siento triste.*
Then cheer up!	*¡Pues anímese!*
They're going to kick him out of the country.	*Lo van a sacar del país.*
What a relief!	*¡Menos mal!*
I can't attend the meeting.	*No puedo asistir a la reunión.*
What a shame! It'll be interesting.	*¡Qué lástima! Va a ser interesante.*
Now I feel very well.	*Ahora me siento muy bien.*
I'm glad of that.	*Me alegro por eso.*
You have to do it every day.	*Tienes que hacerlo cada día.*
From now on I will.	*De aquí en adelante lo haré.*
Come without fail at six in the evening.	*Venga Ud. sin falta a las seis de la tarde.*
I assure you I'll be on time.	*Te aseguro que estaré a tiempo.*
It's necessary to do it as soon as possible.	*Hay que hacerlo lo más pronto posible.*
I'll do it for sure. Don't worry.	*Sí lo haré. No se preocupe.*
There is no remedy for this.	*Esto no tiene remedio.*
What do you mean no remedy!	*¡¿Cómo que no tiene remedio?!*

Performance Challenge

Individual   This activity presented a number of useful openers and rejoinders. Choose at least three of each, and practice them until you can say them without looking at the text. Look for chances to use them in everyday conversations this week.

Performance Challenge

Group   Split the students into teams. Give each team a sentence from the activity. Have them create a story in Spanish that both starts and ends with the assigned sentence. Have them read their stories aloud.

ACTIVITY 67

Needle Soup

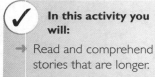

In this activity you will:

→ Read and comprehend stories that are longer.

Disc **6**   Track **4**

INSTRUCTIONS   Read and listen to this vocabulary-building story.

An Old Czech Tale	Un Viejo Cuento de Checoslovaquia
There was once a boy named Sasha.	Había una vez un muchacho llamado Sasha.
His mother was a poor widow.	Su madre era una pobre viuda.
One day her house caught on fire.	Un día la casa se incendió.
She managed to save her son, but she died in the fire, leaving Sasha alone in the world.	La madre pudo salvar a su hijo, pero ella murió en el incendio, dejando a Sasha solo en el mundo.
The only thing he found in the ashes of the house was his mother's needle.	La única cosa que encontró entre las cenizas de su casa fue la aguja de su madre.
Poor Sasha was only ten years old.	El pobre Sasha tenía sólo diez años.
He had no brother or sister, no grandmother or grandfather.	No tenía ni hermanos, ni hermanas, tampoco abuela o abuelo.
Where could he go? What could he do?	¿Adónde podría ir? ¿Qué podría hacer?
He decided to leave the village to make his way in the world.	Decidió irse de la aldea y buscar su camino en el mundo.
Besides the clothes he was wearing and his mother's needle, he took nothing with him.	Además de la ropa que llevaba puesta y la aguja de su madre, no llevó nada más consigo.
He wrapped the needle in paper and placed it in his pocket.	Envolvió la aguja en un papel y se la guardó en el bolsillo.
Because I have no money, I'll just have to live by my wits, he thought.	Ya que no tengo dinero, tendré que vivir por mi ingenio, pensó.
For two days he wandered, cold and hungry.	Por dos días anduvo errante, con hambre y sed.
At last, he came to a village.	Al fin llegó a una aldea.

An Old Czech Tale (cont.)	Un Viejo Cuento de Checoslovaquia
Weak and tired, he knocked on the door of a pretty house near the village gate.	Débil y cansado, tocó a la puerta de una hermosa casa a la entrada de la aldea.
A lady opened the door.	Una dama abrió la puerta.
When she saw the ragged little boy, she thought:	Cuando ella vio al pequeño harapiento [niño] pensó:
Such a ragged child must be a beggar.	Este niño harapiento debe ser un mendigo.
I don't like beggars. I won't give him a thing.	A mí no me gustan los mendigos. No le daré nada.
She was quite selfish and greedy, don't you think?	Ella era bastante egoísta y codiciosa, ¿no te parece?
"Please, ma'am, have you a small crust of bread for a hungry child?" Sasha asked.	"Por favor, señora, ¿tiene un pedazo de pan para un niño hambriento?" preguntó Sasha.
"No," the lady said. "Beggars and thieves have taken all my food."	"No," dijo la dama. "Los mendigos y ladrones se han llevado toda mi comida."
"Don't you have anything left to eat?"	"¿No le queda nada de sobra para comer?"
"I already told you, I haven't even a crumb of bread."	"Ya te dije, que ni siquiera tengo una migaja de pan."
"Very well," said Sasha with a sigh.	"Muy bien," Sasha dijo con un suspiro.
"Then I shall have to have needle soup."	"Entonces tendré que tomar sopa de aguja."
The selfish lady was about to close the door, but the little boy's words made her hesitate.	La egoísta mujer estaba a punto de cerrar la puerta, pero las palabras del niño la hicieron vacilar.
"Needle soup?" she said, wrinkling her brow.	"¿Sopa de aguja?" dijo, frunciendo el ceño.
"Yes, it's really quite tasty, only I've had it three nights in a row now.	"Sí, es realmente sabrosa, sólo que ya la he comido durante tres noches seguidas.
I'd rather have a bit of bread tonight."	Me preferiría comer un poco de pan esta noche."
The lady started to think:	La dama empezó a pensar:
Wouldn't it be nice to know how to make soup from needles?	¿No sería bueno saber hacer sopa de agujas?

Geography of Chile

Chile borders Perú to the north, Argentina to the east, and the Pacific Ocean to the south and west, and also lays claim to the islands of Chiloe, Juan Fernández, and Easter Island, as well as half of Tierra del Fuego, the continent's southernmost island which Chile shares with Argentina. Within the borders of this long, narrow country, a variety of environments flourish. Beautiful beaches dot its lengthy Pacific coastline, while snow-capped Andes peaks mark its border with neighboring Argentina. The Atacama Desert, where some weather stations have never, in their several centuries of existence, recorded rain, separates Chile from Perú. In storm-prone southern Patagonia, glaciers and fjord-like landscapes dominate the scenery. The central region, where the capital city stands, has a Mediterranean climate, which makes it very well-suited to its fruit-growing and wine-making endeavors. Temperate rainforests flourish just south of the central region, as well as on Chiloe and the Juan Fernández islands. Easter Island rounds out Chile's wide assortment of climates with a tropical one. This variety of climates makes Chile home to just as wide a variety of flora and fauna, many of which can be viewed in the nation's extensive national park system. Some plants native to Chile include cypress trees, araucaria (monkey-puzzle trees), the copihue (Chile's national flower), and rare but massive alerce trees. Animals include the vicuña, the Patagonian guanaco, flamingos, pelicans, penguins, otters, sea lions, and a very limited number of Andean condors.

An Old Czech Tale *(cont.)*	*Un Viejo Cuento de Checoslovaquia*
Then I would never want for food.	*Entonces nunca me faltaría comida.*
She smiled at the boy and opened the door.	*Ella le sonrió al muchacho y abrió la puerta.*
"I'm sorry I don't have any food for you, but if you like you may come inside and cook some needle soup in my pot."	*"Lo siento que no tengo comida para tí, pero si deseas puedes entrar y cocinar la sopa de aguja en mi olla."*
Sasha smiled too and thought: I may not have food, but I have my wits.	*Sasha sonrió también, y pensó: tal vez no tenga comida, pero sí tengo mi ingenio.*
Soon a large pot of water was boiling on the fire.	*Rápidamente una inmensa olla de agua estaba hirviendo en la estufa.*
Sasha carefully took the package from his pocket.	*Con mucho cuidado, Sasha sacó el paquetito de su bolsillo.*
He unfolded the paper, took the needle, and held it up for the lady to see.	*Desenvolvió el papel, tomó la aguja, y la sostuvo en lo alto para que la dama la viera.*
He said:	*El dijo:*
"This needle has an especially good flavor."	*"Esta aguja tiene un sabor especialmente bueno."*
Then he dropped the needle into the pot.	*Después él tiró la aguja en la olla.*
The lady watched, her eyes wide open, as Sasha busied himself stirring the pot.	*La dama miraba con sus ojos bien abiertos, a medida que Sasha se ocupaba en revolver la sopa.*
After a moment Sasha said:	*Después de un momento Sasha dijo:*
"With salt and pepper it's especially good.	*"Con sal y pimienta tiene un sabor especialmente bueno.*
Did the thieves and beggars take all your salt and pepper?"	*¿Llevaron los mendigos y ladrones toda su sal y pimienta?"*
"No. I still have plenty of salt and pepper. Here!"	*"No, todavía tengo mucha sal y pimienta. Aquí tienes."*
"Marvelous!" Sasha said, pouring some salt and pepper into the boiling water.	*"¡Maravilloso!" dijo Sasha al poner algo de sal y pimienta en el agua hirviendo.*
Then he stirred the pot some more, smacked his lips and said:	*Entonces él revolvió la olla un poco más, y lamiéndose los labios dijo:*

An Old Czech Tale *(cont.)*	Un Viejo Cuento de Checoslovaquia
"Hmm, smell it! Doesn't it smell good already!	"¡Uhm! Huela. ¿Verdad que huele bien?
It's a pity the thieves and beggars took all of your food.	Es una lástima que los ladrones y mendigos se llevaron toda su comida.
An onion would have given extra flavor to the soup."	Una cebolla le habría dado un sabor más exquisito a la sopa."
The lady said:	La dama dijo:
"Come to think of it, I did save one onion. I'll go get it."	"Ahora que me acuerdo, guardé una cebolla que la voy a traer."
When she returned, she had not one but three onions.	Cuando regresó no tenía solo una, sino tres cebollas.
"Marvelous!" Sasha said, and he peeled them and sliced them and dropped them into the boiling water.	"¡Maravilloso!" dijo Sasha, y las peló, las cortó, y las echó en la olla de agua hirviendo.
Then he continued stirring the pot.	Entonces siguió revolviendo la olla.
After a little while he said:	Después de un rato dijo:
"A bit of cabbage would have really added a good taste.	"Un poco de col le hubiera dado buen sabor de verdad.
What a pity the beggars and thieves took all of your food."	Qué lástima que los mendigos y ladrones se llevaron toda su comida."
The lady exclaimed:	La dama exclamó:
"Come to think of it, they said they didn't like cabbage, so they left two heads of it."	"Ahora que me acuerdo, dijeron que no les gustaba la col, así que dejaron dos cabezas."
As soon as she had spoken, she was off to get the cabbage.	Tan pronto como terminó de hablar, se fue para conseguir la col.
"Marvelous!" Sasha said, and he sliced it with a knife and dropped it into the soup.	"¡Maravilloso!" dijo Sasha, y cortó la col con un cuchillo y la echó a la sopa.
Soon, delicious smells filled the room where the soup was cooking.	Muy pronto aromas deliciosas comenzaron a llenar el cuarto donde se estaba cocinando la sopa.
"What a pity that all of your food was stolen," said Sasha.	"Qué lástima que toda su comida se la robaron," dijo Sasha.
"If it hadn't all been stolen we could have added a carrot or two.	"Si no hubiera sido toda robada, hubiéramos podido agregar una zanahoria o dos.

An Old Czech Tale (cont.)	Un Viejo Cuento de Checoslovaquia
Then it would have been most delicious."	Y así la sopa hubiera sido riquísima."
"Oh, I nearly forgot about my garden.	"Oh, casi olvidé mi jardín.
Just this morning I noticed two carrots ready to pull."	Justamente esta mañana noté que había dos zanahorias que estaban listas para arrancarlas."
She went outside and in a moment came back with two big carrots and a nice big potato.	Ella salió afuera y al momento regresó con dos zanahorias y una papa buena y grande.
"Marvelous!" Sasha said as he peeled and washed them off.	"¡Maravilloso!" dijo Sasha al pelarlas y lavarlas.
Then he cut them up and dropped them into the soup, and as he stirred he said:	Después las cortó en pedazos y las echó en la sopa, y revolviéndola, dijo:
"If the beggars and thieves hadn't taken all your food, we could have had some meat in our needle soup."	"Si los mendigos y los ladrones no se hubieran llevado su comida, hubiéramos tenido un poco de carne en nuestra sopa de aguja."
"Come to think of it," said the lady, "I hid a tiny scrap of meat from them."	"Ahora que me acuerdo," dijo la dama, "Escondí un pedacito de carne."
In a moment she was back with a nice big chunk of beef.	En un momento ella regresó con un buen pedazo de carne.
"Marvelous!" Sasha said as he cut up the meat and dropped the pieces into the soup.	"¡Maravilloso!" dijo Sasha al ir cortando la carne y echó los pedazos en la olla.
Soon the kitchen was filled with a delicious aroma.	Muy pronto la cocina estaba llena de una aroma deliciosa.
Sasha kept stirring the soup.	Sasha seguía revolviendo la sopa.
In a while he said:	Luego él dijo:
"Ma'am, it will soon be ready.	"Señora, esto estará listo muy pronto.
Perhaps you have a nice tablecloth and porcelain bowls and spoons for this special occasion."	Quizás tenga usted un mantel bonito, platos de porcelana y cucharas para esta ocasión especial."
"Indeed I do." The woman put a linen cloth on the table and set her china bowls and glass spoons on top.	"Tienes razón." La mujer puso un mantel de lino sobre la mesa, con platos de porcelana y las cucharas de vidrio.

An Old Czech Tale (cont.)	Un Viejo Cuento de Checoslovaquia
In a few minutes the soup was served in the fine china bowls.	En unos pocos minutos la sopa estaba servida en los finos platos soperos de porcelana.
And the two sat down together and enjoyed the tasty soup.	Y se sentaron los dos juntos y gozaron de la sabrosa sopa.
But the story does not end here.	Pero la historia no termina aquí.
The woman saw that Sasha was a very fine boy.	La mujer vio que Sasha era un muchacho excelente.
"What is your name, little boy?"	"¿Cuál es tu nombre, niñito?"
"Sasha."	"Sasha."
"And where do you live?"	"¿Y dónde vives?"
"I have no place to live. My mother and father are dead."	"No tengo donde vivir. Mi padre y mi madre han muerto."
"So where will you go now?"	"¿Y a dónde vas ahora?"
"Out into the cold, dark night."	"Afuera a la noche oscura y fría."
Now the woman saw her own selfishness.	Ahora la mujer vio su propio egoísmo.
"I live alone here. I don't have any children.	"Vivo sola aquí. No tengo ningún hijo.
I apologize for being unkind to you.	Perdóname por haber sido tan descortés contigo.
Here there is a warm fire.	Aquí hay un fuego caliente.
Won't you stay inside and keep warm?"	¿Te gustaría quedarte adentro y calentarte?"
Sasha stayed. In the morning, the woman gave him chores to do.	Sasha se quedó. A la mañana siguiente, la mujer le dio unas tareas para hacer.
Sasha was very clever, and he was a willing worker.	Sasha era muy listo, y muy trabajador.
He liked the village and found the woman to be really very kind.	Le gustaba la aldea y encontró que la mujer era realmente muy bondadosa.
When he was twenty he was elected to be a member of the town council.	Cuando él tenía veinte años, fue elegido para ser un miembro del consejo municipal del pueblo.
People came to him for advice.	La gente venía a él para pedirle consejo.

ACTIVITY 67

An Old Czech Tale *(cont.)*	*Un Viejo Cuento de Checoslovaquia*
And do you know what he told them?	*¿Y saben lo que él les decía?*
"If you use your wits, you can find a solution to every problem."	*"Si ustedes usan su ingenio, pueden hallar una solución para todo problema."*
Even today, Sasha keeps his mother's needle.	*Aún hoy en día Sasha guarda la aguja de su madre.*
He wears it on his shirt.	*Él la lleva en su camisa.*
And when people ask him why he wears a needle on his shirt, he says:	*Y cuando las personas le preguntan por qué lleva una aguja en su camisa, él dice:*
"One never knows what tomorrow will bring, but as long as I have my wits and this needle, I know I will never go hungry."	*"Nunca se sabe lo que el mañana le traerá, pero mientras tenga mi ingenio y esta aguja, yo sé que nunca tendré hambre."*

Performance Challenge

Individual   This activity presented one of the longest stories you've seen so far in this course. Using the Spanish you've learned, summarize the story and the moral of the story in your own words. Then, try retelling it to a parent, sibling, or friend.

Performance Challenge

Group   Divide the students into groups. Have each group write a new ending for "Needle Soup." Then, have the groups perform or read their creative endings to the other students, in Spanish.

Compound Tenses

INSTRUCTIONS Use these explanations to gain a better understanding of Spanish verbs.

Indicative Forms

Name	Form	Example
Present perfect	has [verb]ed	he has spoken
Imperfective past perfect	had [verb]ed	he had spoken
Preterite past perfect	had [verb]ed	he had spoken
Future perfect	will have [verb]ed	he will have spoken
Conditional	would have [verb]ed	he would've spoken

Examples in Spanish

English	Spanish
I know the child has spoken.	*Sé que el niño h-a hablado.*
I know the child had spoken.	*Sé que el niño hab-ía hablado.*
I know the child had spoken.	*Sé que el niño hub-o hablado.*
I know the child will have spoken.	*Sé que el niño habr-á hablado.*
I know the child would have spoken.	*Sé que el niño habría hablado.*

Subjunctive Forms

- Present subjunctive perfect
- Past subjunctive perfect

In this activity you will:

→ Understand and use compound tenses and conjugations.

History of Chile

Before the arrival of Europeans, Chile was peopled by a variety of tribes and cultures, many of which became subject to the Incan empire when it rose to power. When it fell from power, they went back to their normal ways, until the man assigned to conquer Chile, Pedro de Valdivia, arrived in the Mapocho Valley in 1541. He swiftly established Santiago and went on to found La Serena, Valparaíso, Concepción, Valdivia, and Villarrica. He conquered as far south as the Río Biobío, but there he was stopped by fierce resistance from the Mapuche tribes. Leaving that trouble spot for later, Valdivia returned to the capital and rewarded his followers with enormous land grants that resembled the feudalism he had left behind in Spain.

Mining and business outweighed agriculture in the colonial Chilean economy, but it was the structure of those estates that shaped colonial society. Native populations were decimated by European diseases, and mestizos (the children of Spanish and Indian unions) were used as tenant laborers on the landowners' estates. Many of these estates, with their social structures, remained intact into the 1960s.

(continued)

History of Chile, continued

In the 1820s, Chile was liberated from Spain by Simón Bolívar and José de San Martin. Bernardo O'Higgins, son of an Irish immigrant, became the first director of Chile's fledgling republic. Chile's success in the War of the Pacific (1879-83) expanded its borders to its present size, and Chile soon achieved the political stability and relative democracy needed for significant agricultural and industrial improvements. These improvements empowered the working class and created a level of nouveau riche, who together challenged the landowning oligarchy in a brief civil war in the 1890s.

During the first half of the 20th century, political power swung from right to left, with neither side having enough staying power to enact real reform. Development halted, leading to poverty and over accelerated urbanization. In the 1960s, a party called the Christian Democrats gained power and made successful reforms to housing, education, health services, and social services. Unfortunately, these reforms alienated and offended both extremes of the political pendulum, dividing things badly enough that in 1970, Marxist Allende's union of socialist, communist, and extremist forces was able to come into power. Allende introduced sweeping economic reforms, including state control of many private businesses and wholesale redistribution of income. The ensuing chaos almost bankrupted the nation and angered many of its neighbors and trading partners.

The economic chaos was terminated when a coup, led by a four-man junta which in turn was led by General Pinochet, overthrew Allende. General Pinochet got the country back on its feet economically (and is often credited with paving the way for its current successes), but as many as 80,000 Chilean citizens were imprisoned or killed during his regime. A 1988 referendum led to multiparty elections in 1989, and power passed peacefully from Pinochet to the elected president. Peaceful and democratic elections have continued to be the hallmark of Chilean politics since then, paving the way for Chile's ongoing progress.

Examples in Spanish

English	Spanish
I doubt the child has spoken.	*Dudo que el niño haya hablado.*
I doubted the child had spoken.	*Dudaba que el niño hubiera hablado.*

Conjugating the Verb *Haber*

Because of its use as an auxiliary in forming compound tenses, the verb *haber* is very important.

Note that this verb has various stems: *h-, hab-, hub-*

Present perfect (have or has [verb]ed)			
h-e			
h-as			
h-a	tom-Ado	com-Ido	dorm-Ido
h-emos	tak-en	eat-en	slep-t
h-an			
h-an			

Preterite past perfect (had [verb]ed)			
hub-e			
hub-iste			
hub-o	tom-Ado	com-Ido	dorm-Ido
hub-imos	tak-en	eat-en	slep-t
hub-ieron			
hub-ieron			

Imperfect past perfect (had [verb]ed)			
hab-ía			
hab-ías			
hab-ía	tom-Ado	com-Ido	dorm-Ido
hab-íamos	tak-en	eat-en	slep-t
hab-ían			
hab-ían			

Future perfect (will have [verb]ed)

habr-é			
habr-ás			
habr-á	tom-Ado	com-Ido	dorm-Ido
habr-emos	tak-en	eat-en	slep-t
habr-án			
habr-án			

Conditional (would have [verb]ed)

habr-ía			
habr-ías			
habr-ía	tom-Ado	com-Ido	dorm-Ido
habr-íamos	tak-en	eat-en	slep-t
habr-ían			
habr-ían			

Present subjunctive perfect (have [verb]ed [irrealis])

hay-a			
hay-as			
hay-a	tom-Ado	com-Ido	dorm-Ido
hay-amos	tak-en	eat-en	slep-t
hay-áis			
hay-an			

Past subjunctive perfect (had [verb]ed [irrealis])

hub-iera			
hub-ieras			
hub-iera	tom-Ado	com-Ido	dorm-Ido
hub-iéramos	tak-en	eat-en	slep-t
hub-ieran			
hub-ieran			

Performance Challenge

Individual   This activity presented several compound verb tenses. After carefully reviewing the tenses taught in this lesson, use what you've learned to write several sentences of your own.

Performance Challenge

Group   Split students into groups. Give each group ten Power-Glide Flashcards. Using a stopwatch have them create as many sentences as they can with the flashcards, using the verb forms found in this lesson.

A Geometry Lesson

INSTRUCTIONS   Use these sentences to master geometry-related vocabulary.

🔊

English	Spanish
These three lines are parallel.	*Estas tres líneas son paralelas.*
They are also equally long.	*También son del mismo tamaño.*
Lines AB and CD are far apart.	*Las líneas AB y CD están muy separadas.*
Line AB is next to line EF.	*La línea AB está junto a la línea EF.*
Line AB is between lines CD and EF.	*La línea AB está entre las líneas CD y EF.*
What's the difference between these two lines and these two?	*¿Cuál es la diferencia entre estas dos líneas y estas dos?*
These lines touch but don't cross.	*Estas líneas se tocan, pero no se cruzan.*
This line touches that one but doesn't cross it.	*Esta línea toca esa pero no la cruza.*
These lines are very close to each other but do not touch.	*Estas líneas están muy cerca, la una a la otra pero no se tocan.*
Line AB crosses line CD at point X.	*La línea AB cruza la línea CD en el punto X.*
These lines touch at point Y.	*Esas líneas se tocan en el punto Y.*
Draw a diagonal line about this long.	*Dibuje una línea diagonal más o menos así de larga.*
Then draw a curved line that crosses the diagonal two times.	*Después dibuje una línea curva que cruza dos veces la diagonal.*

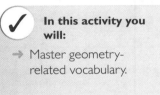

In this activity you will:
→ Master geometry-related vocabulary.

Disc **6**   Track **5**

Sites to See in Chile

Chile's capital city, Santiago, is both a traveler's most likely point of arrival and home to many interesting sites. The top of *Cerro San Cristóbal* offers an excellent view of the city and of the *Parque Metropolitano* in which the hill stands. *Plaza de Armas*, the historical city center, is not distant from the very large *Palacio de la Moneda*, former mint and current presidential palace. *Cerro Santa Lucia* offers another excellent view of the city and also boasts the ruins of a colonial fortress, which are open for visitors to explore. For museums, be sure to check Santiago's Pre-Columbian Museum and the *Museo de Santiago*. The *Palacio de Bellas Artes* also has a fine collection of European and Chilean art. For wonderful crafts, puzzles, woodworkings, and souvenirs, visit *Parque Artesenal Los Dominicos* or the larger but pickpocket-prone parque artesenal at the foot of *Cerro Santa Lucia*. For sports enthusiasts, an hour's drive from Santiago can take you to hiking and mountain climbing adventures in the summer, or to some of the finest skiing in South America in the winter.

(continued)

ACTIVITY 69

Sites to See in Chile (Continued)

Valparaíso, Chile's main port and second-largest city, lies just 74 miles northwest of the capital city, on the Pacific coast. Jammed onto a narrow strip of land between shore and coastal hills, Valparaíso expanded up the hill, with steep stairs, winding cobbled streets, very distinctive architecture, and a city center well-suited to maze-like strolls. Its recently redeveloped pier, *Muelle Prat,* has become a lively market area.

Viña del Mar, Chile's most popular beach resort, is just six miles up the coast from Valparaíso. White sand beaches set off its lovely turn-of-the-century waterfront mansions. *Viña* is also home to Chile's national botanical garden.

Parque Nacional Puyehue is Chile's most popular national park. Situated in the beautiful Lake District of southern Chile, *Parque Nacional Puyehue* features lush mountain forests, awe-inspiring volcanic scenery, nature trails, lake views, thermal springs, and waterfalls, as well as some of Chile's varied wildlife.

Those who enjoy venturing off oft-traveled routes might enjoy *Isla de Pascua,* Easter Island. A full 2294 miles away from the Chilean mainland, *Isla de Pascua* (*Rapa Nui* in the native tongue) is the most remote inhabited island in the world. This speck of land is famous for its hundreds of massive volcanic basalt statues. Around 2000 people live on the island, mostly around the town of Hanga Roa.

English *(cont.)*	Spanish
Then draw another line that crosses both the diagonal and the curved line.	*Entonces dibuje otra línea que cruza y la línea diagonal y la línea curva.*

Performance Challenge

Individual Get a pencil and paper. Listen to the activity again and try to draw what is being described. Have you mastered the vocabulary from this lesson?

Performance Challenge

Group Divide into two teams. Write the words from the lesson on pieces of paper. Attach a word to each student. Play "Red Rover, Red Rover" calling out a word from the lesson to add players to each team. The team with the most players at the end of the game, wins.

The Story of Cinderella

ACTIVITY 70

INSTRUCTIONS   This is an audio-only activity. Listen carefully, trying to understand the Spanish.

Performance Challenge

Individual   Were you able to follow along all right? Listen to the story one more time, then try retelling it in your own words.

Performance Challenge

Group   Rent a DVD of "Cinderella" that can be played in Spanish, and in Spanish with English subtitles. Have students watch the movie (or part of the movie) in English, in Spanish with English subtitles, and then in Spanish alone.

In this activity you will:

→ Listen to a Spanish story and maintain comprehension without a text.

Disc **6**   Track **6**

You have completed all the activities for

**Section 2.3.1
Day Four, 15:45 Hours**

and are now ready to take the section quiz. Before continuing, be sure you have learned the objectives for each activity in this section.

Section Quiz

INSTRUCTIONS Select the most correct answer for the following questions. Check your answers in Appendix D, on page 346.

1. **Fill in the blank in the sentence from the story *Caperucita Roja*: "¿Por qué tienes las orejas tan grandes? ... oírte mejor."**

    A. *Por*

    B. *Para*

    C. *Porque*

    D. *A*

2. **¿Qué significa la frase 'aquí está' en ingles?**

    A. it is

    B. here is

    C. where is

    D. why is

....

INSTRUCTIONS Choose the most correct response.

3. *Fallé en un examen.*

    A. *Fuera de aquí.*

    B. *Me alegro por eso.*

    C. *No me di cuenta.*

    D. *No te preocupes.*

4. **María no puede venir a la fiesta.**

   A. *Si lo haré.*

   B. *Entonces me equivoqué.*

   C. *Qué lástima.*

   D. *Tienes razón.*

5. **Which of the following is NOT a compound tense in Spanish?**

   A. present perfect

   B. present subjunctive perfect

   C. future perfect

   D. past subjunctive

6. **Which verb is used in all of the compound tenses as an auxiliary verb?**

   A. *estar*

   B. *ser*

   C. *tener*

   D. *haber*

7. **¿Cómo se dice 'she will have eaten' en español?**

   A. *Habría comido.*

   B. *Ha comido.*

   C. *Habrá comido.*

   D. *Haya comido.*

8. **¿Qué significa 'hemos hablado' en inglés?**

   A. We have spoken.

   B. We had spoken.

   C. We would have spoken.

   D. We will have spoken.

9. **According to the end of the story *Sopa de Aguja*, what does Sasha keep with him to avoid going hungry?**

   A. *sal y pimienta*

   B. *su ingenio y una aguja*

   C. *cebollas y carne*

   D. *zanahorias y una papa grande*

10. **What is the correct translation for "Draw a diagonal line about this long."?**

   A. *Dibuje un línea diagonal más o menos así el larga.*

   B. *Dibuje un línea diagonal más y menos así de larga.*

   C. *Dibuje una línea diagonal más o menos así de larga.*

   D. *Dibuje una línea diagonal más y menos así el larga.*

Bolivia

N

Chile

Arica

Iquique

Chuquicamata

Antofagasta

Chile

Copiapo

Nevado Ojos
del Salado

La Serena

Viña del Mar

Valparaiso   Santiago

Concepción

Argentina

Valdivia   Villarica

Puerto
Montt   Volcán
            Osorno

Chiloe

Coihaique

Parque Nacional
Laguna San Rafael

Chile

Parque Nacional
Torres del Paine   Punta
                     Arenas

Tierra del
Fuego

Day Five, 07:30 Hours

Disc **6**   Track **7**

Tesoro escondido

🔊

By the time *Araña* reaches the southern city of Puerto Montt, you've finished the last puzzle and caught a few hours sleep. *Araña*, though, is almost too tired to land the plane. He encourages you to finish the case—he'll catch a few winks here in the plane cabin.

Reluctantly leaving your partner behind, you take *el mapa* and *entra a la ciudad*. It's cool, pleasant, and verdantly green. Signs of the city's many German settlers are visible in the local *arquitectura y comidas*. You admire the architecture in passing but don't have time right now to sample the foods. You check local maps and visit the city offices, hoping to find tourism brochures. None of these offer you any useful hints, though. Where are you going to find the *sombrero rojo* that the puzzle told you to seek? You stop walking abruptly and look down the side street you're passing. An old-fashioned sign hangs from the front of a decrepit-looking old building. On that sign, in faded, chipped paint, is the image of a large red hat. Could this be the place you're looking for?

You approach the old building cautiously. You hear angry voices coming from inside the building *pero no puede ver* anyone at all. With your cell phone, you place a quick call to the local authorities and explain the situation. They promise to send someone over as soon as they can, but from their tones, you get the distinct impression they aren't taking you seriously. Those angry voices are getting louder and louder, though, and if the owners of those voices get angry enough to harm *Señor* Espinoza…you shake your *cabeza*. You can't wait. Swiftly, you let yourself into the dark, musty building. You wait for your *ojos* to adjust—you can't risk turning on a flashlight. There, in the corner, you see a staircase going downward. Footprints in the thick dust on the floor suggest that several other people went that way recently.

Your *cerebro* is working furiously, trying to figure how to get yourself, *Señor* Espinoza, *y el diario de* Alonso Hernández out of here unharmed. Looking around the dim, dusty room, you see a number of decaying wooden crates, all labeled in Spanish—*campanillas*, *cuerda*, *riendas*, *herramientas*…. Hmm…bells, rope, reins, tools…it looks like *El Sombrero Rojo* once sold tools and supplies to the farmers and ranchers of the surrounding countryside, *el campo*. You think *que tiene una idea*. Carefully making your way across the room, you retrieve several coils of rope and one box of bells. The shouting downstairs shows no sign of abating. You carefully balance the bells on the top step, then loosely wind the rope around handrails, loose boards, and hanging rafters as you make your way downstairs.

The basement ahead is even dimmer than *el cuarto* upstairs—the kidnappers can't be using more than a single lantern. *¡Perfecto!* You finish descending *las escaleras* and conceal yourself in a dark corner. In front of you, half a dozen people, presumably the kidnappers, are arguing while gesturing at something on the far wall. *Señor* Espinoza sits huddled and miserable on the floor between them and the wall. You tug one of the rope ends in your hand. *La caja* full of *campanillas* topples, and its contents spill down the stairs, making a terrible racket.

"*¿Qué es?*" shouts one kidnapper, whirling around.

"*¡Alguien está arriba!*" shouts another, starting towards *las escaleras*. All but one of the kidnappers follow him. You let them get about halfway up the stairs, then pull the other rope end, tangling and trapping them in a dusty web of old ropes. Hastily securing that rope end around a wooden support pillar, you incapacitate the one who remained standing menacingly over *Señor* Espinoza.

"*¿Señor Espinoza?*" you ask.

"*Sí,*" he replies. "*¿Quién es Ud.?*"

You grin. "*No importa. Estoy aquí para ayudarle. ¿Está bien?*"

"*Más o menos,*" he answers, slowly getting to his feet and wincing. "*¿Encontró mis rompecabezas?*"

You pull the solved puzzles from your pocket. "*Sí, todos.*" You put the puzzles away and wipe the grin off your face. "*Tenemos prisa, Señor Espinoza*—we need to hurry. *No sé* how long those ropes will hold."

"*Sí, tiene razón,*" he agrees. "*Bueno,* go ahead. *Supongo que* the journals can't remain here any more."

INSTRUCTIONS   Put together the last clue then continue when you're ready.

There. You're done. "*El tesoro está detrás del animal que persiguió al gato de la casa de Chuchurumbel,*" you read in a whisper. *El animal que persiguió al gato*…. You think back, remembering the story you studied. Surely *el animal que persiguió al gato* was *un perro*, a dog. Looking at the wall behind *Señor* Espinoza, you notice that the old bricks are carved with different figures. You push on one with the figure of a dog carved on it. That brick disappears, and you hear a scraping sound. A small door opens in the wall. Finally switching on your flashlight, you walk through it. Inside is a small room, with an old-fashioned desk and lamp. On the shelf nearby are stacked volume after volume of journals similar to the one you saw earlier at a museum.

Señor Espinoza comes through after you and closes the door. *"Estos diarios son el tesoro,"* he tells you. "My captors, they did not *entender*. They thought the journal would lead them to lost Incan gold, but it was another sort of treasure I had in mind." He picks up one volume and carefully turns its brittle leaves. "Alonso Hernández was an escritoire, a writer, like me. He kept impeccable records of the people he encountered, the stories and songs he heard, the different and changing cultures as Old World meshed with New World, all the places he visited…as a whole, these *diarios* will provide previously unheard-of insights into life in colonial-era *Latinoamericana*. Scholars the world over will be thrilled by this discovery." *Señor* Espinoza smiles. Forgetting for a moment the danger behind you, you run *una mano* over the worn leather backs of *los diarios*.

You shake your head, returning abruptly to the situation at hand. "Listen, *tenemos que irnos*," you tell *Señor* Espinoza. "Those captors are still out there, and as soon as they get free, they'll be after us again."

"Tiene razón," *Señor* Espinoza says again. *"Vámonos."* He eases the shelf away from the wall and motions for you to take the other end. The two of you proceed up a cobblestoned staircase to a storm cellar-type door, which you easily knock open. Sunlight streams in. As the fresh, warm air hits your face, the nearby sound of sirens reaches your ears. Evidently the authorities listened after all. You go out to the main street with *Señor* Espinoza, where you find several police officers and, to your surprise, Agent *Araña*, who got worried and came looking for you. While several officers enter *El Sombrero Rojo* to arrest the erstwhile kidnappers, you and *Señor* Espinoza each make a full report of what happened. Then you carefully transport the travel journals of Alonso Hernández to the libraries of *la Universidad de Chile* in Santiago, where they can be scanned and preserved for any who wish to enjoy them.

Mission accomplished, you and Agent *Araña* spend some time vacationing in Chile before escorting *Señor* Espinoza safely home and then, at last, heading north to your own homes and a hero's welcome back at the office.

✓ You have completed

**Section 2.3.2
Day Four, 15:45 Hours**

and are now ready to take the section quiz. Feel free to consult Appendix C and the information in the course as needed.

Section Quiz

INSTRUCTIONS   Complete this quiz over the cultural material presented in this course. Check your answers in Appendix D, on page 346.

1. **Panama's national motto is "For the … of the world."**

   A. sake

   B. benefit

   C. pride

   D. inconvenience

2. **What are two popular national foods in Panama?**

   A. rice with beans and tamales

   B. chicken stew and omelets

   C. tortillas and rice with beans

   D. omelets and tortillas

3. **What is Panama's most popular sport?**

   A. rugby

   B. cricket

   C. baseball

   D. American football

4. **When was the Panama Canal completed?**

   A. 1914

   B. 1904

   C. 1880

   D. 1897

5. **Which famous conquistador set sail from Panama's *Isla Taboga*?**

   A. Cortéz

   B. de León

   C. Pizarro

   D. Bolívar

6. **What is the smallest Hispanic nation in South America?**

   A. Paraguay

   B. Guyana

   C. Ecuador

   D. Uruguay

7. **Uruguay was the first South American country to give this group the right to vote.**

   A. women

   B. mestizos

   C. native tribes

   D. loyalists

8. **Which country borders Uruguay to the west?**

   A. Brazil

   B. Argentina

   C. Montevideo

   D. no country—Uruguay's western border is the Atlantic Ocean

9. **In Uruguay, what weather pattern is evenly distributed over both the calendar year and the country?**

   A. frost

   B. rain

   C. snow

   D. tornadoes

10. **Which of the following is not a popular destination in Montevideo?**

    A. *Mercado del Puerto*

    B. *Museo Histórico Nacional*

    C. *Ciudad Nueva*

    D. *Palacio Legislativo*

11. **Which South American nation is home to the world's highest waterfall?**
    A. Argentina
    B. Colombia
    C. Uruguay
    D. Venezuela

12. **Simón Bolívar, famous liberator of much of South America, was born in what nation?**
    A. Venezuela
    B. Peru
    C. Ecuador
    D. Uruguay

13. **What is the capital city of Venezuela?**
    A. Quito
    B. Santiago
    C. Lima
    D. Caracas

14. **What is Venezuela's central grassland plain called?**
    A. *Maracaibo*
    B. *Orinoco*
    C. *Llanos*
    D. *Verano*

15. **Who gave Venezuela its name?**
    A. Alonso de Ojeda
    B. Francisco Pizarro
    C. Cristobal Colón
    D. Simón Bolívar

16. **Asunción is the capital city of which South American nation?**
    A. Uruguay
    B. Paraguay
    C. Chile
    D. Ecuador

17. **What are Paraguay's two official languages?**

    A. Spanish and French

    B. Spanish and Guaraní

    C. Spanish and Aymara

    D. Spanish and English

18. **When did Paraguay declare independence from Spain?**

    A. 1524

    B. 1840

    C. 1811

    D. 1932

19. **Which Native American empire had its capital in Cuzco, Peru?**

    A. Incan

    B. Salinar

    C. Nazca

    D. Tolmec

20. **Which of the following languages is NOT widely spoken in Peru?**

    A. Spanish

    B. Quechua

    C. Aymara

    D. Guaraní

21. **When was Peru liberated from Spain?**

    A. 1824

    B. 1780

    C. 1965

    D. 1572

22. **In what South American nation is Lake Titicaca, the world's highest navigable lake, located?**

    A. Ecuador

    B. Venezuela

    C. Peru

    D. Chile

23. **What is the capital city of Chile?**
    A. Puerto Montt
    B. Osorno
    C. Valdivia
    D. Santiago

24. **Which of the following islands does Chile share with Argentina?**
    A. *Chiloe*
    B. *Tierra del Fuego*
    C. *Juan Fernandez*
    D. *Isla de Pascua*

25. **Who was the man assigned to conquer Chile for Spain?**
    A. Ponce de León
    B. Francisco Pizarro
    C. Pedro de Valdivia
    D. Bernardo O'Higgins

You have completed all the sections for

Module 2.3

and are now ready to take the module test. Before continuing, be sure you have learned the objectives for each activity in this module.

Module Test

INSTRUCTIONS   Choose the correct Spanish translation of the English sentence. Check your answers in Appendix D, on page 345.

1. **We lost the game.**
   A. *Pierde el partido.*
   B. *Perdimos el partido.*
   C. *Perder el partido.*
   D. *Perdí el partido.*

2. **How can that be?**
   A. *¿Cómo puede ser (eso)?*
   B. *¿Cómo puedes ser (eso)?*
   C. *¿Cómo puede estar (eso)?*
   D. *¿Cómo podía ser (eso)?*

3. **I'm sorry for having run over you.**
   A. *Siento mucho por atropellarte.*
   B. *Siento mucho para haberle atropellado.*
   C. *Siento mucho para había atropellarte.*
   D. *Siento mucho haberle atropellado.*

4. **Well, so it goes from time to time.**
   A. *Pues así sucede de vez en cuando.*
   B. *Pues así sucedí de vez en cuando.*
   C. *Pues así sucede de vez a vez.*
   D. *Pues así sucede desde vez en cuando.*

MODULE 2.3

5. **Life gets harder and harder.**

    A. *El vida es siempre más y más dura.*

    B. *La vida está nunca más y más dura.*

    C. *La vida está siempre más y más dura.*

    D. *La vida es nunca más y más dura.*

6. **Keep the faith, brother.**

    A. *Guarda la fe, hermano.*

    B. *Mantiene la fe, hermano.*

    C. *Mantenga la fe, hermano.*

    D. *Mantenga el fe, hermano.*

7. **I'm looking for a person who knows how to draw.**

    A. *Yo busco para una persona que sepa dibujar.*

    B. *Yo busco a una persona que sepa dibujar.*

    C. *Yo busco a una persona que sabe como dibujar.*

    D. *Yo busco por una persona que sepa dibujar.*

8. **And I'm looking for someone who can read Chinese.**

    A. *Y yo busco alguien que pueda leer chino.*

    B. *Y yo busca a alguien pueda leer chino.*

    C. *Y yo busco a alguien que pueda leer chino.*

    D. *Y yo busco a alguien que puede leer chino.*

9. **I'm looking for a Mr. Juan Gonzalez.**

    A. *Busco a un señor Juan Gonzalez.*

    B. *Busca a un señor Juan Gonzalez.*

    C. *Busco un señor Juan Gonzalez.*

    D. *Busco a una señor Juan Gonzalez.*

10. **There's no such person here.**

    A. *La persona no está aquí.*

    B. *No está aquí esa persona.*

    C. *No hay tal persona aquí.*

    D. *No hay esta persona aquí.*

11. **You must be a millionaire.**

   A. *Ud. debo ser un millonario.*

   B. *Ud. debe ser un millonario.*

   C. *Ud. debe estar un millonario.*

   D. *Ud. debe ser una millonario.*

12. **On the contrary, I'm not even rich.**

   A. *En el contrario, ni siquiera soy rico.*

   B. *Al contrario, no soy rico.*

   C. *Al contrario, ni supiera soy rico.*

   D. *Al contrario, ni siquiera soy rico.*

13. **For sure you told me 2+2=5.**

   A. *Seguro que me dijiste que 2+2=5.*

   B. *Por seguro me dijiste que 2+2=5.*

   C. *Seguro que me decía que 2+2=5.*

   D. *Seguro que me dijiste cual 2+2=5.*

14. **Then I was mistaken.**

   A. *Luego me equivoqué.*

   B. *Entonces yo equivoqué.*

   C. *Entonces me equivoqué.*

   D. *Entonces me equivocaba.*

15. **I flunked the exam.**

   A. *Me fallé en el examen.*

   B. *Fallé en el examen.*

   C. *Fallé al examen.*

   D. *Fallé en la examen.*

16. **Don't worry. For sure the sun will come out tomorrow.**

   A. *No te preocupas. Seguro el sol saldrá mañana.*

   B. *No preocuparte. Seguro el sol saldrá mañana.*

   C. *No te preocupes. Seguro la sol saldrá mañana.*

   D. *No te preocupes. Seguro el sol saldrá mañana.*

MODULE **2.3**

17. **You collided with a tree.**

    A. *Chocaste con un árbol.*

    B. *Chocabas con un árbol.*

    C. *Chocaste en un árbol.*

    D. *Chocaste con una árbol.*

18. **I didn't realize it.**

    A. *No lo realizó.*

    B. *No lo di cuenta.*

    C. *No me di cuenta.*

    D. *No me di cuento.*

19. **This is a very important matter.**

    A. *Esto es un asunto mucho importante.*

    B. *Esto es un asunto muy importante.*

    C. *Esta es una asunto muy importante.*

    D. *Esto está un asunto muy importante.*

20. **I'll do it as soon as possible.**

    A. *Lo hace cuando es posible.*

    B. *Lo haré cuanta posible.*

    C. *Lo haré cuando tan posible.*

    D. *Lo haré cuanto antes.*

....

INSTRUCTIONS   True or False: The following phrases or sentences are translated correctly.

21. *Deseo que ella camine.* **= I desire that she walk.**

    A. True

    B. False

22. *El pide que yo hable.* **= He asks that I speak.**

    A. True

    B. False

23. *Queremos que hables chino.* **= They want us to speak Chinese.**

    A. True

    B. False

24. *Quieren que hablemos ingles.* = They want us to speak English.

    A. True

    B. False

25. *Deseamos que ellos coman bien.* = We desire that we eat well.

    A. True

    B. False

You have completed all the modules for

Semester 2

Congratulations on completing this language course. Use Spanish everyday and become a lifelong learner.

Appendix A
Student Answer Keys

Answers to activity questions and exercises are provided for checking the student's own work. Answers to module tests and section quizzes are found in Appendix D and are provided for grading purposes.

Activity Answers

Activity 8: Description

In this picture, there are various houses. In the center of the picture, there is a suitcase. And on one side of the suitcase we see two adults: a man and a woman. On the other side there are two children. To the left on the extreme side of the picture, there are two things. To the right on the other extreme, there are four big buildings. Perhaps it's the center of the city. Above there is an alarm clock. The alarm clock reads 9:05. Below there is a street, and on the street there is a car and a driver. In front of the car, there is a stoplight.

Activity 15: Description

In this picture, there are various objects. On the top of the picture, there is a train that is going from the left to the right. Beneath the train and in the center of the picture, there are three instruments used to communicate over long distances. The instrument to the left of the three is a letter. The instrument to the right is a television. And the instrument in the middle is a telephone. Under the horizontal line, we see two modes of transportation. One is faster than the other. They are an airplane and a truck. The airplane is to the left of the truck and is pointing to the left. The truck is pointing to the right. On the bottom left, we see two

types of arms (weapons); a pistol and a knife. The pistol is to the left of the knife. On the opposite side of the weapons, we see two types of animals; a turtle and a dinosaur. The latter is to the right.

Activity 28: Performance Self Quiz

1. B
2. C
3. A
4. C
5. B
6. A
7. B
8. A
9. C
10. D
11. B
12. A
13. C
14. D
15. C
16. A
17. D
18. B
19. B
20. A
21. C
22. D
23. A

APPENDIX A

24. B

25. C

Activity 39: Performance Self Quiz 1

1. Preterite
2. Imperfect
3. Imperfect
4. Preterite
5. Preterite
6. Imperfect
7. Imperfect
8. Preterite
9. Imperfect
10. Imperfect
11. Imperfect
12. Preterite
13. Preterite
14. Imperfect

Activity 39: Performance Self Quiz 2

1. llor-ó
2. llor-aba
3. cant-ó
4. cant-aba
5. sufri-ó
6. sufr-ía
7. hablaba
8. habl-ó
9. vivi-ó
10. viv-ía

Section Puzzle Answers

Section 1.3.1 Puzzle

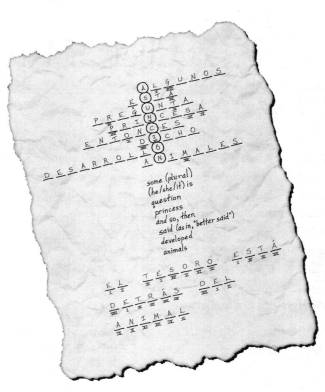

APPENDIX A

Section 2.1.1 Puzzle

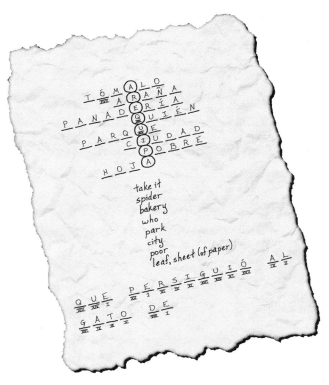

take it
spider
bakery
who
park
city
poor
leaf, sheet (of paper)

Section 2.3.1 Puzzle

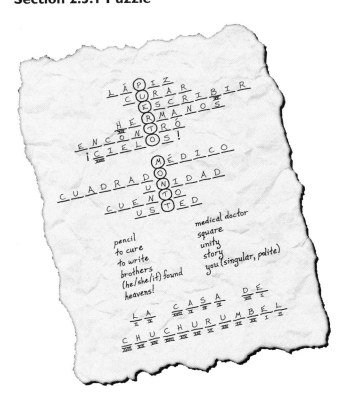

pencil
to cure
to write
brothers
(he/she/it) found
heavens!

medical doctor
square
unity
story
you (singular, polite)

Appendix B
Scope and Sequence

Semester I Module I

Includes the following grammar and content:

Grammar	Content
Pronouns with finite and infinite verbs	Animal vocabulary
Use of negative voice	Telephone conversations
Pronoun verb use	Conversations
Yes/no questions	Asking and answering questions
Object pronouns	Exclamations
The verb *conocer*	Plant vocabulary
Expressing wants	Family vocabulary
Present tense verbs	Giving and following directions
Imperative verbs	Classroom vocabulary
Past tense verbs	Color vocabulary
There is /s there are sentences	Giving explanations
	Geography-related vocabulary
	Geometry-related vocabulary
	Vocabulary related to location
	Review activities
	Pictographs
	Culture information
	Section quizzes
	Module test

Semester 1 Module 2

Includes previous module plus the following:

Grammar	Content
Use of object with the command voice	Additional animal vocabulary
Differences between *le* and *se*	Openers and rejoinders
Past perfect tense	Storytelling practice
Verb distinctions	Identifying objects from descriptions
Imperfect tense	Additional directions
Additional present tense verbs	Additional classroom vocabulary
Dependent clauses	Introductions
Master grammar patterns	Additional conversations
Imperfect, perfect, and past participle verb endings	Additional questions
New aspects of past tense	Additional exclamations
Simple verb tenses without an auxiliary verb	Using conjunctions in storytelling
Reading comprehension	Using verb forms to express distinctions in time
Additional imperative verbs	Bargaining
Future tense verbs	Questions and answers
Additional uses of negative voice	Review activities
Additional infinitive verbs	Culture information
	Self quizzes
	Section quizzes
	Module test

Semester 1 Module 3

Includes previous two modules plus the following:

Grammar	Content
Additional past tense verbs	Additional vocabulary
Sentences with multiple verbs	Additional storytelling practice
There was / there were sentences	Additional conversations
Additional future tense verbs	Suggestions
Additional questions	Giving directions

Grammar *(cont.)*	Content
Should have __	Humorous stories
Verb endings -aba, -ó, and -ado	Giving and following instructions
Comparing past tense forms	Culture information
Indicative forms	Self quizzes
Subjunctive forms	Section quizzes
Indicative modes	Module test
Subjunctive modes	

Semester 2 Module I

Includes previous semester plus the following:

Grammar	Content
Additional past tense verbs	Additional family vocabulary
Additional present tense verbs	Expressing thanks
Additional imperative verbs	Familiar stories
Making requests	Additional ways of giving and following instructions
Passive verbs	Practice with numbers
Prepositions	Additional animal vocabulary
Additional future tense verbs	Minidialogues
Expressing emotions	Reading comprehension
Additional questions	Additional humorous stories
Conditional verbs	Additional geometry-related vocabulary
Additional past perfect tense verbs	Openers and rejoinders
	Weather-related vocabulary
	Poems and ditties
	Culture information
	Section quizzes
	Module test

Semester 2 Module 2

Includes previous module plus the following:

Grammar	Content
Additional dependent clauses	Additional familiar stories
Prepositional phrases	Additional openers and rejoinders
Additional conditional verbs	Making apologies
Additional future tense verbs	Warnings
Additional questions	Additional geometry-related vocabulary
Past participle verbs	Descriptions
Irregular past participles	Additional reading comprehension
Indicative verb forms	Useful words and phrases
Expressing doubt	Making polite requests
	Additional questions and answers
	Additional color-related vocabulary
	Practice with days of the week
	Culture information
	Section quizzes
	Module test

Semester 2 Module 3

Includes previous two modules plus the following:

Grammar	Content
Additional present tense verbs	Additional reading comprehension
Present perfect	Additional openers and rejoinders
Preterit past perfect	Additional family-related vocabulary
Imperfect past perfect	Food-related vocabulary
Future perfect	Additional geometry-related vocabulary
Additional conditional verbs	Vocabulary related to professions
Present subjunctive perfect	Expressing permission
Past subjunctive perfect	Culture information

Grammar *(cont.)*	Content
The verb *haber*	Section quizzes
	Module test

Semester 1 Objectives

→ Understand and use small talk.

Activity 1
→ Comprehend the meaning of a story.

Activity 2
→ Understand a telephone conversation in Spanish.

Activity 3
→ Understand and use small talk.
→ Understand new vocabulary in a conversation.

Activity 4
→ Understand new vocabulary in a conversation or story.

Activity 5
→ Master object pronouns with finite and infinite verbs.

Activity 6
→ Build fluency through repetition.

Activity 7
→ Follow instructions in Spanish.

Activity 8
→ Identify objects from a description.
→ Understand the story of "The Three Bears" in Spanish.
→ Learn Spanish action verbs.

Activity 9
→ Understand the story of "The Three Bears" in Spanish.
→ Describe objects of different sizes and shapes.

Activity 10
→ Expand grammar skills.

Activity 11
→ Understand new vocabulary in a conversation or story.

Activity 12
→ Understand enough vocabulary to comprehend a lesson about geography.

Activity 13
→ Understand enough vocabulary to comprehend a lesson about geometry.

Activity 14
→ Understand pronoun and verb use.

Activity 15
→ Identify and describe objects.

Activity 16
→ Recognize how much Spanish you can comprehend, say, read, and write.

Activity 17
→ Learn Spanish action verbs.
→ Use small talk phrases.

Activity 18
→ Use small talk phrases.

Activity 19
→ Expand your comprehension toward complete understanding.

Activity 20
→ Use objects with command voice.

Activity 21
→ Understand new vocabulary in a conversation.

Activity 22
→ Use the grammar "*le*" and "*se*."

Activity 23
→ Understand past perfect tense.

Activity 24
→ Use more small talk on a formal level.

Activity 25
→ Make distinctions among verbs and use them correctly.

Activity 26
→ Use numbers and math terms in a math setting.

Activity 27
→ Ask and answer questions in imperfect tense.

Activity 28
→ Master grammar patterns.

Activity 29
→ Create a mini-story using both written and oral skills.
→ Expand comprehension, fluency, and use of past and present tense.

Activity 30
→ Build fluency in past tense.

Activity 31
→ Understand new vocabulary and grammar.

Activity 32
→ Expand comprehension, fluency, and use of past and present tense.
→ Follow a conversation and understand its meaning.

Activity 33
→ Understand directions.

Activity 34
→ Follow a story line with full comprehension.

Activity 35
→ Understand new vocabulary in a conversation.

Activity 36
→ Use repetition to gain full comprehension.

Activity 37
→ Master new vocabulary.

Activity 38
→ Use imperfect, perfect, and past participle verb endings.

Activity 39
→ Perform in aspects of past tense.

Activity 40
→ Use the simple verb tenses without an auxiliary verb.

Semester 2 Objectives

Activity 41
→ Increase reading and listening comprehension, and vocabulary usage.

Activity 42
→ Read a dialogue for comprehension and then repeat it.

Activity 43
→ Recognize your ability to understand Spanish.

Activity 44
→ Increase reading and listening comprehension, and vocabulary usage.

Activity 45
→ Increase reading and listening comprehension, and vocabulary usage.

Activity 46
→ Recognize your ability to understand Spanish.

Activity 47
→ Tell a joke in Spanish.

Activity 48
→ Understand and use geometry vocabulary.

Activity 49
→ Read and understand a story in Spanish.

Activity 50
→ Increase the number of useful phrases you can say.

Activity 51
→ Follow a story line with full comprehension.

Activity 52
→ Increase vocabulary through poems and ditties.

Activity 53
→ Listen to a Spanish story and maintain comprehension without a text.

Activity 54
→ Use important phrases.

Activity 55
→ Read a story in Spanish and understand new vocabulary from context.

Activity 56
→ Increase geometry vocabulary.

Activity 57
→ Read to increase all skill levels of language learning.

Activity 58
→ Learn and use important phrases.

Activity 59
→ Read to increase all skill levels of language learning.

Activity 60
→ Learn and use important phrases.

Activity 61

➜ Ask and answer useful questions.

Activity 62

➜ Build comprehension and vocabulary through reading.

Activity 63

➜ Learn and use important phrases.

Activity 64

➜ Gain a better understanding of verb forms.

Activity 65

➜ Build comprehension and vocabulary through reading.

Activity 66

➜ Use important phrases.

Activity 67

➜ Read and comprehend stories that are longer.

Activity 68

➜ Understand and use compound tenses and conjugations.

Activity 69

➜ Master geometry-related vocabulary.

Activity 70

➜ Listen to a Spanish story and maintain comprehension without a text.

Appendix C
Index of Marginalia

Introduction

Culture facts and other interesting information can be found in the margins throughout the course. While not part of your course curriculum, these marginalia provide a fun and educational view into the many exciting facets of Spanish and Spanish-speaking countries.

Index

Culture Notes

As you've worked through the course, you may have been interested in certain countries or interesting facts and histories. Write any notes about people, places, or things that you would like do more research on.

....

....

....

....

APPENDIX C

Appendix D
Grading Answer Keys

Module Test Answers

1.1	1.2	1.3	2.1	2.2	2.3
1. A	1. B	1. C	1. C	1. A	1. B
2. B	2. C	2. A	2. A	2. D	2. A
3. A	3. D	3. C	3. B	3. A	3. D
4. B	4. B	4. B	4. C	4. B	4. A
5. A	5. A	5. D	5. A	5. A	5. C
6. B	6. C	6. A	6. C	6. C	6. C
7. A	7. D	7. C	7. B	7. C	7. B
8. B	8. C	8. B	8. D	8. B	8. D
9. A	9. B	9. D	9. A	9. A	9. A
10. B	10. B	10. B	10. C	10. B	10. C
11. B	11. A	11. B	11. B	11. D	11. B
12. B	12. B	12. A	12. A	12. C	12. D
13. A	13. A	13. B	13. A	13. C	13. A
14. A	14. A	14. B	14. B	14. B	14. C
15. A	15. B	15. B	15. B	15. A	15. B
16. C	16. A	16. A	16. A	16. A	16. D
17. D	17. B	17. A	17. B	17. A	17. A
18. D	18. A	18. B	18. A	18. B	18. C
19. C	19. A	19. A	19. A	19. B	19. B
20. B	20. A	20. B	20. B	20. A	20. D
21. C	21. A	21. B	21. C	21. B	21. A
22. D	22. A	22. A	22. B	22. A	22. A
23. A	23. B	23. D	23. A	23. A	23. B
24. C	24. B	24. B	24. D	24. A	24. A
25. B	25. A	25. C	25. A	25. B	25. B

Section Quiz Answers

1.1.1	1.1.2	1.2.1	1.2.2	1.3.1	1.3.2	2.1.1	2.1.2	2.2.1	2.2.2	2.3.1	2.3.2
1. A	1. B	1. D	1. C	1. C	1. C	1. B	1. B	1. D	1. C	1. B	1. B
2. C	2. A	2. A	2. B	2. B	2. D	2. C	2. A	2. B	2. D	2. B	2. D
3. B	3. C	3. B	3. A	3. B	3. A	3. B	3. A	3. D	3. D	3. D	3. C
4. A	4. C	4. B	4. B	4. C	4. D	4. C	4. B	4. C	4. A	4. C	4. A
5. B	5. B	5. A	5. C	5. B	5. C	5. B	5. B	5. C	5. B	5. D	5. C
6. D	6. A	6. D	6. A	6. C	6. B	6. A	6. C	6. A	6. D	6. D	6. D
7. B	7. C	7. B	7. A	7. A	7. C	7. A	7. B	7. B	7. D	7. C	7. A
8. B	8. D	8. C	8. B	8. D	8. B	8. B	8. B	8. A	8. D	8. A	8. B
9. C	9. C	9. A	9. D	9. D	9. C	9. D	9. D	9. B	9. B	9. B	9. B
10. D	10. A	10. B	10. B	10. C	10. A	10. D	10. C	10. B	10. D	10. C	10. C
											11. D
											12. A
											13. D
											14. C
											15. A
											16. B
											17. B
											18. C
											19. A
											20. D
											21. A
											22. C
											23. D
											24. B
											25. C